TAKING LONDON

ALSO BY MARTIN DUGARD

Taking Berlin

Taking Paris

Killing the Witches with Bill O'Reilly

Killing the Legends with Bill O'Reilly

Killing the Killers with Bill O'Reilly

Killing the Mob with Bill O'Reilly

Killing Crazy Horse with Bill O'Reilly

Killing the SS with Bill O'Reilly

Killing England with Bill O'Reilly

Killing the Rising Sun with Bill O'Reilly

Killing Reagan with Bill O'Reilly

Killing Patton with Bill O'Reilly

Killing Jesus with Bill O'Reilly

Killing Kennedy with Bill O'Reilly

Killing Lincoln with Bill O'Reilly

The Explorers

To Be a Runner

The Murder of King Tut with James Patterson

The Training Ground

Chasing Lance

The Last Voyage of Columbus

Into Africa

Farther Than Any Man

Survivor

Knockdown

Surviving the Toughest Race on Earth

TAKING LONDON

WINSTON CHURCHILL AND
THE FIGHT TO SAVE CIVILIZATION

——

MARTIN DUGARD

DUTTON

DUTTON

An imprint of Penguin Random House LLC
penguinrandomhouse.com

LIBRARY OF CONGRESS CATALOGING-IN-PUBLICATION DATA
has been applied for.

ISBN 9780593473214 (hardcover)
ISBN 9780593473238 (ebook)

Printed in the United States of America
1   3   5   7   9   10   8   6   4   2

BOOK DESIGN BY TIFFANY ESTREICHER

While the author has made every effort to provide accurate telephone
numbers, internet addresses, and other contact information at the time of
publication, neither the publisher nor the author assumes any responsibility for
errors or for changes that occur after publication. Further, the publisher does
not have any control over and does not assume any responsibility for author
or third-party websites or their content.

For the Tough Guy Book Club and the Diamond Dogs
Welcome Ports in a Storm

TAKING LONDON

I think it is well also for the man in the street to realize that there is no power on earth that can protect him from being bombed. Whatever people may tell him, the bomber will always get through. . . .

The only defense is in offense, which means that you have to kill more women and children more quickly than the enemy if you want to save yourselves. . . . If the conscience of the young men should ever come to feel, with regard to this one instrument, that it is evil and should go, the thing will be done. . . .

Well, as I say, the future is in their hands. But when the next war comes, and European civilization is wiped out, as it will be, and by no force more than that force, then do not let them lay blame on the old men. Let them remember that they, principally, or they alone, are responsible for the terrors that have fallen upon the earth.

—BRITISH PRIME MINISTER STANLEY BALDWIN,
NOVEMBER 10, 1932

PROLOGUE

WINSTON CHURCHILL

Winston Churchill obsesses about Adolf Hitler. Even if the rest of civilization does not.

The parliamentary gadfly sits before a new British Broadcasting Corporation Type A microphone. Friday night. Pages of typewritten speech arranged in a neat pile on the small, angled desk before him. Rain pattering out on Portland Place. Brick walls absorb the rumble of Bakerloo line Underground trains one hundred feet below. Churchill removes the cigar from the corner of his mouth. Draws a breath, focuses on the first sentence.

Cries wolf.

"I have but a short time to deal with this enormous subject. I beg you therefore to weigh my words with the attention and thought which I have given them," the fifty-nine-year-old implores the people of Britain. Breath of Hine's brandy, Stilton cheese, the Cuban.

Churchill's career is in reverse. Once the holder of high offices in the government, the politician is now a figure of scorn and ridicule. His jeremiad is unpopular and out of touch with Britain's anti-war sentiment. This makes him only more determined that his message must be heard.

"It is startling and fearful to realize that we are no longer safe in our island home. For nearly one thousand years England has never seen the campfires of an invader. Stormy seas and our Royal Navy have been our sure defense. . . . It is indeed with a pang of stabbing pain that we see all this in mortal danger. A thousand years has been spent to form a state—an hour may lay it in the dust.

"What shall we do?"

. . .

"Causes of War" is the theme of this evening's broadcast, part of a series featuring prominent English thinkers. The first two speakers treated their discourse as an intellectual exercise, fawning over their topic with minutiae about arms manufacturing and flawed treaties. Their focus was a hypothetical conflict, war in the abstract.

Winston Churchill
Picryl/Original photo housed at the Imperial War Museums

But Churchill does not think another great war in Europe *might* happen—he is convinced it *will* happen. And now is the time to prepare.

"Only a few hours away by air there dwells a nation of nearly seventy million of the most educated, industrious, scientific people in the world, who are being taught from childhood to think of war as a glorious exercise and death in battle as the noblest deed for man. There is a nation which has abandoned all its liberties in order to augment its collective strength. There is a nation which with all its strength and virtue is in the grip of a group of ruthless men preaching a gospel of intolerance and racial pride unrestrained by law, by Parliament, or by public opinion. In that country, all pacifist speeches, all morbid books, are forbidden or suppressed and the authors rigorously imprisoned.

"From their new table of commandments they have omitted: Thou shalt not kill.

"It is but twenty years since these neighbors of ours fought almost the whole world and almost defeated them. Now they are rearming with the utmost speed. And ready to their hands is this new lamentable weapon of the air against which a navy has no defense and before which women and children, the weak and the frail, the pacifist and the jingo, the warrior and the civilian, the frontline trenches and the cottage home all lie in equal peril. Nay, worse still, for with the new weapon has come a new method or has come back the most brutish method of ancient barbarism—the possibility of compelling the submission of races by torturing their civil population. And worst of all, the more civilized the country is, the larger, more splendid its cities, the more intricate the structure of its social and economic life."

. . .

CHURCHILL SPEAKS OF Adolf Hitler's Germany.

The strongman's Nazi Party grew from a fringe Bavarian group to national power between 1920 and now. British intelligence estimates the dictator's private army of "storm troopers" numbers more than four hundred thousand. These thugs can be seen roaming the streets of Berlin, beating and whipping anyone suspected of being anti-Nazi. At the sight of Adolf—and no one ever calls him that—these excitable gangs raise their right arms in salute, bellowing "Heil Hitler."

The Nazi leader's response is a simple lifting of his palm in acceptance, a Caesar, his power assured.

As Churchill speaks on the radio tonight, it is just three months since the death of Germany's elected president, eighty-six-year-old Paul von Hindenburg. Hitler, who had served as chancellor, quickly seized control, forming an all-powerful dictatorship. He is not the president, nor the chancellor, but the omnipotent *Führer und Reichskanzler des Deutschen Volkes*—"leader and reich chancellor of the German people."

Or just führer.

Winston Churchill has followed Hitler's violent ascent from a distance. He even attempted to meet the führer during a recent visit to Germany but was denied. Hitler saw no sense in spending time with a man possessing no political power. Now Churchill's personal mission includes keeping careful track of Germany's illegal military buildup, and even constructing a network of informants to spy on the Nazi war machine. In this way, he often shocks the House of Commons by presenting outrageous but true statistics about the growing threat. These figures, which many members of Parliament refuse to believe, are not designed to lead Britain into war, but to build the defenses necessary to protect his nation when war arrives. "To urge the preparation of defense is not to assert the imminence of war," he will tell Parliament on November 28. "On the contrary, if war were imminent, preparations for defense would be too late."

Churchill well knows Adolf Hitler's twisted plans include more than just conquest: All enemies of the German government are being rooted out—lawyers, homosexuals, Roma, Communists, and Jews. Hitler reserves his greatest hatred for all things Jewish, a people he blames for the nation's Great War defeat.

To the citizens of Germany, Hitler makes that outrageous claim, building rabid national sentiment against the very existence of Jewish people so he might one day succeed in their extermination. Already, a concentration camp known as Dachau, devoted to the torture, prosecution, and execution of Jews and political prisoners, opened outside Munich in 1933.

But to the people of Great Britain, Adolf Hitler tells a very different lie: Germany does not want war with Europe. She is a buffer state, protecting the continent against the Soviet Union and the spread of global Communism.

And England believes it.

The British like Hitler.

A lot.

Winston Churchill now asks the nation to wake up and confront reality: "These are facts. Hard, grim, indisputable facts, and in face of these facts, I ask again:

"What are we to do?"

. . .

"I HAVE COME to the conclusion—reluctantly I admit—that we cannot get away. Here we are. We must make the best of it, but do not, I beg you, underrate the risks, the grievous risks, we have to run. I hope, I pray, and on the whole, grasping the larger hope, I believe that no war will fall upon us. But if in the near future the Great War of 1914 is resumed again in Europe after the armistice, for that is what it may come to under different conditions, in different combinations no doubt, if that should happen no one can tell where and how it would end. Or whether sooner or later we should not be dragged into it, as the USA was dragged in against their will in 1917. Whatever happened, and whatever we did, it would be a time of frightful danger for us.

"First, we must, without another day's delay, begin to make ourselves at least the strongest airpower in the European world. By this means we shall recover to a very large extent the safety which we formerly enjoyed through our navy, and through our being an island. By this means we shall free ourselves from the dangers of being blackmailed against our will either to surrender. . . .

"May God protect us all."

R. J. MITCHELL

R. J. Mitchell is dying.

A year and a half has passed since Winston Churchill's "Causes of War" speech. The aircraft designer sits alone in his Rolls-Royce with the butter-yellow door panels, parked to one side of Eastleigh Aerodrome's grass runway. Sandy blond hair combed straight back, tweed coat, and knotted tie, colostomy bag anchored to left hip. Mitchell is forty, too young to leave behind a wife and a sixteen-year-old son but accomplished enough to have been awarded one of Britain's top honors by King George V—and this fancy car from the world-famous auto manufacturer.*

Mitchell draws on his pipe. Never takes his eyes off a fighter prototype purring over the quilted green Hampshire countryside. The aircraft banks to land. Today's test pilot steers toward the airstrip in a wide arc rather than approaching the runway directly. If anyone else was sitting in the Rolls and cared to ask, Mitchell would explain why the two-bladed propeller and the 900-horsepower V-12 Merlin engine in the nose, the fuel tank

---

* The Most Excellent Order of the British Empire was founded in 1917 by King George V to reward contributions to the arts and sciences and for philanthropic service. There are several tiers to this award. Mitchell was named commander of the Most Excellent Order of the British Empire (CBE) on December 29, 1931. Lower ranks are the officer of the Most Excellent Order of the British Empire (OBE) and member of the Order of the British Empire (MBE).

behind the Merlin but in front of the cockpit, and the tail-dragger landing gear make Sussex-born Jeffrey Quill's roundabout pattern necessary.

The answer, Mitchell would point out, is simple—and R.J. is a huge believer in the power of a simple explanation: Quill will be flying blind once the nose tilts upward in the last seconds before touchdown. The flier will be able to look out the canopy to the right and left, but the long forward section of the fuselage will block his frontal view. The approach is reconnaissance, a last full view of the runway to ensure there are no obstacles or other chances for ground collision.

Were he not alone, R. J. Mitchell might also talk at length about the concentric square tubing of the new plane's wing spars, the monocoque aluminum skin, the four Browning machine guns inside each wing, and the eighty thousand rivets holding it all together. And the engineer knows by heart precise reasons why the revolutionary elliptical wing means a pronounced advantage in aerial combat—should the rumored war in Europe ever take place.

But right now it is enough for a solitary Reginald Joseph "Reg" Mitchell to set details aside and simply watch fuselage number K5054 fly. A pilot himself, he scrutinizes this final approach. Mitchell sees it all. The engineer has conceived twenty-four aircraft—everything from flying boats to bombers—since assuming the role of chief engineer at Supermarine Aviation Works in 1920.

This is his first fighter.

And what a warrior she is, arguably the most nimble aircraft to ever take flight. A fighter aircraft's primary role is to attack other planes, and K5054 appears quite prepared to do just that. But R. J. Mitchell knows she is still a far cry from the airborne killing machine he promised Britain's Air Ministry. There is still much work to do.

His pilots disagree.

"Don't change a thing," proclaimed Supermarine's lead test pilot, thirty-one-year-old Mutt Summers, upon completing the maiden flight. High praise coming from a salty career flier who earned his nickname by urinating on the rear wheel before climbing into a cockpit.

That date was March 6, two months ago, back when the new plane was supposed to be a secret. Sharp-eyed Portsmouth residents, so used to witnessing Mitchell's revolutionary designs take flight, made a fuss about the unique appearance. K5054 looks different from anything the locals have ever seen.

And this new plane is fast.

Very fast.

For all the many times the people of Portsmouth have craned their necks upward as the loud and lonely thrum of an aircraft engine pierced the calm of a blue-sky day, this fighter is the closest thing to a speeding bullet they have ever seen.

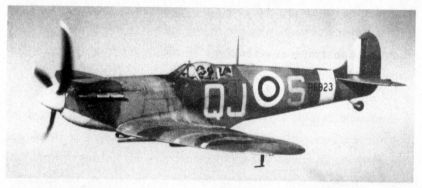

Supermarine Spitfire   *Flickr*

Supermarine has yet to publicly acknowledge the prototype, but as the date for mass production draws near, cryptic advertisements in London newspapers seek men qualified as "bench fitters, sheet metal workers, panel beaters, toolmakers, and assemblers, used to light and actual engineering. Applicants must be able to work to drawings."*

The mystery will be revealed soon enough. Next month's Hendon Air

---

* The accepted date for the first flight of K5054 is March 5, 1936. Yet test pilot and eyewitness Jeffrey Quill states in his autobiography that March 6 is the actual moment in history. Quill restored K5054 in 1983, and it now resides in the Tangmere Museum.

Show in North London will be a coming-out party for K5054. British dailies will write of Mitchell's design: "the abolition of everything which could even slightly retard its speed through the air has been carried to a fine art. The fuselage is slim, the wings are cantilever, and there are no bracing wires at all. The outer covering of the wings as well as fuselage is of metal, and the paint which covers the metal is highly polished, for even a rough surface will produce what is known as skin friction and will reduce the speed."

Even when not in flight, the *Guardian* will add, "the machine as it stood on the ground showed speed in every line."

R. J. Mitchell revels in the praise. The broad-shouldered engineer was an athlete before cancer. Cricket and tennis are no longer part of his life, but he still nurses a deep competitive streak. Mitchell keeps a close eye on rival manufacturer Hawker Aircraft and designer Sydney Camm—at forty-two, two years R.J.'s senior but still undeniably a young man with the same visionary mindset. Hawker is currently working on its own new fighter named the Hurricane.

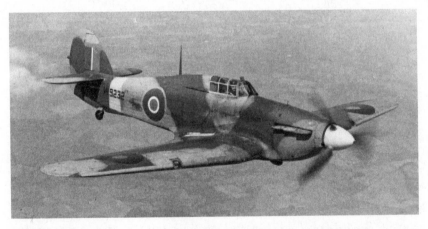

Hawker Hurricane   *Picryl/Original photo housed at the Imperial War Museums*

But Mitchell enjoys being one step ahead. Though similar in appearance to K5054, Camm's design is slower, a throwback to a previous era when cockpits were open to the wind and rain; when landing gear was fixed into position, not folding neatly into the undercarriage after takeoff;

when wings were stacked one on top of the other, wrapped in canvas, braced with wires and struts. Indeed, the wood-framed Hurricane is based on a biplane known as the Fury. Five years into its military service, Fury is already obsolete.

R. J. Mitchell has the design edge over Hawker for now, but only as long as he continues making K5054 better. There are nuances to perfect before transitioning from prototype to mass production: the piston-driven engine tends to stall in a steep dive, the fuel tank's forward position represents a fire risk to the pilot, 20mm cannon might be a better choice than .50-caliber guns, and so on. Mitchell will find his answer by questioning test pilot Quill about today's performance after he lands, then retreating into his office at Supermarine. His personal secretary Vera Cross will halt all visitors and hold all calls until the designer emerges with a solution. "His mood is not right," Miss Cross will warn. "Better leave it until later."

Yet design changes trouble Mitchell far less than the name his corporate bosses are giving the new creation.

Mitchell prefers the "Shrew."

Shrews are mammalian killing machines, some of the most voracious predators on earth.

No matter. Supermarine's sobriquet is infinitely more evocative: "Spitfire."

It's what Supermarine chairman Sir Robert McLean calls his daughter Ann.*

Reg Mitchell loathes the name.

---

* Ann McLean was twenty-four at the time, soon to marry actor Robert Newton (*Black Beard the Pirate*; *Oliver Twist*; *Treasure Island*). Her actual childhood nickname was "Little Spitfire." Coincidentally, as design work began on the aircraft in 1934, the Katharine Hepburn film *Spitfire* was released, perhaps reminding the Supermarine chairman of his daughter's childhood moniker. When Annie Penrose, as she was known in later life, turned a hundred years old, a plane trailing a banner flew over her Falmouth home bearing the message "Happy 100th Birthday Spitfire Annie." It's worth noting that Sir Robert's choice for the aircraft's name might have been quite different if he had chosen the nickname of his younger daughter, Evelyn: Bunny.

. . .

SALT BREEZE BLOWS in from the Solent. Sky robin's-egg blue. The air inside Mitchell's Rolls is a cloying blend of pipe tobacco and stoma, humming with the full-throated growl of K5054's approaching Merlin.*

Mitchell sucks on his pipe. The diagnosis was a shock. There is no known correlation between smoking and cancer. What began as a single rogue cell became many, growing into tumors, multiplying as the disease traveled through bloodstream and lymph nodes to invade internal organs.

Surgery seems to have solved the problem. Doctors tell Mitchell there is a good chance his sickness will not return if he is cancer-free a year from August.

That's a long way off. So the designer focuses on the Spitfire instead of worst-case scenarios. Britain's need for a fighter that can dive, climb, and turn with the very best in the world is immediate. For just like the destruction visited upon R. J. Mitchell's body, a cancer has also made its presence known on the European continent. What began with Adolf Hitler's rise to power in Germany has resulted in that nation's military and societal overhaul. The country once crushed by World War I reparations has rearmed—secretly, at first, then openly and defiantly. Hitler commands one of the most powerful military forces in the world—and is bent on putting that juggernaut to use.

Aerial warfare will play a defining role.

On March 16, 1935, in defiance of strictures against German airpower that had been in place since the end of the Great War, Hitler militarized the nation's aircraft industry.

The Nazi Luftwaffe—"air weapon"—was not so much born as it came out of hiding. Pilots, manufacturers, and designers assumed a wartime

---

* Rolls-Royce named its aircraft piston engines after birds of prey: Eagle, Falcon, Hawk, Kestrel, Peregrine, Goshawk, Condor, Buzzard, Vulture, Griffon, and Merlin. Naming shifted to Greek gods, mythology, and rivers during the jet age. In 1969, Rolls-Royce broke with those evocative traditions by not using any name at all for the engine initially powering the 747 passenger aircraft, simply calling it RB211.

footing. Even as Reg Mitchell studies K5054's flight right now, German designers like Willy Messerschmitt and Kurt Tank are fine-tuning fighter aircraft of their own. Their expectations for the Bf 109 and Focke-Wulf 190 are no less demanding than Mitchell's.

And it's not just fighters. Britain and Germany are also racing to produce long-range bombers.

There is a vast difference between these two types of aircraft: it can be argued that fighters are defensive in nature, a deterrent, a protector.

Bombers don't protect anything.

Bombers drop fire and brimstone from the heavens, raining instant destruction on a horrific scale.

An ordinary British citizen—even the aviation-minded people of Portsmouth—would be hard-pressed to identify a single German aircraft on sight right now. Yet in time, they will distinguish a Heinkel bomber from a Dornier from a Junkers. Not just by silhouette, but also by speed and wasplike engine drone and size and weight of bombs spilling out their bellies. For these warplanes are the greatest threat to England's security and sovereignty in more than a century.

The people of Great Britain well know their nation has never been safe from attack. Invaders from Europe have assaulted the island nation numerous times:

Julius Caesar and the Romans landed in 55 BC.

Vikings from Scandinavia raided for five centuries beginning in the eighth century.

William, Duke of Normandy, the illegitimate son of an unmarried French duke and his mistress, famously landed in 1066. William turned the Roman settlement of Londinium into his personal stronghold, building the fortress that would later become known as the Tower of London.

Seven centuries after William was crowned king, London's population was more than five hundred thousand. A century after that, its large port and magnificent buildings such as St. Paul's Cathedral made London the island's centerpiece. In 1707, the Kingdom of England, which included

Wales, joined with Scotland to form the United Kingdom of Great Britain. Ireland would join the union in 1801.*

Raids along the English shoreline never ceased, but successful invasion and conquest of Great Britain ended with William the Conqueror, as the bastard became known.

Naval power made the difference.

Initially slow to grasp the notion of strength on the seas, England was transformed by the establishment of the Royal Navy in 1546. A kingdom united by name and treaty became even more joined by the defensive wall provided by naval force. The English Channel and the North Sea—the cold, dark, watery bodies separating Great Britain from Europe—became the world's most impregnable moat. The British slept well, assured no foreign power would surprise them in the middle of the night.

Then came aircraft.

In January 1915, Kaiser Wilhelm of Germany authorized the aerial bombardment of England. The first attack on London was that May, killing twenty-eight people and wounding sixty. On September 8, 1915, motor-driven German Zeppelin L13 dropped a half ton of bombs on Central London. The Royal Navy's defensive cordon meant nothing, particularly to the twenty-two Londoners in Aldersgate who died that day. By the end of May 1916, five hundred fifty Britons had been killed by German bombs.†

The terror of being killed from the skies was so great that the Treaty of Versailles, signed to end the Great War, specifically forbade Germany from possessing aerial weapons of war.

---

* Ireland would become divided into the north and south in 1922. The newly formed Republic of Ireland would leave this kingdom after a war of independence. Northern Ireland would remain loyal to British rule, forcing a name change to the United Kingdom of Great Britain and Northern Ireland.

† A ham bone was also dropped by parachute. The bone was inside a small bag. A drawing of a zeppelin dropping a bomb on UK foreign minister "*Edwart Gray.*" On the other side: "A memento from starved-out Germany."

Too late. No treaty could diminish mankind's thrall for strategic bombing.

In the abstract, *strategic* means factories, bridges, barracks, airfields, and all other targets connected with military power. Inevitably, those German bombs also fell on churches, libraries, grocery stores, pubs, and people out for a Sunday stroll, turning ordinary citizens into pink vapor. This shattering of civilian morale gave a new definition to strategic.

But as the British learned in the summer of 1916, when their fighter aircraft used incendiary bullets to set Zeppelins ablaze over London, strategic also means stopping bomber aircraft from releasing their payloads by shooting them down first.

Thus, the Spitfire.

One month from now, on June 3, 1936, Britain's Air Ministry will order 310 Spitfires from Supermarine. Visionary Royal Air Force air vice marshal Hugh Dowding, leader of Britain's Fighter Command, is making the Spitfire, the Hurricane, and a new discovery known as "Radio Direction Finding" the cornerstone of his island defense.*

A triumph.

Yet in the midst of this crowning moment, R. J. Mitchell's doctors have news: His cancer has returned.

---

* Radio Direction Finding was the first proven method of detecting incoming enemy aircraft. RDF was later surpassed by Radio Acquired Detection and Ranging—RADAR—which became the popular term in 1942. Radar is now commonly used in lowercase to describe any sense of advance warning or intuition. In keeping with historical chronology, the term "RDF" will be used throughout *Taking London*.

FOUR PILOTS

The Boy

MARCH 20, 1939
LONDON, ENGLAND
10 A.M.

The next hour could forever change Geoffrey Wellum's life.

Or he might just be sent home.

The nervous boy walks from the Tube station at Holborn. Left toward the Thames. Bustling Kingsway is uninspiring: bankers and clerks and secretaries, briefcases and pocketbooks with lunch tucked neatly inside, copies of the *London Times* and the *Daily Telegraph* folded under elbows. Headlines report Adolf Hitler's invasion of Czechoslovakia five days ago, though none of the commuters show the slightest concern about what might come next.

"Heads down, intent on another day at the office, the same sort of day as yesterday and no doubt a similar day tomorrow," judges brown-haired Wellum, so young he still has one term left at the Forest School.

Warm sun on his face. Small white clouds scudding across the sky, not sure whether or not they want to rain. Tomorrow is the first day of spring. Wellum combats his stomach full of raging butterflies with a single bold thought, shoving aside any notions of family tradition and parental expectation of a career in banking or some other deskbound profession:

"I'd rather fly if they'll have me."

At the corner of Aldwych, Wellum steps left into towering Adastral House, home of Great Britain's Air Ministry. Crossing the threshold dampens his nerves. The seventeen-year-old looks like a lost child in this Monday morning hub of grown-up bureaucracy. Wellum knows this. He buttons up his courage.

A man in uniform asks his business.

"I'm here for an interview with the selection board for pilots in the RAF," the teenager blurts.

Room 21 on the third floor is filled with almost two dozen aviator candidates. Not everyone will be accepted. An impatient Geoffrey Wellum grows annoyed as one young man "speaks non-stop in spite of the fact that nobody is really listening," detailing his solo flying experiences. A mood of competition settles over the waiting area. One by one, the would-be pilots are ushered alone into a conference room. When his turns comes, Wellum enters and hears the door close behind him. He sees a large table. Three "distinguished looking men" sit on the other side studying his imperfections. One stiff wooden chair faces the officers.

So this is what a selection board looks like.

Wellum is told to sit.

He thinks the gentleman in the middle looks pleasant. The man on the right appears "harmless enough." But the officer to the left looks fond of asking hard questions.

The interrogation begins.

Geoffrey Wellum is wrong—all three grill him like he is a murder suspect. Every aspect of his life is fair game, from the newspapers he reads to military knowledge. Detailed mathematical queries. Interest in cricket. Education. Wellum finds he is more well versed in the ways of the world than he realized, even knowing that the Royal Navy has no battleships on station in the Far East, only cruisers. Where that bit of trivia comes from is anyone's guess.

Finally, "Thank you, Mr. Wellum, for your time." He is given a slip of blue paper and ordered to hand it to an officer outside the door.

Then Wellum is, indeed, sent home.

There he waits for a letter that may never come. His flight dream seems over. But then, just after Easter, "comes the welcome news that I have been accepted for pilot training." Included in the packet are instructions to read a very specific set of books and to bring a dinner jacket on the day he reports.

"I am going to be a pilot, and that is all that matters," he rejoices.

The blue chit he was given, it turns out, means he passed the interview. A pink slip would have meant a formal letter, beginning with "The Air Ministry regrets . . ."

On July 28, 1939, Geoffrey Wellum presents himself at the No. 7 Elementary and Reserve Flying Training School in Desford, Leicestershire. Two hundred acres in the Midlands devoted to all things flight: hangars, mess, quarters, classrooms, gun range, squash courts, pub.

"The Boy," as the teenager is nicknamed, is nine rigorous months from earning his wings. He will master bureaucracy, aviation law, military discipline, navigation, armament, aerial photography, and flying—or be sent home.

"Failure," he writes, "doesn't occur to me."

Handsome Richard

JULY 28, 1939
LYMPNE, ENGLAND
DAY

Richard Hillary is Below Average.

And that is becoming a problem.

On the same date Geoffrey Wellum begins flight training, a cocksure Hillary is close to washing out. Everything in the Australian's life has come easy—until now. "A very casual pupil who has been slow to learn, he lacks keenness and I do not consider that he has any real interest in flying," writes Royal Air Force flight lieutenant Peter Dicken Cracroft, commander of the Oxford University Flying Squadron.

The assessment form offers Cracroft the choice between designating Hillary as Exceptional, Above Average, Average, or Below Average. The thirty-one-year-old lieutenant has spent two years training college boys to become pilots. Observing young men under extreme duress qualifies him as an expert in character judgment.

Cracroft writes a bold *YES* next to the last choice.

Richard Hillary is nineteen. Two years into Oxford. Rows crew. Known for his sexual appetite. Proudly wears his hair too long for RAF regulations, over his ears and collar, like at school. Asked to describe himself on the Royal Air Force Volunteer Reserve application, Hillary writes of being just over six feet tall, possessing a thirty-seven-inch chest, blond hair, gray eyes, and a scar under his chin from a childhood accident.

Richard Hillary
Shrewsbury School

That will not be the last blemish on his otherwise unmarked face.

The young pilot pens stories for the university newspaper and longs to be a writer. But that career must wait. With war looming, his immediate ambition is to fly in the RAF. "In a fighter plane, I believe, we have found a way to return to war as it ought to be, war which is individual combat between two people, in which one either kills or is killed," he tells a friend who plans to sit out the war as a pacifist.

"I shan't be sitting behind a long-range gun working out how to kill people sixty miles away. I shan't get maimed. Either I shall get killed or I shall get a few pleasant putty medals and enjoy being stared at in a night-club."

Hillary's blasé affectation and entitled behavior have long been his downfall, and he doesn't care. Despite the enormous charm he shows beautiful women, the pilot trainee was thrown off a Trinity shell for "lack of enthusiasm and cooperation." Hillary himself admits to being "disillusioned and spoiled." As Flight Lieutenant Cracroft's assessment shows, those habits now threaten Sergeant Hillary's chances of earning his pilot's wings.

Yet while he does not show it on the surface, a powerful new motivation grips Richard Hillary:

Reality.

Below Average will not see him pilot a single-seat fighter aircraft. Women will not smile seductively at him in nightclubs, marveling at the silver wings on his chest and the tailored drape of his air force blue tunic. There will be no aerial jousting. Instead, he will be sent to bombers, with their big crews of men squeezed inside a long, narrow fuselage, or to a squadron of two-man, open-cockpit Fairey Swordfish, a torpedo bomber and suicide machine so outdated that Wilbur and Orville Wright might have sketched its original design.*

That is, if Hillary gets his wings at all.

---

* Air force blue is actually azure, a color said to represent the sky on a clear day. However romantic that might be, the hue was initially chosen by the Royal Air Force due to a surplus of twill fabric of that color in the United Kingdom during World War I. This had been intended for export to Russia for use by Czar Nicholas's cavalrymen. The Russian Revolution ended the czar's reign, and with it the need for blue herringbone twill. The fabric, suddenly inexpensive and coincidentally perfect to differentiate pilots from ground soldiers, was put to use by the RAF. Air forces around the world use blue to this day.

The Veteran

Flight Lieutenant Peter Townsend is ready.

Hurricane pilot. Twenty-four. Joined the RAF nine years ago. Destined to be involved in a scandal not of his making.

The mood at 43 Squadron here in West Sussex is calm. Countryside. Close to the ocean. Yet war has arrived. Pilots are always at the ready. Planes fueled. Guns primed. Anticipation carries on the wind, informing every word, thought, and action.

Townsend and 43 went through the same drill one year ago, sleeping in tents near the runway, working with ground crews to belt ammunition, and improvising camouflage by slathering their silver aircraft with brown and green paint. This application increases drag and slows the planes, but sun bouncing off the skin of a shiny metal fuselage is a beacon to enemy fighters. Townsend believes this necessary desecration of their beautiful Hawker Furies was "an act of vandalism."

The squadron's work was for naught. British prime minister Neville Chamberlain visited Adolf Hitler for what became known as the Munich Conference. The squadron set aside their paintbrushes to stand down as Chamberlain returned to England with a promise of "peace in our time."

Hawker Furies are lithe biplanes with fixed landing gear and a top speed of 210 miles per hour. German fighters are 100 knots quicker, and able to climb higher and dive faster. The Fury is not a weapon but "a delightful plaything," in Townsend's words, the sort of plane a civilian gentleman flies for fun on a peaceful Sunday afternoon. "The Fury was sensual, thrilling, like a lovely girl, perfect in looks and manners," he now remembers fondly. If it had come to war, odds are that Townsend and his Fury would be shot from the sky.

Salvation arrives two months after Chamberlain's appeasement of Hitler. Gone is the Fury, and with it the fantasy that biplanes are still relevant in aerial combat. In its place, Hawker's muscular new weapon of war, the Hurricane, a broadsword to the Fury's penknife. Flight Lieutenant Townsend was immediately smitten.

Townsend revels in flying the "Hurry." The difference from the Fury to his audacious new fighter is that leap from flying fast in pleasant sporting fashion to balls-in-his-throat power. Top speed 6 miles per minute—almost twice as fast as the Fury. Maximum ceiling thirty-six thousand feet. Range six hundred miles. Retractable landing gear. The flight officer with an easy smile—whom some consider shy and others dashing—admits that the Hurricane lacks "the speed and glamour of the Spitfire." Yet he delights in his aircraft, a devout believer in its performance characteristics.

"The Hurricane," he argues like an apostate, is "a thoroughly war-like machine." In terse pilot tongue: "Rock solid as a platform for its eight Browning machine guns, highly maneuverable despite its large proportions, and with an excellent view from the cockpit."

Still, the Hurricane punishes bad pilots. The unforgiving nature of its design demands precise handling, especially at low altitude. At night, the Merlin in the nose blinds the pilot by shooting blue flame from the exhausts—a color that turns to yellow when the engine loses all power, as it is prone to do. Townsend has personally endured a loss of hydraulic brakes and witnessed a fellow pilot crash and burn when misjudging a night landing.

For Pete Townsend, that is a regretful part of getting to know his airplane—and preparing emotionally for battle.

In Germany, the Luftwaffe High Command is developing a five-point plan for waging an air war against England. The most pertinent items for Townsend and 43 Squadron are the first and last: (1) gain total air superiority over the Royal Air Force; and (5) take London after winning the air war.

Yet as armed conflict appears imminent once again, the veteran pilots of 43 have complete faith the battle will go their way.

"It was the Hurricane, really, which gave us such immense confidence," Townsend believes. "With its mighty engine, its powerful battery of guns, and its feel of swift, robust strength and the ability to outdo our enemies."

Townsend adds: "The Hurricane was our faithful charger and we felt supremely sure of it and ourselves."

The American

AUGUST 30, 1939
NEW YORK, NEW YORK
6:37 P.M.

Billy Fiske needs to get out of the country.

Before it's too late.

Long day of waiting. Fat gray clouds and a quarter inch of drizzle. Squall looming off Connecticut. The daredevil playboy stands on the main deck of RMS *Aquitania* in the muggy summer air. Sixty-nine degrees. Humid. Manhattan glides past. The Empire State Building rising above a horizon of rooftops.

Fiske might never see these sights again.

Hard not to think like that.

This is the last good time to sail for Europe. A French vessel, *De Grasse*, fled New York yesterday, carrying just thirty-four passengers. Flying a bright red Nazi swastika from her bow, *Bremen*, the name trimmed in gold, raced for Germany thirty minutes ago. *Normandie* remains tied to the end of Pier 88. The most glamorous ship in the world. Her French owners don't want to hemorrhage money by sending an empty liner across the Atlantic—and perhaps lose their majestic vessel to submarine attack.

They should have put to sea. *Normandie* will never leave New York again.*

Aquitania arrived yesterday from Southampton. She now turns right back around to make course for England before it's war. Windows blacked out, she slips her berth seven hours late because of a customs search. Lots of empty cabins. The manifest shows 434 passengers on a ship that can transport 2,200. Sir Ronald Lindsay, British ambassador to the United States, is on board, sailing into retirement. John Rhodes Cobb, a Briton who set the world land speed record of 367 miles per hour one week ago in Utah, also travels in first class.

This complement of minor celebrity includes Billy Fiske. Twenty-eight. American. Old-money wealthy. The two-time Olympic bobsled gold medalist served as US flag bearer during the 1932 Winter Games. Founded the first ski resort in a former silver mining town known as Aspen. Champion of the icy headfirst Cresta sled run in St. Moritz, where he is known to leap from the bar chandelier at Badrutt's Palace Hotel in a tuxedo. Actor Cary Grant was so jealous of Fiske's friendship with his wife that he once bribed operators at a Beverly Hills hotel to listen in on the playboy's phone calls. Fiske's 1938 wedding to Rose Bingham, titled Countess of Warwick during her first marriage to English aristocracy, made the society pages.†

Yet none of those are the most significant items on William Meade

---

* *Normandie* and her French crew will remain in New York, then the ship will burn and capsize in 1942. Foul play was suspected. RMS *Aquitania* was smaller and older than *Normandie* and *Bremen*. However, her nine hundred feet from bow to stern made her thirteen feet longer than *Titanic*, launched one year before *Aquitania* in 1911.

† Grant's wife was actress Virginia Cherrill, best known for her role with Charlie Chaplin in *City Lights*. Fiske produced the 1934 film version of *White Heat*, starring

Lindsley Fiske's résumé. Nor is the ironic coincidence that he was born on June 4, the same date as Great Britain's George III, who lost the American colonies during the War of Independence.

As he leaves America, perhaps forever, it is Fiske's willingness to fight for England that matters most. He attended Trinity Hall at Cambridge and worked as a banker in London. Dillon, Reed & Co. called him home to their New York office for his own safety as Americans fled Britain.

Now Billy Fiske is going back.

"The English have been damn good to me in good times so naturally I feel I ought to try and help out if I can," he writes to his sister, Peggy. "There are absolutely no heroics in my motives. I'm probably twice as scared as the next man, but if anything happens to me I at least feel I have done the right thing in spite of the worry to my family—which I certainly couldn't feel if I was to sit in New York making dough."

Billy Fiske has an elaborate plan to join the Royal Air Force and fly fighter aircraft. He is already a trained pilot, inspired by the movie *China Clipper* to take flying lessons in California three years ago. He refreshed that training last year at an airfield outside London, and was awarded an Aviator's Certificate by the Royal Aero Club of Great Britain. The daredevil currently has ninety solo hours to his credit.

Fiske has friends in the Royal Air Force's exclusive 601 Squadron. Formally known as the Royal Auxiliary Air Force Squadron, it is more often called the "Millionaires' Squadron" for its affluent membership. The 601 was just called up for war. Fiske attempted to join the unit one year ago, but the RAF refused, noting America's neutrality and stating that "it was not yet in the best interests of Britain to enlist American citizens."

So this time, Billy Fiske is pretending to be Canadian. As a member of the British Commonwealth, Canada is an active participant in the fighting. Now he just needs to convince an RAF selection board.

Cherrill and David Newell. She and Cary Grant divorced in 1935, after just one year of marriage.

Aquitania glides out into the Atlantic. Billy Fiske lingers on his final views of home.

Wall Street. Brooklyn.

Statue of Liberty backlit by the setting sun.

Next stop: England.

And, hopefully, a chance to wage war.

SINISTER TRANCE

1

THE LUFTWAFFE

SEPTEMBER 1, 1939
WIELUŃ, POLAND
4:40 A.M.

The Second World War begins now.*
Right now.
Six years since the "bomber gets through."
Five years since Winston Churchill warned England this would happen.
Three years since R. J. Mitchell and his gorgeous first Spitfire.
One year since four RAF pilots began the transition from young men to Nazi hunters.
And this embodiment of "sleepy little town" is defenseless, because despite many official British promises, those fliers and hundreds of RAF pilots just like them are sound asleep, not even dreaming in their wildest nightmares of flying to this sleepy little town's rescue.
Wieluń is wonderful. Idyllic.
And the most alone village in the entire world.

. . .

FRIDAY MORNING. TWENTY minutes to sunrise. Empty sidewalks. Spires and chimneys looming over the village square. Homes and shops and

---

* The precise time is still a matter of great debate. Some say the aerial bombing began as early as 4:30 that morning. However, the accepted moment of 4:40 for the dropping of the first bombs on Poland at Wieluń is five minutes before the artillery shelling of Westerplatte by German ground forces.

offices rise side by side without an alley. Catholics and Jews coexisting just as easily. The town baker, fine white flour coating fists and forearms, kneads morning rye in his warm, cramped shop. Night-shift Bernardine nuns who've given their lives to Jesus and nursing insert bedpans between sheets at *Szpital Wszystkich Świętych*—All Saints Hospital.

Nothing military about Wieluń.

Just a village.

But Wieluń stands between the German border and Poland's seat of power in Warsaw. Twenty unfortunate miles in one direction and one hundred twenty in the other. The centuries have been horrible. Wieluń has been attacked, pillaged, burned, and wasted by plague. A common thread to those tragedies was a portent of doom before tragedy descended.

Not this morning.

Two air wings of Junkers Ju-87B Stukas took off from the asphalt runways at Nieder-Ellguth airfield in Nazi Germany at 4:02 a.m. and flew east. As Wieluń's baker slides shaped loaves into his fiery ovens and the Bernardines collect morning ordure from their patients, whose lives they have taken a vow to protect, *Hauptmann* Walter Sigel guides twenty-nine aircraft from *Sturzkampfgeschwader* 76 and *Sturzkampfgeschwader* 2 *Immellman* toward pale orange rays of sunlight limning the horizon. Sigel is a man with high ambitions, proud in the knowledge that leading this morning's flight is an amazing honor. Easy smile, honest face, almost too tall for the cockpit.

Each Junkers *Flugzeug-und-Motorenwerke AG* Ju-87B-1 *Sturzkampf-flugzeug* ("diving combat aircraft") is fitted with an 1,100-pound *spreng dickwand*, or high-explosive device, designed to punch through concrete; two 110-pound SC50 fragmentation bombs; two wing-mounted MG-17 machine guns; and a single rear-facing 7.92mm machine gun operated by the second part of the two-man crew.

Piloting a Stuka is not a serene experience. In addition to the relentless thrum of a twelve-cylinder engine, the aircraft is outfitted with a wind-driven siren so loud, it can be heard thousands of feet below. Pilots privately complain about this apparatus affixed to their landing gear. Yet the banshee wail is synonymous with death itself. Terror on the ground is almost as horrific as the bombs to follow, a profound psychological trauma the Luftwaffe learned while carpet-bombing civilians during the Spanish Civil War. It is the private domain of all pilots, no matter the nation or airplane, to gripe among themselves about their aircraft. Outsiders have no say. Non-fliers have never been joined as one with such a machine, miles above the earth, diving and rolling and slashing through the sky like a saber, fist wrapped tightly around stick, feet tapping ballet on rudders, loins and legs and torso and brains above all else coursing with danger and adrenaline and something very much the opposite of sex—but far more immediate in the most heated moments.

And that's not even when another pilot is trying to shoot him from the sky.

So Walter Sigel grins broadly and revels in the din of his beloved Stuka's infamous sirens, particularly on this lovely morning over Wieluń, for he knows quite well the wail is waking the Polish people with a confusion they have never in their lives imagined.

. . .

THE STUKA IS also not pretty.

Nor fast.

But the thick, low-slung inverted gull wings are sturdy enough that a pilot can dive vertically and drop his payload at the least possible altitude.

Stukas almost never miss. The Zeiss gyro-stabilized bombsight is so precise that most bombs hit the target directly. Even the worst drops are within a hundred feet—easily inside blast radius.

Two weeks ago, at a demonstration of the Stuka's prowess for top Luftwaffe officials, *Hauptmann* Sigel put on an unplanned show of his own expertise. Weather reports that morning showed cloud cover beginning at an altitude of six thousand feet and descending to a base of twenty-five hundred, where the skies would become clear for the viewing party to witness the legendary dive-bomber drop cement practice bombs fitted with smoke flares.

Two miles above the ground, the thirty-three-year-old from Baden-

Stukas in flight
Heinrich Hoffman/Wikimedia Commons/Original image housed at the German Federal Archives

Württemberg maneuvered his formation of fourteen Stukas into position. After running the nine-step predive checklist, Sigel rolled the aircraft 180 degrees, dropping into a near vertical plunge. Descending close
to the aircraft's maximum speed of 373 miles per hour, Sigel's Stuka raced
toward earth at 9.5 seconds for every mile.*

Sigel entered the thick white cloud bank at six thousand feet, as predicted. His altimeter confirmed the height. Seven years' experience as a
pilot told Sigel that his aircraft would reemerge into daylight in just four
or five seconds. The veteran airman would then drop his bombs on the
test range at fifteen hundred feet, giving him plenty of time to pull out of
the dive.

Five seconds passed.

Then six.

Seven.

---

* Landing flaps at cruise position, elevator at cruise position, rudder trip at cruise position, contact altimeter on, contact altimeter set to release altitude, supercharger set to
automatic, throttle closed, cooler flaps closed, dive brakes open.

Eight.

The weather reports were very wrong.

"Pull out!" *Hauptmann* Sigel screamed over the radio.

Sigel's Stuka burst into daylight just three hundred feet off the ground. The stunned pilot yanked back hard on his steering column, simultaneously toggling a small knob to initiate the automatic pullout mechanism. Gravity pushed Sigel down hard into his seat and cut off blood flow to his brain. Thick gray haze settled over his eyesight. Less than ten feet off the ground, Sigel finally pulled out of the dive and regained altitude. The *hauptmann's* quick reaction saved his life and that of his gunner.

Thirteen other Stukas were not as lucky. Sigel's warning came too late. Twenty-six aircrewmen slammed into the ground, the rear-facing gunners barely knowing death was coming as the planes nosed in. Smoke rose through the clouds as aircraft exploded. Thousands of feet above the test range, a circling second wave of Stukas heard Sigel's scream over the radio and saw the ascending black columns, then called off their own dives.

The Neuhammer Stuka Disaster, as the tragedy became known, might have ended the career of a lesser wing commander. The gathered generals insisted on canceling further demonstrations and even disbanding Sigel's air wing. But a military tribunal cleared him of all responsibility, placing the blame on rapidly changing weather conditions.

So it is that *Hauptmann* Walter Sigel now begins the nine-step predive checklist once again, this time over Wieluń. Real bombs slung beneath his fuselage. The same military tribunal clearing him of responsibility for the Neuhammer Stuka Disaster is expecting the wing commander's aircrews to use Wieluń as a proving ground. The failed demonstration at Neuhammer will instead take place right now. Sigel's mission is to test an improved version of the Stuka, now outfitted with a new 1,150-horsepower engine twice as powerful as its predecessor.

Left unsaid is that the Luftwaffe plans to bomb civilians in this war. Sleepy little Wieluń, population sixteen thousand, is a dry run for larger cities with populations in the millions.

Walter Sigel's view through his Zeiss bombsight window on the cockpit floor is not that of a test range, but an actual town. No clouds to hide the target. No obstacles to mission success.

Nothing but pale blue dawn.

And a convenient bull's-eye.

Sigel focuses on the bright red cross painted on the roof of All Saints.

Speaking into the radio, he orders his pilots to make the hospital their primary target.

Luftwaffe protocol holds that the commander's aircraft leads order of attack. Walter Sigel will drop the first bomb.

World War II will not begin with a gunshot, like the Sarajevo assassination launching the First World War. It will commence with an explosive, free-falling quietly to earth, launched by *Hauptmann* Walter Sigel.

Flipping his Stuka into a half roll, Sigel stands the aircraft on its nose and dives on Weiluń like a peregrine falcon dropping on a field mouse.

.   .   .

SIX-YEAR-OLD JAN TYSZLER dreams of Stuka sirens.

Waking from a deep sleep, he jumps from bed in confusion. A handsome child with close-cropped brown hair and a big sister named Maria, who wears hers in a single long braid.

"At first, I didn't know what it was," he will remember as an old man. "I saw my parents out on the balcony. My mother told my father it was probably a test. My father agreed and wondered why they were doing it at such an early hour."

Then the bombs begin to fall.

All Saints is flattened, killing the six nurses and twenty-six patients. Nothing left but a crater the size of a small building. Nearby, St. Michael the Archangel Catholic Church, built in the fourteenth century, is also reduced to rubble.

Jan Tyszler and his family run from their home as bombs rain down. His father is a mechanic, and the family takes refuge in his garage, hiding in the car inspection pits.

As residents flee the city on foot, eight-year-old Josef Musial takes a last look at Wieluń's city center. The synagogue is in ruins, but some walls still stand. The small hotel and school are completely gone.

It's not just buildings. The death toll is more than twelve hundred men, women, and children.

"Everywhere lay corpses and body parts torn off: arms, legs, a head," young Musial will long remember.

Yet bombing is not enough for *Hauptmann* Walter Sigel.

Sigel did not fly in Spain. This is his first taste of total war. Just to make clear to his superiors that he is well aware total annihilation is part of the German fighting philosophy, the wing commander orders his crews to strafe civilians fleeing the bombings. The peasants of Wieluń don't have a chance, cut down at rooftop level by Stuka gunners.

Sigel and his crews fly back to base without the loss of a single plane. They land just after 5 a.m., in high spirits, bragging about their accuracy and reveling in the wonderful feeling of doing their jobs from the skies in such perfect weather.

"Objective destroyed. Fires observed," Sigel writes in the after-action report. His words are blasé, professional, inhumane.

"No particular enemy movements seen."

2

CHURCHILL

Great Britain breaks its promise.

A betrayal that should be corrected in the next few minutes. *Should* be.

Saturday night. Nine hundred miles west and thirty-eight hours since the bombing of Wieluń. House of Commons. Emergency session. Grim and irritated assemblage. Sidewalks outside Parliament throng with anxious citizens awaiting the news. Late last night, Great Britain issued Adolf Hitler an ultimatum demanding that Germany leave Poland or face war with England and France. No time limit was given for a response, but British government policy is to allow twenty-four hours before admitting rejection.

No news so far.

It has been a long day of waiting and delay for members of Parliament. Commons debated the National Service Act this afternoon, preparing for tonight's expected declaration of war. The bill would make all men, married and single, between eighteen and forty-one, liable for military service. Prime Minister Neville Chamberlain was not in attendance for that session, preferring to wait until this evening to announce his big news.

England quivers with anticipation.

Yet the declaration of war Chamberlain is sure to deliver should not be a surprise.

Progress toward conflict has been slow and then sudden. Ten days ago in Moscow, Germany and the Soviet Union signed the Molotov–Ribbentrop Pact, each party agreeing not to attack the other. This freed up both countries to invade Poland, one from the west and one from the east.

Right here in London, Britain and Poland then signed an "agreement of mutual assistance" in case of such an attack. England promised to provide "all the support and assistance in its power": planes, tanks, ships, artillery, soldiers. The British Army was once the greatest fighting force the world has ever seen. "In its power" speaks of a might that can stop the German Army in its tracks. An irritated Berlin pronounced this protection a British "blank check."*

Yet absolutely no action has been taken thus far.

More than four hundred members of Parliament jostle for space on the padded green benches of the eighty-seven-year-old chamber. Many spent the last three hours sucking on cigarettes and gin—a *lot* of gin—as they awaited the historic declaration. "The nervous house, chafing under delay, and genuinely distressed, some of them, by our guarantee to Poland having been immediately operative, quenched their thirsts in the Smoking Room, and when they returned to hear the PM's statement, many of them were full of 'Dutch Courage,'" parliamentary private secretary Henry Channon observes. "One noticed their flushed faces."†

It *has to be* war.

How else can Britain stop Adolf Hitler?

And if there is no war, why is London on wartime footing?

---

* The "agreement of mutual assistance" provoking the German "blank check" comment came two days after the August 25 agreement between Britain and Poland, Article I, of which reads: "Should one of the Contracting Parties become engaged in hostilities with a European Power in consequence of aggression by the latter against that Contracting Party, the other Contracting Party will at once give the Contracting Party engaged in hostilities all the support and assistance in its power."

† The forty-two-year-old Channon was Chicago born, but moved to the United Kingdom in 1920 to attend university. His nickname was "Chips." Channon made his fortune by marrying Lady Honor Guinness, heiress to the brewery of the same name. Channon's diaries recounting his decades in Parliament are considered some of the most insightful of his time.

All across England, the nation takes the extreme measures required of a nation ready to be attacked. Headlines scream, "Imminent Peril of War." The government is asking Britons to leave Germany for their own safety. Americans are being told to depart Great Britain for the same reason. The contrary US ambassador Joseph Kennedy remains in London but is about to send his children home. Medical students take breaks from surgical residencies to stack the sandbags protecting their hospitals from explosive ordnance. Ten thousand men train in London's parks to launch enormous antiaircraft barrage balloons. Forty-four million gas masks—a figure that includes children under the age of two—have been issued to civilians in case the Luftwaffe drops poison gas. Signs throughout London remind citizens that the sound of hand rattles will signal poison gas. The all clear is the ringing of handbells.

Air raid wardens are being trained in first aid, the extinguishing of small fires, and management of unexploded bombs. But there are plenty of other defense jobs for which volunteers are needed. "Men Wanted For Stretcher Parties," reads one handbill, "And They Are Wanted In Thousands For A Real Man's Job."

Every British citizen is required to know the location of their local air raid shelter. Lacking toilets, London's cavernous Underground stations are currently off-limits to escape potential bombings, though there is popular pressure to change that government decision.

Yet preparation turned to reality with yesterday's invasion of Poland. Great Britain is now in a state of nighttime blackout. Householders and businesses will be fined for not using drapes, paint, plywood, or cardboard to prevent light from escaping their homes and factories, which could potentially alert Luftwaffe bombers to precise target locations.

A heartbreaking plan known as Operation Pied Piper also commenced yesterday, young children wrenched from their parents and sent to live in the countryside for the duration. Germany will undoubtedly bomb London. Separation is for the good of Britain's next generation. The boys and girls will live with strangers paid for the inconvenience. Return and reunion are months, perhaps years away.

Per government edict, each child carries "a handbag or case containing the child's gas mask, a change of under-clothing, night clothes, house shoes or plimsolls, spare stockings or socks, a toothbrush, a comb, towel, soap and face cloth, handkerchiefs; and, if possible, a warm coat or mackintosh."

But farewell is messy, even in the best-organized circumstances. In the trauma of saying good-bye, not knowing precisely where their child is bound, tearful mothers press a sack lunch into their hands for the journey and pin luggage labels listing name and school to their child's coat.

Sobbing. Hugs. Long last squeeze.

Young faces pressed to windows as trains chug out of stations. Small hands waving good-bye, curling into fists, rubbing tear-filled eyes.

Great Britain is divided into three zones based on their relative safety: Evacuation, Neutral, and Reception. Pregnant women, mothers of babies or preschool children, and the elderly are also among those rallying at 1,589 assembly points, then boarding trains, buses, and ships for Reception. A train packed with children leaves London every nine minutes.

Evacuation is not compulsory. Yet such is the love of these British parents that they would rather endure separation than utter devastation: the unimaginable thought of their young child's body broken and mangled into the lifeless and unrecognizable by a German bomb.

So it is that a total of 673,000 schoolchildren, 406,000 mothers and preschool-aged children, and 3,000 expectant mothers will be relocated within the first three days, lest these families suffer the same grisly fate as the villagers of Wieluń.

Meanwhile, Poland burns. No trains whisking children to safety. No gas masks. Absolutely no need for blackout orders because the Luftwaffe controls the skies and Stukas dive-bomb in broad daylight.

Is this fate to befall London?

. . .

A HOSTILE HOUSE of Commons is called to order. Prime Minister Chamberlain takes his seat, knowing what he is about to say will be unpopular. Seventy, six feet two inches tall, clipped gray mustache, deep-set eyes, nose bent like a hawk's beak. Upright. Idealistic. Doomed. Officials in the

French government privately mock him as *faible* and *lâche*—weak and a coward.

Six months ago in this very chamber, with tension rising between Germany and Poland, Chamberlain offered his first assurance to the Poles: "In the event of any action which clearly threatened Polish independence," the prime minister vowed, "His Majesty's Government would feel themselves bound at once to lend the Polish Government all support in their power."

A solemn promise but just words, as it turns out.

And Adolf Hitler knows it.

The führer has played Chamberlain for a fool. All the world—except the British leader—seems aware. The two famously met one year ago in Munich, concluding with an agreement guaranteeing peace between Britain and Nazi Germany. In exchange, England would not contest Hitler's claims on Czechoslovakia.

Chamberlain called the pact "peace with honor."

"You were given the choice between war and *dis*honor," shot back one enraged member of Parliament. "You chose *dis*honor and you *will* have war."

That man is the fallen politician, Winston Churchill.

Winston Churchill   *Flickr*

Just yesterday, Neville Chamberlain invited him to join his new War Cabinet, a first step in Churchill's return from professional embarrassment. The sixty-four-year-old sits in the House tonight. Black bow tie, crisp white shirt, black suit dusted in cigar ash.

For almost a decade, Churchill has warned his nation that Hitler is a threat. Yet no one listened. The people of England, still reeling from the horrible death toll of the Great War, saw Churchill as a warmonger.

"There was a general readiness to believe that the Fuhrer," wrote the London *Daily Telegraph* about 1933 and Hitler's first days in power, "might show statesmanship and some respect for pledges which he gave in that office. The pledges were certainly encouraging. Europe was told that Herr Hitler rejected the use of force as a means of removing differences between states."

Hitler is uncouth but dynamic, a small, scowling former soldier and failed watercolor artist famous for his flamboyant speeches and Charlie Chaplin mustache. *Time* magazine called him "bristle-lipped, slightly pot-bellied," seeing no reason to fear the new German leader. They put him on the cover and named him "Man of the Year."

David Lloyd George, a former British prime minister, called Hitler the "George Washington of Germany," and paid a 1936 visit to the führer.

Edward, Prince of Wales, was filmed teaching his seven-year-old niece, Princess Elizabeth, how to deliver a straight-armed Nazi "Sieg heil" salute in 1933, three years before he ascended to the throne as King Edward VIII, only to abdicate eleven months later.

But Winston Churchill, who visited Germany during Hitler's rise to power and even read the führer's *Mein Kampf* manifesto, which advocated a German nation based on race and espoused hatred for the Jews, implored the people of Britain not to believe the *grosse Lüge*—"Big Lie."*

Great Britain refused to arm for the great war prophesied by Churchill.

---

* "If we want to score a victory, we must actively make use of lies. They have to be big. The bigger the lies the quicker people will believe them," Adolf Hitler stated, coining the term "Big Lie." Hitler used the Big Lie to spread untruths about Germany's Jewish population. Dictator Joseph Stalin didn't much like Hitler, but he appropriated the Big Lie to

The British scoffed when he predicted time after time that this day would come, so caught up were they in their fondness for Adolf Hitler and all things Nazi that Churchill became a national joke. A nation decimated by the staggering loss of its young men in the Great War was in denial about the threat, believing pacifism and appeasement of the Germans could prevent war.

Britain's greatest fear was the violent Communists of the Soviet Union. Hitler and Nazi Germany were a deterrent to that threat, a model for industry, prosperity...

...and peace.

Nothing said "peace" like Nazi Germany. The führer's avowed policy is "peace, reconciliation, and agreement as a basis of all decisions and every undertaking." Great Britain once believed him. Chamberlain believes him still. Yet Hitler has invaded Austria, Czechoslovakia, and now Poland.

Tonight, finally, the prime minister can reverse years of supplication.

All he has to do is find backbone.

Neville Chamberlain rises to address the House of Commons. The time is 7:44 p.m.

One Chamberlain loyalist is privy to what is about to come.

Chief Whip David Margesson is beside himself with laughter:

"I'd give a hundred quid to be present when Winston is told that there is to be no war."

---

explain purges of Soviet citizens. In America, almost a century later, the Big Lie is now woven into the fabric of daily political discourse.

3

CHURCHILL

SEPTEMBER 2, 1939
LONDON, ENGLAND
7:44 P.M.

Commons quiets.

"The PM rose, was cheered, but not over-much, and then he read out his statement, which was ill-conceived," private secretary Henry Channon, the American-born Chamberlain loyalist, will write.

"Ill-conceived" because Chamberlain does not declare war.

He ignores his own ultimatum. Instead, the prime minister states that if Nazi Germany "should agree to withdraw their forces, then His Majesty's Government would be willing to regard the position as being the same as it was before the German forces crossed the Polish frontier."

But Chamberlain gives no deadline for this withdrawal. Does not dictate consequences for failing to pull back. Instead, the prime minister states that Britain would be happy to mediate peace talks.

Neville Chamberlain's unfortunate speech lasts three minutes.

Howls fill the incredulous chamber. No one applauds, not even members of the prime minister's Conservative Party. Fury. A punch thrown but not landed. Two members vomit.

Chamberlain sits down.

"The House, thus prepared to unsheathe the sword, was aghast when it was hinted peace might yet be saved. I have never seen such an ugly exhibition: there were roars of disapproval; Duff Cooper, I hoped, would have an epileptic fit, as his cheeks, like an angry frog's, began to swell," adds Channon, speaking of an avowed Chamberlain opponent.

The opposition Labour Party is given a chance to respond.

Arthur Greenwood rises from the front bench. Not a great speaker. Not even a good speaker. Not even Labour Party's leader. He's filling in for Clement Attlee, who is in the hospital for prostate surgery. A lean fifty-nine-year-old with a thick Yorkshire accent and the gimlet squint of a longtime smoker, Greenwood is unsure and nervous. His prepared speech affirming Labour's favorable view of a war declaration is suddenly irrelevant.

Greenwood is utterly at a loss for words.

A helpful voice cries out.

"Speak for England!" yells sixty-five-year-old Leo Amery, an outspoken opponent of appeasement. One day soon, Amery will deliver the most important speech of his life. Chamberlain himself will state that in all his years in Parliament, he has never heard words land with such impact. But that is ten months from now. On this night, Amery exhorts Arthur Greenwood to seize this pivotal moment in British history and find the words for a great speech of his own.

The time is 7:48 p.m.

Arthur Greenwood finds the words.

"I am speaking under very difficult circumstances with no opportunity to think about what I should say, and I speak what is in my heart at this moment," states Greenwood.

"I am gravely disturbed. An act of aggression took place thirty-eight hours ago. The moment that act of aggression took place, one of the most important treaties of modern times automatically came into operation. There may be reasons why instant action was not taken," the temporary Labour leader says, references to Poland and Chamberlain plain.

"That delay might have been justifiable, but there are many of us on all sides of this House who view with the gravest concern the fact that hours went by and news came in of bombing operations, and news today of an intensification of it, and I wonder how long we are prepared to vacillate at a time when Britain and all that Britain stands for, and human civilization, are in peril."

Greenwood's voice grows more sure with every passing syllable.

"Tomorrow we meet at twelve. I hope the Prime Minister then—Well, he must be in a position to make some further statement—"

"Definite!" members of Parliament cry out, seconding the need for firm words.

"And I must put this point to him. Every minute's delay now means the loss of life, imperiling our national interests—"

"Honor," corrects a new voice from the Conservative side, that of Bob Boothby, an unwavering friend of Winston Churchill's.

But Arthur Greenwood will not be corrected.

"Let me finish my sentence.

"I was about to say: imperiling the very foundations of our *national honor*, and I hope, therefore, that tomorrow morning, however hard it may be to the right honorable gentleman—and no one would care to be in his shoes tonight." Here Greenwood speaks carefully of Neville Chamberlain, following parliamentary protocol by not using his actual name. "We shall know the mind of the British Government, and that there shall be no more devices for dragging out what has been dragged out too long.

"The moment we look like weakening, at that moment dictatorship knows we are beaten. We are *not* beaten.

"We *shall not* be beaten.

"We *cannot* be beaten.

"But delay is dangerous.

"And I hope the Prime Minister—it is very difficult to press him too hard at this stage—will be able to tell us when the House meets at noon tomorrow what the final decision is, and whether then our promises are in process of fulfillment, for in my mind there can be no escape now from the dilemma into which we have been placed. I cannot see Herr Hitler, in honesty, making any deal which he will not be prepared to betray.

"Therefore, thinking very hurriedly in these few moments, I believe that the die is cast, and we want to know in time."

· · ·

PARLIAMENT ADJOURNS. GREENWOOD'S words resonate, so powerful that he privately tells other MPs Chamberlain will lose his job in the morning unless war is declared.

Winston Churchill has remained silent throughout the two speeches. He is revered for his brilliant oratory but has chosen not to speak tonight. As a fellow conservative, it would be inappropriate to publicly rail against the prime minister at such a raw moment.

Yet Adolf Hitler must be confronted.

And Winston Churchill well knows the power of private conversations.

Leaving the din behind, Churchill steps out into the utter darkness of blacked-out London. His flat at Morpeth Mansions is just a half mile away. The night is young for an energetic aging man like Churchill, so fond of working past midnight. His polymath mind darts to and fro, lost in a bold new plan of his own invention. Even as he walks home, bodyguard a few feet back, Churchill organizes those thoughts.

The nighttime air smells like rain. Strong winds buffet his pale cheeks.

Winston Churchill wants to fight back against Adolf Hitler. Starting tonight.

And he is determined to find a way.

4

CHURCHILL

Air raid warnings pierce London.

For the first time.

Hardly the last.

Sunday morning. One instant after Great Britain declares war on Germany. Winston and wife, Clementine, just heard the announcement on the BBC. He is due in Parliament in little more than half an hour. Unlike last night, Churchill will take the floor and speak. Yet now his departure is delayed. Perhaps there will be no Parliament at all when this enemy raid is over.

How is it possible that German bombers can be here so soon? Britons have been told an air raid warning will be "a succession of intermittent blasts sounded by hooters and sirens." Or they may hear the sound of a "fluctuating or warbling signal of varying pitch"—both of which may or may not be accompanied by "sharp blasts on police whistles."

Yet Churchill will long remember "a strange, prolonged, wailing noise, afterward to become familiar," he will write. "My wife came into the room braced by the crisis and commented favorably on the German promptitude and precision."

"You know, you've got to hand it to Hitler," Winston responds in reference to the sirens. "The war is only a half-hour old and already he has bombers over London."

The couple hurries for the air raid shelter. Their flat is in a redbrick apartment building. Top two levels. Elevator from the lobby to the fifth floor, with its entrance hall, kitchen fit for a very small sailboat, and a study so cramped Churchill writes standing up. A narrow circular staircase spirals up to the sixth-floor bedrooms.

History was made in these rooms last night. This air raid warning is a direct result. As a freak deluge of rain lashed London, the lightning and thunder crackled and boomed so loud and so close, they felt like a rifle firing from inside his own skull, Churchill flexed a political muscle that had withered for a decade.

He fought for, and received, this confrontation. Not because he is a warmonger but because the safety and future of his nation depend upon it.

Last night, right here in Number 11, Churchill and a rogue band of politicians gathered to foment rebellion. Two hours after Parliament adjourned, Churchill summoned his gang of five to Morpeth Mansions—Anthony Eden, Duff Cooper, Bob Boothby, Brendan Bracken, Duncan Sandys. In a sharply worded letter, written by Churchill and delivered to the prime minister after midnight, the furious coalition demanded Chamberlain finally stand up to Nazi Germany. If not, they would find the votes to remove him as prime minister.

As with Adolf Hitler, Neville Chamberlain bent the knee.

That voice the Churchills were listening to on the radio was the prime minister's. Chamberlain's speech lasted five minutes. He spoke in a slow, deep tone, every carefully articulated syllable projecting a note of apprehension. Rather than inspire Britain in this time of crisis, Chamberlain's words were tinged with fear, as if he—and by proxy Great Britain—were powerless to stop the unpredictable Adolf Hitler and his mighty war machine.

"Now may God bless you all," Chamberlain said in closing. "May He defend the right. For it is the evil things that we shall be fighting against—brute force, bad faith, injustice, oppression, and persecution—and against them I am certain that the right will prevail."

The air raid sirens wail just after Chamberlain utters "prevail."

Like all Londoners, the Churchills have been told in advance where to seek safety. Their neighborhood bomb shelter is a basement one hundred yards down the street. Residents of Morpeth Mansions are already hurrying from their apartments and racing for underground refuge.

But Winston Churchill wants to see the Germans with his own eyes.

Winston and Clementine climb up to the "flat top of the house to see what was going on," he will write. As top-floor residents, they have the only apartment with access to the roof.

Despite the grave risk, Inspector Walter Thompson, the lanky forty-nine-year-old former Scotland Yard detective recently rehired to serve as Churchill's bodyguard, has no choice but to join them.

·   ·   ·

THE WARM MORNING air smells like vindication.

Low black wrought iron railing lines the top of the mansard roof. Towering chimney to the left. Winston and Clementine scan the eastern skyline, craning their heads up into the clear blue morning, searching for the first wave of German bombers. Seeing none, Churchill finds himself taken with this unusual view. "Around us on every side, in the clear, cool September light, rose the roofs and spires of London. Above them were already slowly rising thirty or forty cylindrical balloons."

Square tower of the Catholic cathedral just across the street striped in red brick and white stone. Beyond the main sanctuary's great vaulted roof, the icons in profile: Big Ben, Parliament, Westminster Abbey.*

Winston and Clementine agree that the sudden appearance of inflatables meant to halt low-flying aircraft proves England is adequately prepared for war.

Churchill gave a name to his experiences during the 1930s, spent as a figure of scorn and ridicule: the Wilderness Years. The man who has held every major cabinet office except foreign secretary and prime minister

---

* The Catholic church is known as Westminster Cathedral, first opened in 1903. Though both share a similar name, this magnificent structure is separate and distinct from the Church of England's nearby Westminster Abbey.

was reduced to a powerless parliamentary backbencher with no political currency beyond his words and beliefs.

Now those Wilderness Years are over.

The resurgent Winston Churchill standing on the roof of Number 11 is robust, short, pugnacious. Light red hair reduced to a tonsure. Omnipresent cigar and impish smile in the place of his normal scowl.

Clementine is opposite in almost every way: a head taller, ten years younger, hair gone gray, not given to excess.

Winston and Clementine Churchill in London   *Flickr*

He is prone to his "black dog" of depression. She can be anxious. Their love is built on loyalty and respect, although Clementine found her future husband a "boor" the first time they met. Yet the couple is not without romance. Clementine's first impression was replaced by a loyalty so fierce, she once saved his life by pulling him from the path of an oncoming train. An irate suffragette had pushed him into its path. Winston Churchill missed death by inches.

Churchill's fall began during the war in 1915, when he resigned his cabinet position as first lord of the Admiralty, in part due to his role in the disastrous Gallipoli assault.* Leadership of the Royal Navy was a job Churchill deeply adored for the chance to craft policy and strategy, as well as to spend time on board ships at sea. Hours were spent scrutinizing complicated maps laid out in his office, tracking the precise locations of the British fleet. But after four years in power, Churchill was first lord no more. His reputation in shambles, he left his sea charts hidden behind a secret panel in his private office and departed London for the frontline trenches.

Through the next fifteen years, he struggled to maintain his place in government, leaving Parliament between 1922 and 1924 before seeking election once again. But it was the loss of prestige and position and his near financial ruin during the 1930s that brought Churchill to his lowest ebb.

Yet the charismatic politician was not without friends. After Churchill lost much of his fortune in the Wall Street Crash of 1929, more than 140 friends pooled their money to buy him a new car. Among those contributing to the purchase of a black 1932 Daimler landaulette limousine were the Prince of Wales, Charlie Chaplin, and economist John Maynard Keynes.

The Wilderness Years were not just hard politically, but also the roughest of the thirty years the Churchills have been married. Finances are an issue. Their rows are epic. Divorce has quietly been placed on the table, then just as quietly removed. The couple has four children but sleep in separate rooms, are rarely seen together in public, and don't even vacation together—Clementine preferring the British shore, while her husband adores the Mediterranean. He is public, while she is private. He is keen to spout his opinions, and she is unafraid to tell him he is wrong. So great is Clementine's wrath that Winston often refers to her as

---

* The withdrawal from the Gallipoli Peninsula on December 15 to 20, 1915, came after British and Commonwealth troops failed to break through by land to open the narrow and strategically vital Dardanelles Straits to Allied shipping. One hundred and fifteen thousand soldiers were killed or wounded—of whom half were British or Irish. Winston Churchill was the architect of this doomed offensive.

"She-whose-commands-must-be-obeyed"—as he did in 1913, because he was learning to pilot airplanes, then gave up flying altogether when she demanded he stop out of fears he might kill himself.

Yet it is impossible to imagine Winston's perseverance without Clementine's steel.

For all these reasons, and countless more, the Churchills delight in each other.

The sirens are replaced by silence. But there is no "continuous signal at a steady pitch" designating "all clear" in the words of official government warnings.

Winston and Clementine remain in the open air. The clear, lovely morning shows no sign of last night's political donnybrook. Inspector Thompson hovers. Clementine resents his intrusion into her marriage, soon to refer to the detective as a "perpetual annoyance."*

Minutes pass. Not a Stuka in sight. Nor a Dornier. Nor a Heinkel. It's all looking more and more like a drill. Yet "Raiders Passed," as the all clear is formally known, has yet to sound. The couple chooses to take no further chances. Stepping down from the roof, "we made our way to the shelter assigned to us," Churchill will remember of that reluctant descent, with its quick stop at his liquor cabinet for supplies, "armed with a bottle of brandy and other appropriate medical comforts."

But even as he makes light of what appears to be a drill or false alarm, the man so fond of all things British looks at the empty streets and has a grim vision of what is to come. A governmental Committee of Imperial Defence recently announced that London should expect at least sixty days of Luftwaffe bombing, resulting in 600,000 dead and 1.2 million

---

* Inspector Thompson first served as Churchill's bodyguard from 1921 to 1935, when Thompson retired to open a small grocery store. On August 22, 1939, Churchill sent the detective a telegram requesting his immediate return to service. Thompson would go on to serve throughout the war. The two men became great friends, and Thompson later published books about their time together. W. H. Thompson died of cancer on January 18, 1978, at the age of eighty-seven.

wounded. Burial forms and papier-mâché coffins are already being produced for this tragedy.

Winston Churchill has been a member of Parliament for almost forty years. His syphilitic father served two decades before him and very nearly became prime minister. Thus these are not anonymous roads and paths but neighborhoods of which Churchill is deeply fond. The prescient politician knows every building and steeple; he has taken every shortcut, driven every street, walked every sidewalk. This heartbeat of Central London—from Buckingham Palace to the River Thames, Trafalgar Square to Big Ben, seat of British power for centuries—holds a unique place in Churchill's breast. So, as he looks at these streets with the new eyes of a man whose nation is not only at war, but sure to see destruction rain down from the skies, the black dog takes hold.

For he knows all that is about to come is his doing.

"My imagination drew pictures of ruin and carnage and vast explosions shaking the ground," he will write of this moment.

"Of buildings clattering down in dust and rubble, of fire brigades and ambulances scurrying through the smoke, beneath the drone of hostile aeroplanes."

That premonition, as Churchill well knows, will most surely come true.

Yet while he has the political clout to force a war, Winston Churchill remains subordinate to Neville Chamberlain and lacks the authority to take the fight to Adolf Hitler.

For now.

5

CHURCHILL

Parliament is silent, grim, tardy.

"Echoes of the first 'all clear' signal had only just died away when the House of Commons assembled," London's *Daily Herald* will report. "The sitting, timed for noon, was a few minutes late."

Full house. Press, diplomats, strangers, and MPs "packed in like sardines," Soviet ambassador Ivan Maisky will tell his diary.

For good reason. The Commons Chamber is intimate for acoustical purposes, a cramped seventy-five feet long, forty-five feet wide, and forty-one feet high. Oak paneled walls. Stained glass windows. Green.*

Speaker of the House of Commons Edward FitzRoy presides over debates from a chair so tall, it requires a footstool. This stately throne of carved wood, padded in green morocco leather, faces a wide aisle. The party in power sits to FitzRoy's right, facing the opposition across the aisle on his left. Their benches are also upholstered in green. Members

---

* In medieval times, green represented nature's bounty and fertility. The shade of green did not matter. English archers all wore green, which added a military symbolism. Green became the predominant color for fabrics, painting, and other decoration of royal palaces and Parliament, a tradition dating back to the twelfth century. This later carried over into other aspects of daily life, many which survive to this day. The term "green-room" derives from the color's theatrical use, meaning a place to wait before going onstage. And to this day, billiards tables and card tables are covered in green.

wishing to change political affiliation publicly stand and walk from one side to the other. This powerful statement is such a fixture of British life that "crossing the aisle" is synonymous with changing one's mind.

There will be none of that drama this afternoon.

Yet the focus is still on the aisle. The Table of the House—also covered in green leather—fills the center. This will be the hub of today's action. This is where each speaker will stand. The five-foot-long ceremonial mace signifying the power to govern rests on top. Three clerks sit at the far end of the desk, facing the speaker. Black silk robes, white bow ties, bobbed white wigs. These gentlemen referee and record all decisions made in the chamber each day, their chairs also upholstered in green morocco.*

Tiers of seating rise above this lower level. Guests are separated by role, power, and sex: Reporters' Gallery above the speaker's chair. Ladies' Gallery behind the journalist. The Ambassadors Gallery, Distinguished Strangers' Gallery, and Ordinary Strangers' Gallery look down over the far end of the chamber.

Commons has seats for only 460 of the 615 members, yet on this most dramatic day, every MP fights to be in attendance. They press together on the benches, bodies close enough to smell coffee breath, Pears Transparent bath soap, Geo. Trumper's "Eucris." None of yesterday's drunkenness. The desperate clamor for seats, the air raid drill keeping the chamber empty until minutes ago, and Parliament's first session of the war require no alcohol to fuel aggression.

Ambassador Maisky observes the mood is "heavy, menacing, and oppressive."

In the Ambassadors Gallery, United States diplomat Joseph Kennedy makes a point not to sit next to his Soviet counterpart.†

---

* The clerk's record of decisions is separate from Parliament's Hansard, an official verbatim record of all that is said. The speaker of the House of Commons is an elected member of Parliament, but the clerk of the House is a civil servant. This is to maintain impartiality.

† There are several galleries in the House of Commons, many with interesting stories. The Ladies' Gallery was hidden behind a brass grille until 1917. And until 2004 it was

Kennedy is fifty. Awful. The kind of man who brings his mistress on a family vacation. Round owl eyeglasses, hair slicked straight back, bow-legged. Staunch isolationist, stars in his eyes for Adolf Hitler, hopes to run for president in 1940 on an anti-war platform. Kennedy makes no apologies for admiring the Nazi regime over the Communist ideology of the Soviet Union. One British Foreign Office official, Robert Vansittart, believes Kennedy's publicly expressed views make the ambassador "a very foul specimen of double-crosser and defeatist."

Yet Kennedy's opinions are popular in America, espoused by isolationists Henry Ford and Charles Lindbergh. The transatlantic pilot, who believes President Roosevelt, Jews, and the British are trying to force America into the conflict, thinks war "would be the greatest disaster this country has ever passed through."

These men are far from alone: Americans are overwhelmingly opposed to fighting another European war. Even with Europe on the verge of disaster, Congress is reluctant to approve funding to expand and update the American military. A series of three congressional "Neutrality Acts" severely restrict President Franklin Roosevelt from assisting the British.

A scowling Joe Kennedy gives up his prestigious front row seat to perch one row behind Maisky rather than give the appearance of alignment. Behind him, his wife, Rose, and adult children, Joe Jr., John, and Kathleen, take seats in the Strangers' Gallery, where there is no class separation. On this important afternoon, everyone is "Distinguished."

Session comes to order. Five minutes of housekeeping. Standing ovation from the backbenchers as a weary Prime Minister Chamberlain strides slowly into the chamber and sits front row right.

Little to discuss. That which divided the House last night is no longer an issue. Yet speeches must be made: Chamberlain's emotional admission

---

parliamentary custom to refer to someone physically present in the House of Commons but not a member of Parliament or a parliamentary official as a "stranger." The statement "I Spy Strangers" was the traditional request for members of the public to leave the galleries so the chamber could sit in private. That term was abolished by a modernization committee in 1998. The Strangers' Gallery is now known as the Public Gallery.

Joseph Kennedy
Wide World Photos

that "everything that I have believed in during my public life has crashed into ruins."

Greenwood confirming that Labour will go to war.

Liberal Party leader Sir Archibald Sinclair reaching for an original cause and settling on solidarity with France, most likely the next nation on Hitler's invasion agenda.

Now Winston Churchill has something to say.

Joseph Kennedy pays attention. The two know each other well. Even before becoming ambassador, Joe and Rose visited Churchill's country home, Chartwell. This past July, the Kennedy family was invited to a lavish coming-out party for the debutante daughter of Churchill's cousin. One guest was overheard commenting that Churchill was a "poor old has-been" and a "potential troublemaker."

Ambassador Kennedy is keen to hear what trouble Churchill plans to make. The two men have had conversations about a "special relationship" between America and Britain through which the nations would stand side by side as the world's great powers. For Kennedy, this bond does not include war. He considers Hitler unbeatable.

Members hush, anticipating the mesmerizing peculiarities of Churchill's speaking voice: nasal, small lisp, a bleat, a bark. His words will matter.

Always, the words.

Winston Churchill is not yet a heavy man and hardly a tall man. Nor a powerful man, though that is changing before Parliament's eyes. Certainly, a complex man.

The black, chalk-striped suit. The gold Breguet pocket watch no. 765 his children call "the turnip." The cigar.

Always, the cigar.

Churchill is the voice of his nation. Has been for quite a while. No one thought so until right now—though in hindsight, these men and women who disparaged him as a has-been are admitting to themselves they knew it all along.

The time is 12:21 p.m. One hour since the air raid siren. Churchill provides a new kind of warning, this one couched in idealism and perseverance.

"In this solemn hour it is a consolation to recall and to dwell upon our repeated efforts for peace. All have been ill-starred, but all have been faithful and sincere. This is of the highest moral value—and not only moral value, but practical value—at the present time," Churchill begins.

"Outside, the storms of war may blow and the lands may be lashed with the fury of its gales, but in our own hearts this Sunday morning there is peace. Our hands may be active, but our consciences are at rest," he continues, artfully weaving last night's gale and this morning's blue skies into a subtle reminder that Britain did not ask for this war.

Churchill reminds the crowd why their nation must win.

"We are fighting to save the whole world from the pestilence of Nazi tyranny and in defense of all that is most sacred to man. This is no war of domination or imperial aggrandizement or material gain, no war to shut any country out of its sunlight and means of progress. It is a war, viewed in its inherent quality, to establish, on impregnable rocks, the rights of the individual, and it is a war to establish and revive the stature of man."

Churchill closes with a reminder of the hardships to come for Britain and the hope for a bright tomorrow for the whole world: "We look forward to the day, surely and confidently we look forward to the day, when our liberties and rights will be restored to us, and when we shall be able to share them with the peoples to whom such blessings are unknown."

The speech lasts all of five minutes. MP's rise from the packed benches and surround him, eager to shake Churchill's hand in congratulations.

The transformation from scolding prophet to visionary leader is almost complete.

. . .

THE PRIME MINISTER beckons Churchill to 10 Downing Street. Clementine waits in the Daimler. Both Churchills know Neville Chamberlain may offer him an even more prominent role in the war effort.

Winston steps through the shiny black Georgian front door, following in the literal footsteps of great Britons like William Pitt the Younger and the Duke of Wellington. Heavy oak. Brass letter box. The zero on the door number is actually the letter "O."

Churchill returns moments later.

"It's the Admiralty," Winston tells Clementine, stepping into his limousine's passenger compartment.

Nothing more needs to be said.

Yet the Royal Navy has something to add. At the direction of the Admiralty Board, an emphatic message of warning, surprise, and exclamation flashes to all British ships around the world, in port or at sea, about the returning first lord.

Churchill gets right to work. "I therefore sent word to the Admiralty that I would take charge forthwith and arrive at six o'clock."

He is saluted as he steps into the Admiralty building for the first time in twenty-five years. Churchill eagerly bounds up a stairway to his former office and heads straight for the hidden panel where he left his sea maps so long ago.

They remain untouched.

In the midst of his enthusiasm, Churchill is told the precise wording of the Royal Navy's message to the fleet. He could not be more amused.

The missive is three short words:

"Winston is back."

6

DOWDING AND 85 SQUADRON

SEPTEMBER 6, 1939
BENTLEY PRIORY, ENGLAND
6:30 A.M.

Stuffy is in charge.

For now.

German bombers vector toward London. The Filter Room is alive. Calm, busy. Quiet chatter. Blue uniforms around the big map table. Bumping and jostling, but politely. Plotters, filterers, range cutters, controllers, tellers. Everyone knows their job. Half-smoked cigarettes ignored in ashtrays. Morning tea going cold. *"New raid appearing,"* a teller begins the outgoing transmission in a calm, efficient voice. Speaks into a headset telephone. Sequence is always the same: raid number, alpha identifier, big-map grid reference, direction, number of aircraft, "Angels" for altitude.*

Like this: *Hostile 12, Beer William four niner, zero two, Northwest, thirty-five aircraft, Angels twenty thousand.*

The message is phoned to Biggin Hill, North Weald, Debden, Duxford, Hornchurch. Fighter Groups 11 and 12. Pilots sprint through thick fog from tents pitched twenty paces from their aircraft. Boots for warmth at altitude, kapok vest for flotation in case of ditching in the Channel. Some still in pajamas beneath their flight uniforms. Parachutes waiting at

---

* Plotters from the Women's Auxiliary Air Force (WAAF) will join their male RAF counterparts in the Filter Room beginning on September 19.

their planes. Almost no man older than twenty-five. A few younger than twenty.*

. . .

BACK IN THE Filter Room, Air Marshal Dowding looks down on the action from the gallery. Crisp uniform, peaked cap with RAF badge and gold braid. Unsmiling lips beneath a salt-and-pepper mustache. Uncomfortably direct gaze.

Air Marshal Hugh Dowding
Picryl/Original image housed at the Imperial War Museums

---

* Kapok is a moisture-resistant fiber obtained from the seedpods of silk-cotton trees. It is five times more buoyant than cork. The first true parachute for fighter aircraft was invented by American pilot Floyd Smith in 1914. Smith designed what would become known as a "rip cord," which allowed the pilot to deploy his chute by pulling a handle attached to his harness. Smith's young wife, Hilder, first tested the new design over the Pacific Ocean that year. The nonswimmer, not knowing her husband had dropped her over water to adjust for the drift toward land, grabbed back clumsily at the plane after jumping, causing a fast spin that twisted her lines upon deployment. She recovered and landed safely, barely missing the upper masts of naval vessels in Los Angeles Harbor.

Plotters like croupiers setting down markers of the approaching attack—blue circles, yellow triangles, and red squares. On the wall, a list of every squadron. A red light shows those in flight (Committed). Green for standby (Reserve). Everything Dowding needs to know in one glance. The widower has strategized three years for this moment. Converted a windowless ballroom into the hub of England's top secret air defense network. To all the world, this is just a stately pale green mansion and deer park in northern London. Cedar forest, complicated gardens, rolling green hills. Barbed wire, sandbags, and sentries standing guard give it away to passersby on the Stanmore road. Dowding's sister, Hilda, keeps house for him in a large residence in town known as Montrose House. Air Marshal Dowding walks the mile and a half to work each day.

Hard man to know, though the *Guardian* does its best: "The man in the street is mainly concerned with the Fighter Command, which is charged with the protection of the said man and his hearth and home against enemy bombers," writes the *Guardian*. "Its A.O.C.-in-C is Air Chief Marshal Sir Hugh Dowding.[*]

"In the service he is known as 'Stuffy,' but nobody can tell how this nickname arose, for he is a genial as well as an able man of 57. He commands the fighter aircraft, the A.A. guns and searchlights, the barrage balloons, and the Observer Corps."

Adds the newspaper: "He is a strong believer in the superiority of air defence over attack."

Dowding is also a confirmed believer in spirits and fairies. That is for his private life, yet many within the British military find his faith in fighter defense just as suspect. Airplanes were a sidebar to the last great war. Many still believe Britain should rely on the navy for protection, which Dowding finds laughable. "Battleships?" he responded when told that money spent on new airplanes should instead fund more dreadnoughts. "Luftwaffe bombers are shooting off the assembly lines in

---

[*] Air Officer Commanding-in-Chief.

Germany, and you think battleships are going to keep them out of the skies over England? Are you mad?"

Dowding knows Hitler's Luftwaffe outnumbers the Royal Air Force in fighters, bombers, and pilots by a ratio of almost three to one. His faith in the Spitfire's and the Hurricane's ability to intercept and shoot down sleek, multi-engine bombers is complete, and he disbelieves that "the bomber will always get through."

It is Dowding who oversaw development of those fighters. Pushed for the construction of all-weather runways. When his demand for bullet-proof windscreens was rejected by the Air Ministry as too expensive—and he was told that his pilots should instead be "more nimble" in their flying—an unruffled Dowding responded in typically direct fashion: "Well, the way I see it, if Chicago gangsters can have bulletproof glass in their cars, my pilots will have bulletproof glass in their fighters. The only thing standing between your houses and loved ones will be the willing-ness of my fighter pilots to close with German bombers, something they will be more than glad enough to do if they just had a fighting chance to stay alive."

Dowding got his glass.

Yet even as war begins, Stuffy's career is already over—three years from retirement age but being forced out. Dowding is unwavering in loy-alty to his pilots, and they, in turn, revere him as their leader. But this has political cost. He says things he shouldn't say and angers people he shouldn't anger. "I have never accepted ideas purely because they were orthodox," he freely admits. "Consequently, I frequently found myself in opposition to generally accepted views."

Dowding was supposed to be gone in May, but no one was ready to take his place. "In view of the importance of . . . Fighter Command," read the letter asking him to stay on, "it has been decided to ask you to defer your retirement until the end of March 1940."

That gives Dowding just seven more months to perfect his air defense network.

England's Bomber Command is separate and distinct, under the authority of an air marshal with an entirely different military mindset. But Hugh Dowding *is* Fighter Command. Stuffy is the first and only man to lead this newest branch of the Royal Air Force and seems to be the only individual who understands that German bombings will lead to German invasion.*

Great Britain's air defense network is even known as the Dowding System.

. . .

THE DOWDING SYSTEM ends with fighters.

Three squadrons per air base. Each squadron numbers twelve aircraft. Split into two flights of six ("A" flight and "B" flight), which then branch into two formations of three planes coded by color—Red, Yellow, Blue, and Green.

One flight at a time is launched. This is important: scramble too many aircraft, and Fighter Command runs the risk of losing all its meager resources to one massive Luftwaffe raid.

Upon sighting the enemy, a pilot radios the cry "Tallyho" and engages.

What happens next is up to the pilot.

. . .

THE DOWDING SYSTEM divides Great Britain into four geographical air groups.

For reasons no one can explain to Stuffy Dowding, these are numbered 10, 11, 12, 13. London and England's southeast coast are 11 Group. Midlands is 12 Group. Wales is 10. Scotland and the North lucky 13.†

Each Group has its own Operations Room and map table.

---

* Air Chief Marshal Sir Edgar Rainey Ludlow-Hewitt led Bomber Command until he was replaced in April 1940 for what was considered an overly cautious use of bombers. In addition to Fighter and Bomber, the RAF also had Coastal and Training Commands.

† Actually, there is an explanation. Bomber Command controls Groups 1 to 5. This subtle prioritizing of bombers over fighters shows the predominant tactical thinking of the Royal Air Force that would continue throughout the war. It was also thought that only bombers needed concrete all-weather runways. Dowding bristled at this mindset.

Each Group is divided into Sectors, centered around individual air-fields.

Each Sector also has an Operations Room and map table.

Information flows from Dowding's Filter Room to the Group Operations Room down to the Sector Operations Room.

Information becomes orders.

.   .   .

The Dowding System begins with advanced warning.

Coastal Radio Direction Finding towers pick up enemy bombers and fighters, and flash their position, strength, height, and estimated direction back to Fighter Command in Bentley Priory. Coastal watchers using binoculars confirm the attack to Fighter Command, adding precise numbers and heading.

Fighter Command Headquarters *filters* this information in the Filter Room. The centerpiece is an enormous table map showing Britain and its coastal approaches. Filterers specially trained to process raw data have two minutes to triangulate current location, number of enemy aircraft, altitude, and anticipated target. One filterer for each RDF tower. Even a few seconds more will cost pilots precious time in advancing toward the enemy and climbing to a fighting altitude. Aerial combat is chess on a multidimensional blue board, sprawling dozens of miles to the left and right, 6 miles up and down, and every angle in between. At 5,000 feet on a brilliant day a man can see 85 miles. At 10,000 feet, 120 miles. But at 20,000 feet, that range expands to 170 miles, far enough to see from London to a horizon point deep in France. Better to get up high and wait on the enemy—preferably with the sun at your back.

Yet the filterer's decision must not be rushed. Poor filtering means German bombers might be flying in a completely different direction—and not be found at all when a clear-blue-sky flying day becomes a maze of clouds, haze, blinding sunshine, and lighting refraction caused by dense layers of cold air forming above the warmer surface of the English Channel.

So it is that the filterer makes furious mental calculations with the clock ticking.

Then tells the teller.

Who tells the Operations Rooms in each Group and Sector.

Which scramble fighter pilots.

Who take to the skies and shout "Tallyho!"

. . .

THE DOWDING SYSTEM fails on September 6, 1939.

This debacle is what Stuffy Dowding now witnesses from the Filter Room gallery.

. . .

A SEARCHLIGHT BATTERY in the Thames estuary. Low, thick gray pre-dawn coastal soup. Watchers hear a plane somewhere overhead but cannot verify type, altitude, or direction. The sighting is not a sighting at all, just the ominous drone of an unseen aircraft flying in the vague direction of London. In these panicked first days of war, that is enough.

The intruder's presence has not yet been confirmed by the special three-hundred-foot-tall steel transmitter masts installed at Air Marshal Dowding's insistence, utilizing the new Radio Direction Finding technology. Code-named Chain Home, these RDF stations along Britain's southern and eastern coasts detect incoming aircraft eighty miles away.

RDF triggered the air raid warning that sent Winston Churchill to his rooftop and thousands of panicked Londoners into basement bomb shelters three days ago.

The enemy on Sunday morning turned out to be a French military attaché returning to London after a weekend in Paris. Captain François de Brantès had not bothered to file a flight plan. Only dumb luck saved him from being blown out of the sky by Stuffy's Spitfires scrambling from Biggin Hill.*

---

* Captain François Marie Joseph Abel Henri Sauvage de Brantès, Count de Brantès, would join the French Resistance movement later in World War II. He was captured by the Germans and deported to the Mauthausen concentration camp, where he died in May 1944. His daughter, Anne, eleven at the time of her father's death, would grow up to

A second test takes place hours later. At 3 a.m. on September 4, RDF confirms enemy planes approaching Suffolk. Spitfires and Hurricanes scramble to intercept. The Identification Friend or Foe (IFF) radio signal to differentiate good guys from bad guys is not yet operational. These intruders turned out to be Wellington bombers returning home in bright moonlight from Bomber Command's first attack of the war, the pounding of shipyards in Northern Germany. As with Captain de Brantès, what remained of their luck was on the bombers' side. All three aircraft are allowed to land without incident.

The declaration of war makes it unlikely any pilot is taking off without a flight plan today. Yet despite lack of visual confirmation, the fact remains that at least one mystery plane has been heard flying over England at this very moment.

The order goes out: find that aircraft.

In these early days of war, pilots are rested and keen to fight, not at all the exhausted and burned-out versions of themselves they will soon become. So, the admonition to launch just a single six-aircraft flight at a time is forgotten. Eleven and 12 Group scramble squadron after squadron. Within an hour of the coastal sighting, 116 Spitfires and Hurricanes are in the air. Dozens more stand by on the ground, pilots itching to get up while the killing is good.

They are directed into combat by Chain Home stations facing out toward the English Channel, sending radio waves in a 360-degree rotation to detect incoming enemy. A special electronic barrier nullifies signals coming from the English landmass behind the towers. This prevents confusion in the Filter Room. RAF fighters flying from their bases as they roar into action will not be detected and mistaken for enemy.

But this morning, at the Chain Home station at Canewdon, near Southend-on-Sea, that electronic block fails. Every plane in the sky is

---

marry Valéry Giscard d'Estaing, later to become president of France. Anne-Aymone Giscard d'Estaing would serve as France's first lady from 1974 to 1981. Her husband died in 2020, but she is still alive at the time of this writing.

now visible on cathode ray screens. So many in the air at the same time present a formidable silhouette. Fighter Command does not know about the malfunction. They assume that every aircraft is German.

Panic seeps into the Filter Room. Phlegmatic Stuffy Dowding grows uneasy.

More fighters launch, compounding the error. More Luftwaffe fighters and bombers loom over England.

New waves of Spitfires and Hurricanes climb into the sky to shoot them down. Pilots eagerly study the horizon for enemy. Antiaircraft batteries open fire. Barrage balloons at thirty thousand feet. Air raid warnings in London. In the Essex countryside, citizens look up into the sky and witness the aerial carnival.

Two planes plummet to earth.

Yet nobody on the ground or in the sky knows the silhouette of German fighters.

The unthinkable is happening.

. . .

STUFFY DOWDING STUDIES the big map from his seat. The Filter Room is warm from body heat and nervous energy. He has yet to remove his peaked cap. The air marshal sits at attention, eyes riveted on the board with the most casual face he can manage, so as not to worry the filterers and plotters.

Yet these dedicated men see what he sees: red lights for every squadron. Stunningly, a new blow.

Stuffy's pilots are out of gas. Spitfires and Hurricanes, their operational range the same, are desperate to return to base. Pilots who sweated through their first combat now facing the hard reality that patriotism and bravado matter nothing without gasoline. The young brave men have little choice but to land. What matters now is time. Dowding has no control over how quickly ground crews can refuel entire squadrons, but England is defenseless until those planes get back up in air.

Yet for every Spitfire and Hurricane now on the ground, there are fewer blips on the RDF screens. More planes land. Surprisingly, the

German threat continues to ebb. Then the Luftwaffe attackers disappear from RDF screens altogether. Yet there are no reports of bomb damage.

Nothing makes sense.

Then Air Marshal Dowding's second monumental shock of the morning: the king of England chooses this, of all days, to say hello.

In person.

George VI is ushered into the Filter Room, gas mask slung over his shoulder in a khaki container. "The King, wearing the pale blue uniform of Marshal of the Royal Air Force, paid a surprise visit to the secret headquarters of the R.A.F. fighter command," the *Daily Telegraph* will report. "The King went into the control rooms and studied the entire organization."

"Studied," as in witnessing with his own eyes the strained faces of Filter Room professionals who understand for the first time that the bomber always gets through.

Despite the ongoing emergency, a stunned Hugh Dowding is his polite best. He guides the sovereign through the grand halls of Bentley Priory, still unsure what is happening in the skies of Southeast England. The mystery deepens as the two men make small talk, but the king makes no mention of bomber sightings over London. "I fear he must have found me a very distrait host," Dowding will write. "For I was itching to find out what it was that had gone wrong."

Stuffy and the king step outside. London media record the visit; then George VI is on his way. Yet none of the photographers taking pictures of the two men standing side by side in the sunshine remark about any sort of German attack.

There is, however, great curiosity among the press about this morning's air raid sirens. All seem to be false alarms. As the *Telegraph* will note: "We must have time to adjust to the system . . . the organization of air raid warnings will be perfected in a very short time."

. . .

THE MYSTERY UNRAVELS with a top secret phone call. Dowding hears sobering news.

The Hurricane of Pilot Officer F. C. Rose of 56 Squadron has been shot down. Rose managed to crash-land in a field near Ipswich. He is alive.*

Not so Pilot Officer Leslie Montague "John" Hulton-Harrop, also flying for 56, killed instantly by a .50-caliber machine-gun bullet through the back of his head when his Hurricane is attacked from behind. Dowding's bulletproof glass protects only the front of the cockpit.

Both men were blasted from the sky by Royal Air Force fighters, ordered to do so by the Dowding System. Among the fliers in the sky during the deadly shooting is twenty-year-old Spitfire pilot Derek Hugh Tremenheere Dowding. He flies for 74 Squadron out of Hornchurch.

Air Marshal Dowding's only son lands safely, alive to fight another day.

. . .

THERE ARE NO Luftwaffe aircraft over England this morning. Never have been. The lone plane thrumming over the Thames estuary at 6:15 was a lost Dutch civilian. Every plane wheeling through British airspace is a Royal Air Force fighter. The faulty Chain Home tower in Canewdon bears some blame, but the entire Dowding System has been exposed as unreliable.

Quite the embarrassing start to the war for Stuffy Dowding and Fighter Command.

In the words of one Hurricane pilot: "A truly amazing shambles."

The system must be perfected—and in a very short time.

Air Marshal Dowding has until his forced retirement in March to fix this system.

But if he doesn't get this right, there might not be an England by then.

. . .

AND THE DOWDING System isn't Stuffy's only problem.

September 9. RAF Debden. One by one, the sixteen Hurricanes of 85 Squadron taxi down the runway, propellers spinning, long noses waggling

---

* Rose was among those flying in his pajamas due to the early start. Though he survived the friendly-fire incident on September 6, he was be shot down and killed by the pilot of a German Messerschmitt Me 110 *Zerstörer* (Destroyer) over Brebières, France, on May 18, 1940. PO Leslie Montagu "John" Hulton-Harrop is buried in Row 1, Grave 1 at St. Andrew's Churchyard in Essex, England.

back and forth so each pilot can see the plane in front of him. Squadron code VY painted on the side of each fuselage, followed by a single letter identifying individual aircraft—VY-X, VY-C, and so on. This allows 85's pilots to know at a glance whether a Hurricane they encounter in the sky is from their squadron and the name of the pilot at the controls.

The 85 is temporarily moving squadron headquarters to France. The British Expeditionary Force, that military ground army being sent to aid Britain's ally, needs air cover in case of German attack. Stuffy Dowding has reluctantly agreed to base four Hurricane squadrons in France, among them 85. Yet he does so with trepidation: Fighter Command is far short of the aircraft required to defend Britain from aerial attack.

The 85 will be based in France for an undetermined amount of time. Most men are prepared to be away for Christmas. Some think it might be much longer.

Even after the fighters take off today, there is great work to be done. The logistics of moving the men and matériel of an entire squadron across the English Channel to their new base in Boos, just outside Rouen, are enormous.

Until last week, weekends and nights were a constant party in London for the pilots of 85. The British capital was just forty miles away from base. Now the entire unit is off to war. From here on out the partying will be in Paris, if at all. The declaration of war has sobered the unit, which switched from biplanes to Hurricanes just one year ago. There is a new tension to their days as the world awaits the Nazis' next move.

Yet less than an hour later, as the formation descends on its new base, France doesn't seem so bad after all. There is no sign of war. "I shall never forget the countryside," one 85 pilot will write. "With its orchard in the sunshine, in the fields just across the river to the north of Rouen."*

So it is that 85 lands and waits, not knowing when—or if—they will fly home to Mother England.

---

* These observations were written by Flight Officer John Hemingway. He would serve in the Royal Air Force throughout the war, and was shot down four times. Born in 1919, the Irishman is still alive at the time of this writing, making him the last surviving airman from the Battle of Britain.

7

THE AMERICAN

Billy Fiske is stone-cold sober.

"Needless to say, for once I had a quiet Saturday night," he writes in his journal. "I didn't want to have eyes looking like bloodstained oysters."

Monday. London is a cool 66 degrees with a hint of rain. Fiske is on his way to the War Cabinet offices just off St. James's Park for his pilot-training interview. Nine hundred miles away, German bombers level Warsaw. The husks of devastated cathedrals and synagogues rise in silhouette against a daytime sky orange with flame. Streets are covered in rubble, glass, and stiff human corpses waiting to be hauled away. Dead, bloating draft horses fill the air with the smell of rot, a stench made worse by the odor of toilets that cannot be flushed for lack of running water. Surviving residents have no heating oil. If it is the Nazis' intent to forever destroy Warsaw and its large Jewish population, they are succeeding. The German Army is just days away from occupying the medieval city.

Adolf Hitler says the Poles had it coming.

So will the English, if they do not do as Hitler pleases.

But London is not Warsaw. Not yet.

Billy Fiske smells the coming autumn, the exhaust of red double-decker buses and black taxicabs careening through Piccadilly Circus. He navigates packed sidewalks. Regent Street is open for business. Since he's been in town, he knows that every night except Sunday theatergoers stop off for a quick one at the pub before their show; gentlemen stand in tight circles, pint in hand, laughing about life in their black-and-white evening wear, complete with bow tie. The war is a headline glimpsed while walking past a Green Park newsstand, nothing more.

But England knows it's coming. And it's not just about sending soldiers to fight Hitler on some far-off battlefield. London being bombed like Warsaw is the greatest threat the city has known in its history, a shadow cast over every dawn. This fear is compounded by an awareness that the Royal Air Force might not have enough planes and pilots to stop Luftwaffe bombers.

Which is why England needs Billy Fiske.

The American stepped off the *Aquitania* in Southampton two weeks ago. He has spent the time in London lobbying his many well-connected friends for a chance to join the RAF. Fiske meets today with Wing Commander William Elliot, a thin, long-necked flying ace from the previous war, currently spending his days as an assistant secretary to Neville Chamberlain's new War Cabinet. Fiske is now on his way to Elliot's office.

The interview has been arranged through "Ben," a British friend from Fiske's bobsledding days in St. Moritz. Coincidentally, Wing Commander Elliot was educated in Switzerland. As Fiske approaches his interrogation, the would-be fighter pilot imagines how he will explain the odd truth that he possesses a logbook showing ninety hours of actual flight time but, quite mysteriously, no Canadian passport. How Fiske managed to step onto English soil at all is a question that cannot go unasked.

The American must find a clever way to lie about his nationality without actually lying about his nationality—a gentleman's honor being only as good as his word. This seems an impossible task given his popularity and reputation in London. He may have been a teetotaler on Saturday night, but Billy Fiske has been a regular at exclusive clubs like White's, less than a mile from the London plane–lined street where he now hustles to see Wing Commander Elliot. Americans in London are scarce. Billy Fiske stands out in any crowd. His nationality is quite well known.

Of course, the St. Moritz set is not your average group of winter-sport enthusiasts. "Ben," as Fiske calls his fellow member of the Cresta, is actually Benjamin Bathurst, Second Viscount Bledisloe, a thirty-nine-year-old barrister whose family can trace its peerage back centuries. Bathurst's father, a Conservative politician, was most recently colonial governor-general of New Zealand. Ben attended Eton and Magdalen College at Oxford.

Billy Fiske is well aware that a man as ensconced in the British establishment as Wing Commander Elliot will be predisposed to waving a magic wand and suspending all belief to accept the pretense that Fiske, with his broad Chicago accent tinged ever so slightly in polished nasal Cambridge, has no American roots at all, and is, in fact, a Canadian citizen.

Given that scenario, admittance to the Royal Air Force is a given.

The greater problem is that Billy Fiske wants to fly for the 601. This is hardly a low-profile posting. And the Millionaires' Squadron—with their colorful flying scarves, open top tunic buttons, and flight jackets lined in red silk—flies fighters.

Wing Commander Elliot may turn a blind eye to the dodge about Fiske's nationality, but with a war on, he has his own career to think about. His reputation will suffer among RAF peers if he recommends an unworthy individual for flight training. So, even if Elliot does agree that the American has the right stuff to join the Royal Air Force, he will certainly be passing judgment as to whether or not Fiske has *enough* of the right stuff. A poor interview could see Fiske flying coastal patrol in the back seat of a biplane.

Thus, Fiske has already played an early round of golf in Roehampton this morning to increase the healthy glow in his cheeks. And he has rehearsed answers to any potential questions, finding the right words to establish his Canadian bona fides without uttering a flat-out lie. "Having no identification papers other than an American passport, I had to make up some very watertight answers for any questions they might be expected to ask me—which was of no use at all."

Fiske knows the loopholes in the US Neutrality Act of 1939. It does not specifically prevent American citizens from fighting for a foreign nation. Claire Chennault and the famous Flying Tigers have been battling the Japanese for China since 1937. Instead, the law warns that the United States cannot offer protection to men like Chennault and Billy Fiske.

Step one was getting out of New York. Step two was arranging today's interview. Step three is a commission.*

Billy Fiske steps inside the War Cabinet offices and asks to speak with Wing Commander Elliot. Fiske has a way with people, a mixture of charm and sincerity that others notice every time he introduces himself. Not William. Not the more casual Bill. But Billy, a youthful term that says he's his own man but doesn't take himself too seriously.

The would-be RAF pilot dazzles Elliot. Billy finds the right words to every question. By meeting's end, Elliot makes a snap decision, not needing to run this touchy situation up the flagpole: The American is admitted to the Royal Air Force. Fiske is to report to the No. 10 Elementary and Reserve Flying Training School in Yatesbury, Wiltshire, an hour west of London. Given his fondness for driving his Bentley at extraordinarily high speeds, Fiske should make the journey in half that time.

"I believe I can lay claim to being the first US citizen to join the RAF after the outbreak of war," he will write in his journal six weeks from now, having made his first official solo flight as a member of the Royal Air Force. "I don't say this with any particular pride, except perhaps in so far as my conscience is clear, but only because it has some bearing on the course of my career. My reasons for joining the fray are my own."

---

* Some sources claim the meeting was with Chief of Air Staff Sir Cyril Newall at the Air Ministry office.

8

HANDSOME RICHARD

Richard Hillary is now a commissioned officer in the Royal Air Force.

Yet pilot's wings are still a long way off.

His new posting is at Hastings, a former seaside resort. The ocean is angry, whitecapped, and a most unattractive shade of green. Drizzle. No tourists on the promenade. Parade drills underneath the covered carport on rainy days. "It is a desolate gray picture," one of Hillary's fellow trainees will write of Hastings. "The scene evokes in me, for the first time to any degree, an atmosphere of foreboding."

Promoted from Volunteer Reserve to full standing in the RAF, Hillary and former college classmate Frank Waldron drove Waldron's coupe down from Oxford at the end of summer. Past Reading, then Windsor, keeping to the outskirts of London, then south to East Sussex through rolling green countryside. The Alvis Speed 25 was built for drives like this, its long bonnet and leather seats and winged hood ornament the very embodiment of a proper "luxury touring car." Yet while the Alvis has been in production only since 1937, the vehicle has seen its share of college high jinks—Hillary writing of the "battered old Alvis" in his journal.

The symbolism of learning to defend England at the very location the nation was last successfully invaded is lost on Hillary. But of all the hundreds of young officers now assembling at this waterfront training base, only he and Waldron can lay claim to defeating Germans in head-to-head competition. The victory came one summer ago, during a rowing competition on the River Lahn, in Bad Ems, Germany. A four-man British crew, using a shell borrowed from a local boathouse, came from behind to win Hermann Goering's "Four Square" trophy.

But the award lost its luster as war neared and Nazis became the enemy. "It was a gold shell-case mounted with the German eagle and disgraced our rooms in Oxford for nearly a year," Hillary writes of the statue named for the Luftwaffe commander, "until we could stand it no longer and sent it back through the German Embassy."

Hillary is now a member of Initial Training Wing 1, an eight-week course in parade drill, regulations, RAF history, and calisthenics designed to make an officer of him. The would-be pilots are divided into training groups of roughly forty. Seaside boardinghouses and hotels requisitioned by the government serve as quarters. Veteran sergeants lead the rigorous daily training, barely hiding their contempt for the college boys under their command. "Almost every insult was permissible, as long as the regulation compliment was paid at the end of each diatribe," fellow trainee Geoffrey Page will remember, adding an example in a drill sergeant's voice: "'When I say right turn, I mean right turn—*air force* right turn—not some fancy university right turn . . . SIR!'"

Yet being upbraided does not bother Richard Hillary as much as his less-than-luxurious living conditions. "I had never believed in the legend of seaside boarding-houses, but within two days I was convinced," he writes sarcastically, still intent on someday becoming a journalist. "There it all was, the heavy smell of Brussels sprouts, the aspidistras, the slut of a maid with the hole in her black stockings and a filthy thumbnail in the soup, the communal table in the dining room which just didn't face the sea, the two meals a day served punctually at one o'clock and seven-thirty."

This is the glamorous life of a would-be pilot.

Throughout this training, Hillary and his new circle of friends do not see an airplane, let alone set foot inside a cockpit. There is no flying. That comes next. He considers the rules "child-like" and admits to a lack of tact in refusing to accept discipline. Their instructors are more interested in deportment, drill, and proper hair length. Some men sneak out for evenings in London, racing to make it back before morning formation. An impromptu boxing match provides a rare break from routine.

There is an utter lack of hurry. These smart young souls wearing tailored blue uniforms and marching in formation lockstep, destined to fly high over this very spot to defend the glory of Britain, cannot help their nation one iota if that attack comes today.

Or even by Christmas.

The training is intentional and slow because Britain is not under attack. Early panic has been replaced by waiting and dread. The conflict in Europe is settling into a period of inactivity some are calling the "Phony War," as if the invasion of Poland were the end of it. Common sense is setting in as technical realities ensure the safety of the British people. London, for instance, is just over three hundred miles from Northern Germany. Launching from bases in that region, Luftwaffe Dornier Do 17 and Heinkel He 111 bombers, each having a range of more than seven hundred miles, could easily strike the city and return to base.

But those German bombers must first fly over France, Belgium, and Holland. None of those nations has much of an air force, but the Luftwaffe armadas would still be attacked en route to the target by antiaircraft guns on the ground, and then by the Royal Air Force over the Channel.

A fighter escort will not help. The Luftwaffe Me 109 has a range of less than four hundred miles, just enough to take off from Germany and splash into the English Channel on the way home, provided the Dowding System doesn't send up a wave of Spits and Hurricanes to do the job first.*

---

* The Messerschmitt Bf 109 and Me 109 are the same plane. Designer Willy Messerschmitt had a long misunderstanding with Erhard Milch, the architect of the Luftwaffe,

Of course, should the Germans invade France, Belgium, and Holland, and should those buffer nations between Germany and England fall, the Luftwaffe will move forward to the coast. There they will launch fighters and bombers from captured bases on the English Channel. Range will not be an issue.*

That is unthinkable: The French have one of the most powerful armies in the world. Their defensive fortresses along the German border are impregnable. The hulking Char B1 tank is among the most powerful on earth. And the landmass of France, stretching six hundred miles north to south, and the same from east to west, is almost as vast as the enormous American state of Texas. In all of Europe, only the Soviet Union is larger.

Most of all, the French are passionate about their nation. The Germans fought four years to conquer them in the First World War—and failed. If fighting takes that long this time around, every flight candidate here in Hastings will have a few thousand hours in their logbook. The Royal Air Force will be more than prepared.

So, for now, the lengthy training process feels unrushed, even as the would-be pilots eagerly anticipate the next phase in the pipeline. They spend evenings in the pub, chatting at insatiable length about airplanes, aerodynamics, and a longing to fly into the fight before the war ends.

And sex.

Richard Hillary has a girl, though Anne Mackenzie is slowly putting an end to their yearlong relationship. But most trainees have come straight from college or living with their parents. They know zero about

---

preventing him from purchasing *Bayerische Flugzeugwerke*, the "Bavarian Aircraft Works," until July 11, 1938. Thus, early models were "Bf," for the aircraft company's initials. Upon Messerschmitt's purchase, the prefix shifted to "Me." For simplicity, "Me" will be utilized for the remainder of *Taking London*.

* The Luftwaffe divided Germany into four geographical "Air Fleets." Each had its own command, communications, administration, and bases. If, and when, France and the Low Countries were conquered, the plan was to maintain the number of Air Fleets at four, expanding each so they stretched from Poland in the east all the way west to the English Channel.

flying and even less about intercourse—"and yet we held forth with the authority of Socrates," one young pilot candidate will write. "Our parents would have been left speechless had they even caught snatches of the conversations."

The sad undercurrent, for those lacking experience, is the horrifying notion of dying before this longing can be requited.

. . .

RICHARD HILLARY WILL remember his time at ITW 1 as "a fortnight" rather than two monotonous months. But the time serves its purpose. Hillary's emotional bond shifts from Oxford University to the Royal Air Force and the men with whom he now tests himself. He gets better about following the rules because he must. His cocksure spirit is not squashed. If anything, he is even more brash. "We were expected to be superior," he will write of the struggles for Oxford pilot candidates to fit in. "We were known as weekend pilots. We were known as the Long Haired Boys. We were to have the nonsense knocked out of us."

So Richard Hillary is ecstatic when he receives orders for flight school. He and several others will report to No. 14 Flying Training School. The course is six months long.

Hillary knows the location only as "a small village on the northeast coast of Scotland." The location is RAF Kinloss, a remote installation far up the Scottish coast on the rugged Moray Firth.

"None of us had ever heard of it, but none of us cared," believes Hillary.

"As long as we flew, it was immaterial to us where."

9

CHURCHILL

Winston has had an auspicious day.

An auspicious week, actually.

And now he is one phone call away from its crowning moment.

"5:30. Dinner at the flat," reads the barely legible handwritten notation in his engagement calendar. Today the first lord is a pencil man, though Churchill is just as likely to use pen when jotting down his schedule. A simple evening in cramped Morpeth Mansions with friends in uniform from the Admiralty. Just getting dark outside but still warm enough to keep the windows open. Clementine remains at their new Admiralty House apartment, remodeled under her direction since Winston's appointment as first lord. The Churchills moved in two weeks ago. Morpeth Mansions is closer to Parliament, thus this choice of dinner locations, but Churchill has no intent of staying the night. The Admiralty is his center of power, allowing him to track every British ship at sea, anywhere in the world, military or otherwise. He is briefed on the location of German ships, too.

As the rest of Europe awaits Adolf Hitler's next move, Winston Churchill plays chess on the high seas every single day. In addition to vessels currently engaged around the world, Great Britain is rushing a new group of five modern destroyers into the war. The namesake vessel of the

King George V class was launched February 21, one week after Nazi Germany's equally powerful *Bismarck*. HMS *Prince of Wales* launched May 3. *Duke of York, Anson,* and *Howe* are just months from completion. Despite those ships being the length of two soccer pitches and having enormous guns that can hit a target over the horizon and armor fifteen inches thick in places, Churchill is aware that their day may be coming to an end. Aerial warfare has come a long way since the last war. The time is now for prioritizing aircraft carriers over destroyers and battleships. A single aircraft can sink a *George V*–class vessel with a well-placed bomb or torpedo.

Yet Great Britain has just one modern aircraft carrier, the *Ark Royal.* Six more are under construction but will not be ready for sea duty for as long as three years. The other six vessels in the Royal Navy's air fleet when war was declared are not true carriers but Great War battle wagons retrofitted with a flight deck. None is capable of launching Spitfires or Hurricanes.

Even those numbers have already been diminished: HMS *Courageous,* a Great War battle cruiser rebuilt as a carrier in the 1920s, was torpedoed and sunk by a Nazi U-boat on September 17.

Germany will continue to show its control of the high seas in the weeks to come. The battleship HMS *Royal Oak*—"The Mighty Oak"—will be sunk inside its anchorage at Scapa Flow by a German submarine on October 14. Eight hundred thirty-three British officers and sailors will go down with her in those icy waters off the Scottish coast.

·   ·   ·

TODAY BEGAN WITH Churchill's usual morning briefing from Captain Richard Pim of the Royal Navy. But the afternoon has been a series of irregular events: public celebrity, chilled champagne, a nibble of ice cream, a terse hour in the House of Commons, and one very emotional ritual. Reads today's only other calendar entry: "Mr. Randolph's wedding, 1. St. John's. Smith Square."

Winston and Clementine were in attendance as Randolph Churchill, their besotted only son, a twenty-eight-year-old army lieutenant, married the well-heeled nineteen-year-old beauty Pamela Digby.

The couple met three weeks ago, an apparent love-at-first-sight encounter. Randolph proposed the next night, which would sound romantic were it not for the fact that he had already asked a half dozen other women to marry him since his father pushed the country into war. As of this week, British troops are being sent to defend France. Should Randolph join them and die quickly in battle like so many young men during the First World War, he would first like to sire a male offspring—a *legitimate* male offspring.

Miss Digby, a social climber even at her young age, foresaw the advantages of wedding the first lord's son. She quickly said yes.

Her parents, Lord and Lady Digby of Dorset, do not approve. Randolph's fondness for womanizing and double brandies gets around.

Yet on September 29, the father of the groom agreed to the hasty nuptials. That was that. "I expect he will see action in the early spring," Churchill explained to the Duke of Westminster, a longtime friend. "And, therefore, I am very glad he will be married before he goes."*

On the afternoon of their wedding, there was no hesitation as the couple walked up the gray stone steps of St. John's. Two hundred years old. Awkward English Baroque design. Charles Dickens once labeled the church a "petrified monster, frightful and gigantic."

A beaming Randolph wore workaday subaltern attire rather than the more elaborate full dress uniform. Lavish spectacle is not in keeping with wartime austerity, particularly by the son of a War Cabinet member. Even men not in the military dressed down, refraining from wearing top hats, standard accoutrement of society weddings.

Randolph's winsome betrothed, clutching a bouquet of pink and white orchids, also downplayed her attire.

"A wartime bride," one commentator will state of Pamela's simple frock and velvet hat, "dispenses with flowing gowns and trains and veils,

---

* Sixty-year-old Hugh Richard Arthur Grosvenor, Second Duke of Westminster, was one of the wealthiest men in the world. He was the hero of a First World War POW rescue of British personnel held 135 days at Bir Hakeim, in the Libyan desert. A second major engagement at Bir Hakeim during World War II is detailed in *Taking Paris.*

but still manages to look charming and radiant. This bride wore navy blue, very appropriately."

Hundreds gathered outside St. John's to watch famous members of Parliament, lords and ladies, and London luminaries file into the church. Churchill's son-in-law, Vic Oliver, a famous forty-one-year-old stage comedian, drew cheers. But the arrival of Winston and Clementine drew the most enthusiastic applause and roars, faces in the crowd agape at the sight of the great Winston Churchill in person. The couple walked close together, Clementine a half step ahead in hat and long fur coat, bodyguards just behind.

"Mr. Churchill Attends His Son's Wedding," one movie newsreel will trumpet on the title card, showing images of a grinning Winston stepping out of his black Daimler. The commentator for Gaumont News refers to Churchill as "the man the Nazis hate and fear" in a nod to the first lord's growing public adulation.

After, Churchill hosted a small reception at the Admiralty. From there it was on to Parliament, which convened at 2:45 p.m. He finally returned to Morpeth Mansions an hour ago. Among his guests was Rear Admiral Bruce Fraser, third sea lord and controller of the navy. The business at Parliament had much to do with funding for recruitment and promotion, so despite a long day and a well-deserved evening of relaxation, this meal had the undertones of a working dinner.

It is always that way now. The fate of England is never far from Churchill's busy mind. This preoccupation could be seen immediately after the wedding ceremony, his easy smile upon entering the church replaced by a tight-lipped scowl as the first lord stepped back down the stone steps. During the reception, Churchill declined an offer to raise a toast to his son, who appeared too overcome to speak on his own behalf. The first lord worked the room, making jokes about his fondness for eating. This temporary suspension of concern about the fate of England saw Churchill looking calm and almost playful. Then it was on to Parliament and a series of dry questions that demonstrated his power of recall but was as far from jubilation and church bells as the wedding ceremony was from bureaucracy and matters of state.

It is one thing to be a voice in the wilderness, predicting calamity. It is another to be a puppet master assembling a coalition capable of bringing down the British government if its demands are not met. But to actually lead in such uncertain times is an all-consuming pursuit that is invading Churchill's personal life, thoughts, and professional ambitions even when he would prefer a slight respite. Anything can happen at a moment's notice. He is prepared to set all else aside when that time comes. Churchill has even begun traveling with a small pistol and a suicide pill hidden inside a pen, in the extreme event of a Nazi kidnapping.

Like it or not—and Winston Churchill likes it a great deal, though saying so publicly would be perceived as a grievous lack of loyalty to Prime Minister Chamberlain—he is becoming the worldwide symbol of British resistance.

Just three nights ago, Churchill once again visited the BBC studios on Portland Place and gave a radio briefing about the state of the war. Rather than Prime Minister Chamberlain expounding on the European conflict, it was Churchill who spoke openly about the two threats to the east: Adolf Hitler and Joseph Stalin. He called the Soviet Union "a riddle wrapped in a mystery inside an enigma," questioning its own invasion of Poland and sowing seeds of doubt about its tenuous relationship with Germany.

But Churchill being Churchill, a simple update did not suffice. He also spoke as a cheerleader, encouraging listeners to ignore talk about the Royal Navy being crushed by Germany's undersea fleet of U-boats. Churchill pointedly refuses to admit the reality that England has its back against the wall and is almost certain to lose its empire and become a Nazi island. He uses words like "zeal" and "relish" to hearten listeners, and promises a conflict of at least three years before eventual victory.

"It began when he wanted it," Churchill will state of Adolf Hitler's war. "It will end only when we are convinced he has had enough."

But now, during this simple dinner in his flat, Churchill can unwind. He is not the voice of a nation right now, just a sixty-four-year-old man whose son has finally gotten married. The Churchills have grave concerns about Randolph's spending habits and entitled behavior, but now is a time to set all that aside and bask in the glow of being father of the groom.

Then the phone rings.

10

CHURCHILL

Winston ignores the ringing.

Churchill's butler answers the phone in a nearby room, then steps into the dining area to inform the first lord that there's someone on the line. Churchill, who considers the telephone a necessary evil, asks who's calling.

"I don't know, sir."

"Say I can't attend to it now."

The butler hesitates. He knows Churchill's moods and is loath to set him off. "I think you ought to come, sir," he says firmly.

An exasperated Winston Churchill leaves the dinner table to take the call.

Rear Admiral Fraser cannot hear the entire conversation, but the flat is cramped. Snippets can be heard from the dining room table. Surprisingly, Churchill is showing great deference, which is most unlike him. "Yes, sir" is followed by patient listening. "No, sir."

Churchill bursts back into the dining room.

"Do you know who that was? The president of the United States.

"It is remarkable to think of being rung up in this little flat in Victoria Street by the president himself in the middle of this great war," the starstruck first lord gushes. His mother, the wealthy socialite Jennie Jerome, was American. He has traveled widely in that nation, even conducting lecture tours in major US cities—the most recent being a 1929 journey with a teenage Randolph that was notable for many reasons, among them the younger Churchill trying to sneak into the bedroom of William Randolph Hearst's daughter-in-law—only to find that he had mistakenly crept into his father's bedroom instead.*

A phone call from President Franklin Roosevelt would carry great heft under any circumstances. But tonight's transatlantic discussion also brings an element of intrigue, which is catnip to the first lord. Churchill does not question how the White House switchboard got his phone number.

Without another thought, Churchill tells his guests to let themselves out. "This is very important," he states, mind focused once again on England and his top secret conversation. "I must go and see the prime minister at once."

. . .

IN WASHINGTON, DC, President Roosevelt can't help but congratulate himself. The master politician is a fifty-seven-year-old political genius, elitist, and wheelchair-bound chain-smoker. Polio has withered his legs, but his shoulders are broad from two decades of pushing up out of his chair. Some describe his head as overly large. A grave new crisis has forced this urgent phone call.

Yet this is precisely why the president opened a line of communication with Churchill three weeks ago. FDR did so concealed in the spirit of friendship, sending congratulations on Churchill's promotion to the Admiralty.

"My dear Churchill," Roosevelt wrote on September 11. "It's because you and I occupied similar positions in the World War that I want you to

---

* William Randolph Hearst was a billionaire media baron. He is the inspiration for Charles Foster Kane, title character in the Orson Welles film *Citizen Kane*. Hearst despised this ruthless interpretation of his life and attempted to stop its distribution. The film's key plot device is the word "Rosebud," used to describe a child's sled in the film but also a pet name for Hearst's lover, Marion Davies, in real life. Hearst died in 1951 at age eighty-eight.

know how glad I am that you're back again in charge of the navy, although I know there are new problems. I want you and the Prime Minister to know that I'd be happy for you to keep me informed of anything important that's happening. You can always send sealed letters directly to me.

"I'm glad you finished writing the first parts of your history book before this war started—and I've much enjoyed reading them." The president is referring to a biography about the Duke of Marlborough, written by Churchill himself.

"With my sincere regards,

"Faithfully yours,

"FRANKLIN D. ROOSEVELT"

Roosevelt was America's assistant secretary of the navy during World War I, a position almost equal to Churchill's posting as first lord during the same conflict. His compliments about Churchill's writing are an act of seduction, the president possessing a strong dislike for reading books, particularly a multivolume history that Churchill gave him six years ago—a time when there was a decided rift between the two men. Roosevelt will later claim that he and Churchill met decades before, and initiated the period of ill feeling then, though his British counterpart does not remember that occurrence.*

Churchill dutifully reported the high-level missive from Washington to Neville Chamberlain. The prime minister, finding the weight of leading England growing heavier by the day, gave permission for the first lord to open a line of private correspondence with the American leader. The War Cabinet was also notified and gave their approval. Great Britain needs all the help she can get.

As a nod to their old friendship, Churchill then told Ambassador

---

* Roosevelt is correct. The two men met on July 29, 1918, at a dinner for the War Cabinet at Gray's Inn, in London. From Roosevelt's perspective, the meeting did not go well. He carried a grudge about that day for many years afterward but never stated exactly what went wrong. "I always disliked him [Churchill]," Roosevelt will recall, "since that time I went to England in 1917 or 1918. At a dinner I attended he acted like a stinker."

Joseph P. Kennedy of his new relationship with Roosevelt. But the Boston businessman did not bless this budding partnership. He was petulant and frosty, retreating to the privacy of his journal to vent his unhappiness.

"I resented this bypassing of me and my position as the Ambassador. I lost none of that resentment when Churchill two days later asked me over to the Admiralty and read me the letter from the President recalling their association from the last war and inviting Churchill to communicate directly with him."

·   ·   ·

THE PERSONAL HAPPINESS of Joseph P. Kennedy is of absolutely no interest to FDR. In fact, he enjoys making the ambassador squirm. Now, on this Wednesday afternoon in Washington, Franklin Roosevelt continues his artful seduction of Churchill. The call to Morpeth Mansions is the president informing the first lord that Admiral Erich Raeder, head of the German Navy, is warning of a suspected British plot to draw the United States into the war. A merchant vessel known as the SS *Iroquois* has just sailed from Ireland. On board are hundreds of Americans racing home.

The Germans claim Churchill has ordered a bomb hidden on board. Sinking the vessel will put an end to America's isolationist thinking. Admiral Raeder is concerned about the explosion being blamed on a Nazi submarine.

There are two logical ways President Roosevelt might play this issue: He could place a call to Prime Minister Neville Chamberlain and, as the leader of a neutral nation, warn the head of a country at war that a great catastrophe is imminent; or Roosevelt could order the United States ambassador to Great Britain to personally request an urgent meeting with the prime minister to sort out the matter through diplomatic channels.

In no scenario does the president of the United States place a personal phone call to the Royal Navy, no matter how high-ranking the recipient might be.

Strengthening relations with Chamberlain, who once stated of Roosevelt's administration that "it is always best and safest to count on nothing from the Americans but words," is also not in the president's interests.

And Franklin Roosevelt does not like Joseph P. Kennedy in the slightest, and named him ambassador to the Court of St. James only to send him far away from America and prevent him from running for president.

FDR believes Winston Churchill will one day be prime minister of Great Britain. This is the man with whom he prefers to deal. "I'm giving him my attention now because of his possibilities of becoming PM," Roosevelt will admit to Ambassador Kennedy in a rare moment of candor. "I'm willing to help them all I can," the president will add in reference to the British, "but I don't want them to play me for a sucker."

Yet Franklin Roosevelt knows this new relationship is about far more than one side taking advantage of the other. America needs Great Britain just as much as Britain needs America.

Like Churchill, Roosevelt knows the Nazi threat will not end with the fall of Europe.

If anything, Adolf Hitler will be more emboldened when that day comes, since he will have full possession of the continent's navies, factories, mines, and men. The Nazi leader will be more than capable of attacking any nation on earth, even the United States.

America must one day enter the war on the side of Great Britain. Or, should England fall before that day arrives, stand alone against Adolf Hitler.

. . .

LONDON. 5 A.M. Midnight in Washington. Winston Churchill returns President Roosevelt's call. The hour is late, even for the nocturnal first lord. The crisis about the *Iroquois* heightens, and with it the global implications of an American ship sunk in open waters, with no proof of who is committing this atrocity.

In Washington, Franklin Roosevelt is also awake. He takes the call in the White House residence. The phone is black metal with a suede-lined cradle. There is no rotary dial. No bell. Being president means picking up the telephone and talking to anyone, anywhere in the world, anytime he wants without the irritation of phone book or jangle.

Roosevelt already knows how to fix the situation. Talking strategy with Churchill was a kindness. America may be neutral, but now is the time to build alliances. Like it or not, the United States is getting pulled toward war—and much too soon for the president's political timetable. Roosevelt hopes to forestall American involvement until he is reelected for a third term next year.

But Churchill goes one step beyond Roosevelt's plan. The first lord urges the president to make the *Iroquois* situation public. He is not the leader of England, but Winston Churchill acts on behalf of his nation in a manner no less authoritative than Roosevelt's. For the first time since they have known each other, Churchill and Roosevelt dig into the delicate business of solving a volatile international issue.

A partnership is born.

"*Iroquois* is probably a thousand miles west of Ireland," Churchill tells Roosevelt over the phone. "U-boat damage is inconceivable in these broad waters. The only method is a time bomb planted in Queenstown. We think this is not impossible."

Churchill continues. "Action seems urgent. Presumed you have urged the *Iroquois* to search the ship?"

He follows up hours later with a more gently worded telegram, ending with the words: "We wish to help you in any way in keeping the war out of American waters."

Only when the matter is completely settled with President Roosevelt does Churchill present himself before Ambassador Kennedy to discuss the *Iroquois*. It is now the morning of October 5 at 10:45 a.m.

The American public already knows about the beleaguered vessel. Roosevelt has followed Churchill's advice. Beginning with words that will ring ironic to Kennedy—"It is felt that there is no reason for with-holding the following facts from the public"—a statement released five hours ago by the White House tells of the plight of *Iroquois*. It speaks of a US naval convoy now sailing to its location with the intent of escorting her home, and the thorough search for an explosive device currently underway on board the ship.

The statement does not mention German accusations that Winston Churchill and the Royal Navy might be involved.

Churchill sits down with Kennedy in the American embassy on Grosvenor Square and is stunned to learn that the ambassador has not seen the statement. In fact, he knows nothing about *Iroquois*, in spite of the fact that the nation under his diplomatic purview has been accused of planting a bomb to incite war. "It was an embarrassing moment for me," an enraged Kennedy will write in his journal. "Churchill naturally assumed that the president had kept me aware of the situation, whereas I was completely ignorant of every fact.

"Another instance of Roosevelt's conniving mind, which never indicates he knows how to handle any organization. It's a rotten way to treat his Ambassador and I think shows him up to the other people. I am disgusted."

So grows the divide between Joseph Kennedy and Franklin Roosevelt. Kennedy disagrees with the president's pro-Britain policies and is determined to make his own views known by any means possible. Through no fault of Winston Churchill's, Ambassador Joseph Kennedy's animus toward all things British grows.

And the Boston businessman's pro-Hitler leanings will become only more fervent.

11

THE BOY

Pilot Officer Geoffrey Wellum is barely hanging on.

The Cotswolds is the Britain of postcards: country houses built of honey-blond stone, ancient castles, thick forests igniting in a riot of color as the seasons change, woolly white sheep dotting stout green hillsides, and ancient Roman roads so narrow that it is necessary to pull onto the verge when two cars approach from opposite directions. Towns define themselves by prepositions, hyphens, natural nouns: Stow-on-the-Wold, Bourton-on-the-Water, Moreton-in-Marsh.

Now eighteen and still very much living up to his nickname, the Boy sees these sights only from the air. The rest of his world is Little Rissington's one-year-old training base. Redbrick buildings. Grass runways. Two men to a room in cramped dormitories but a thoroughly modern mess, where warm beer on tap waits each evening—for those willing to pass up study time. Days are spent marching, flying, and sitting in lectures. Nights are for memorization and knowledge, preparing for the minefield of written exams each trainee must pass to earn his wings.

Wellum's veteran flying instructor is Flight Sergeant Eddy Lewis. The boy pilot will never forget his first impression: "thinning, short, slightly sandy hair; a thin, hollow-cheeked face and a small, neat mustache. His uniform is pressed and immaculate."

Surprisingly, Wellum is one of the few candidates selected to train in the Harvard. He has no idea why his childlike self has been chosen for this American-made, single-wing, two-seat trainer painted bright yellow. The aircraft is known as a proving ground for future assignment to fighters—and a dangerous machine that kills perfectly good pilots.

In the earliest days of the course, as Geoffrey Wellum sat in the Harvard's two-man cockpit for the first time, he was overwhelmed by the dazzling array of gauges, dials, and switches. Learning their names and functions seemed impossible. But Lewis convinced Wellum that he must commit to this knowledge if wanted to become a true-blue RAF pilot. "Only total and complete understanding is adequate," Lewis tells him with no trace of sympathy. "You must be able to find your way about the cockpit layout blindfolded."

Under the flight sergeant's sometimes prickly leadership, Wellum memorizes the control panel—and much more: "fuel systems, hydraulics, data concerning the engine, the correct revs and manifold pressure (whatever that is) to fly for climb and cruise, take-off and landing procedures and drills."

Wellum soon flies solo, one of aviation's hallowed milestones. The event gives him purpose. "I get the feeling that I'm beginning to understand aeroplanes and there is no doubt in my mind I'm beginning to like the Royal Air Force," he thinks, his memory going back to that warm March morning when he interviewed to become a pilot. "The walk down Kingsway when going for my interview and the sight of the hurrying businessmen worrying their way to their various offices seems a long time ago.

"There is no question about my having made the correct decision."

Yet Geoffrey Wellum is barely eighteen. Despite moments of confidence, he feels like an impostor. Wellum wonders if he belongs in this world of grown men—some married, some with careers, some more than a decade older. "Is the whole thing going to be too big for me?" he worries. "I feel alone and unsure."

And flying solo does not mean Wellum has completed flight school. That accomplishment is a jumping-off point for much more rigorous flying—aerobatics, formation, cross-country, nights, clouds, instruments.

Wings are not guaranteed. In fact, it seems just the opposite to Wellum, as if the RAF is trying to find ways to send him home. Every trainee is on probation. The penalty for failure is total: fly right in the sky and pass written exams in the classroom, or go home and explain to embarrassed loved ones what went wrong. Geoffrey Wellum has no doubt what this tragic moment in each failed man's life looks like, for he has personally witnessed such a departure.

"As I go into the mess for tea," Wellum observes one gut-wrenching morning, "I see a solitary lonely figure in civilian clothes complete with bag and baggage, getting into a taxi waiting at the mess entrance. The expression on his face and the way in which he carries himself is, to me, frightening."

Wellum dreads "the weeding out process rearing its ugly head," terrified his name might be on the list of suspended. "My uniform looks naked and ashamed without those most elusive RAF pilot's wings. Is there any badge anywhere in the world more coveted?"

The thought of taking off his tailored blue uniform and returning to civilian life haunts Wellum's every action as he progresses deeper into training. Yet he knows the challenges will only get tougher. "Things won't let up until we leave this bloody place," he sighs.

The workload increases. So does the pressure. Tankards of ale in the mess help take the edge off. But Wellum's test results slip. Then he all but flunks a navigation exam.

The chief ground instructor takes notice. Flight Officer Wellum is asked to appear in this commander's office. The young pilot's right knee trembles as he stands at attention in his cleanest uniform. The senior officer stares at the young man for what seems like a very long time.

"Do you know why I have sent for you, Mr. Wellum?"

The senior officer is an old-school pilot, commissioned in the years of biplanes and open cockpits. He knows that sloppy aviators kill themselves—and others. He has seen it all. The chief ground instructor's face is stern and disapproving.

"Yes, sir," Wellum replies.

"Well, I should damn well hope so."

The officer launches into an embarrassing five-minute reprimand. He uses words like "unsatisfactory" and "frightful" and "unacceptable."

Wellum takes advantage of a brief pause to apologize. He promises to do better.

"Be quiet!" the commanding officer barks, eyes burning with contempt. The Boy is young enough to be his own son.

"I do not recall giving you permission to speak, Wellum."

The chief ground instructor resumes his scathing critique. Geoffrey Wellum realizes he will be asked to leave. He prays for the speech to end. His flying career is over. Perhaps, if there is a war, he will join the fight as a regular soldier. Wellum wants no more abuse. He just wants to hear the words. Then the Boy will scoot out the door, change into civvies, call a taxi, and flee as quickly and quietly as possible to the bedroom of his childhood home.

"Now, listen to me most carefully," the chief ground instructor snarls.

"You must start to think about growing up, Wellum. The RAF wants men, not boys," the officer tells him. "The Royal Air Force is not a club. It is a fighting service and it has no time or room for people such as you are at the moment."

The speech continues: "You are existing here on a knife-edge. Now go away and think about what I have said. Get down to it and do a little hard work for a change or else . . .

". . . or else.

"If you have the sense to try, we might yet make an RAF officer of you.

"That's all.

"Now go."

12

THE VETERAN

Flight Lieutenant Peter Townsend sprints like the devil is on his heels.

Hurricane at the ready. Coast of Northern England. Calm voice on the dispersal hut phone with a message loud as a starter's pistol: "Sector ops, here. Blue section 43 scramble base. Angels 1." RAF Acklington is black steel hangars and old brick buildings, a blustery World War I relic reopened last year in case of attacks just like this.

Flight Lieutenant Peter Townsend (left) and Caesar Hill (right)
Courtesy of the Imperial War Museums

Incoming Germans. Unable to strike London, 250 miles south, Luftwaffe Heinkel bombers are launching from bases in Germany's far north. Their mission is to sink British merchant vessels plying the cold dark waters between England and Norway. The Danby Beacon Chain Home station 85 miles south picked up the intruders when the Nazis were still fifteen minutes from land, proof the Dowding System now works.

A winded Townsend reaches his Hurricane. The paint scheme is dark green and brown camouflage, applied in a way that does not reduce speed or increase drag. The aircraft will be all but invisible as it flies low over water or land. A rigger helps him into his parachute.

Meanwhile, Townsend's "fitter" starts the engine and departs the cockpit, jumping down off the wing to make room for the pilot.

The flight lieutenant steadies his left hand atop the windscreen before stepping down into the cockpit. Elbows poke into ribs as he squeezes into his seat. Townsend eases thick, fleece-lined boots down onto the rudder pedals, his bent knees just inches below the black control panel. "Snug," he calls it. The fuselage walls and armored headrest are painted pale lime RAF interior green. Throttle and starter button to the left. Control column rises between his legs, crowned by a circular metal ring wreathed in vulcanized rubber. A brass "gun button," also known as the "tit" for its similarity to a woman's nipple, is affixed to this spade grip at eleven o'clock.

He clips into his Sutton safety harness, pulling the webbing down over the shoulders of his sheepskin flight jacket and kapok life vest before fastening the pin-release buckle.

Flight Lieutenant Peter Townsend and his Hawker Hurricane fighter aircraft are now one.

Townsend reaches right arm back to slide shut the canopy, engages the rudder to take off the parking brake, and taxis toward the snow-covered runway.

The Hurricane launches.

Elapsed time: ninety seconds.

Forming up with the other two Hurricanes of Blue section, Townsend aims away from the safety of the English coast, vectoring east over the churning North Sea.

The three fighters drop down to wave-top altitude, throttles wide open. The windswept ocean is a roiled landscape of deep troughs and towering crests. Spume flecks Townsend's windscreen. Camouflage matches the piss-green chunder of this charmless sea. The Hurricanes fly into the bleak, overcast outline of the rising sun.

Not so the two-engine Heinkels flying one thousand feet above, with telltale glazed glass nose bubbles and swastikas painted on the tails, their own dark paint a sharp contrast against light gray clouds.

Townsend's eyes strain upward, searching.

Then back to the horizon. Down to his instruments. Skyward again. Over and over. Constant rapid retinal scan.

The veteran pilot's greatest concern is finding bombers. Yet if his lone Merlin engine fails, he will ditch in the turbulent soup just a few feet below his wings, from which there can be no escape. Friends have died like this. There is no room for a raft in his Hurricane, and swimming miles to shore is a fantasy. The life jacket will keep him bobbing just long enough for what he refers to as the "immense wastes of the sea" to slowly freeze, suck into the depths, and drown him.

Townsend flies lead. Flight Officer Patrick "Tiger" Folkes and Sergeant Pilot Herbert James Lempriere Hallowes trail just off his left and right wings. Both are veteran pilots with hundreds of hours in the cockpit. H. J. L. Hallowes, now twenty-seven, has almost fifty years to live. Twenty-two-year-old Tiger, with his red hair and deep blue eyes, will be forever lost in these waters two months from now.

"Vector 190, Bandit attacking ship off Whitby, Buster" comes the radio report.

"Bandit" certifies the aircraft is hostile. "Buster" screams *as fast as possible!*

Townsend corrects course. The 43 Squadron was transferred to these remote northern airfields just before Christmas. Fashionable London—now enduring the bite of war as butter, bacon, and sugar are rationed nationwide—is a stark contrast to this frozen tundra. But the flight lieutenant finds the hardship ideal preparation for the conflict to come—"toughening us to the notion that we were to fight and possibly die," he will remember. "We became more rugged, coming to readiness in the icy dawn before flying out to sea, more often than not in the filthiest weather, to patrol above the coast bound convoys."

. . .

THERE HE IS.

Peter Townsend spies a lone German Heinkel 111 trying to hide in the clouds. Top speed almost 80 miles per hour less than a Hurricane—even slower with a full bombload. Machine guns in the nose, belly, and upper fuselage even the fight.

"Tallyho!" the flight lieutenant shouts into his radio. "Two o'clock."

Townsend climbs hard and banks right, followed by Folkes and Hallowes. Fists clutch the hard rubber of the circular spade grip. Both hands wrench the plane skyward. Camouflage means nothing as the Hurricanes close on the Heinkel.

The Germans see him.

"*Achtung!! Jaeger!*" shouts Rudolf Leushake, the flight observer inside the Heinkel, warning his fellow crew members that there is a hunter in their presence. These young men have flown together since August, and they bombed Poland on the opening day of the war. They have sweated, grumbled, cheered, endured, pissed, shit, argued, farted, and spent hours watching the world pass beneath the windows of this narrow tube. Now all that is over.

Rudolf Leushake has spoken his last words. With a simple twist of his gloved left fingers, Townsend rotates the gun button casing from "safe" to "fire." He depresses the trigger for two seconds, sending a burst of .50-caliber bullets into the bomber from above and behind. *Unteroffizier* Karl Missy calmly returns fire from his position in the Heinkel's top rear gun.

Townsend remains unscathed.

The Hurricanes are new to this game, but they press the attack, firing at close range. On land, enthralled witnesses watch the battle turn back toward England. "One fighter was firing at the tail from below, another was shooting at it from above, and the third was circling around it," a local resident will tell a reporter.

Observer Leushake is shot through the skull. *Unteroffizier* Missy's legs are shattered. Flight mechanic Johann Meyer presses blood-covered hands to his bullet-riddled stomach.

Flight Lieutenant Townsend doesn't need to give the order: Blue Sector stops shooting.

Pilot Hermann Wilms flies on, even as black smoke pours from his Heinkel's tail. The German aims for farm country, hoping to set the bomber down rather than crash into the sea. His path takes him directly over seafaring Whitby, where the great British explorer Captain James Cook began his career two centuries ago. "People on a cliff-top heard what was evidently the last burst of machine-gun fire from the fighters," the *Observer* will report in tomorrow's Sunday edition. "The British planes then drew off and made no further attacks when the raider was seen to be crippled and fast losing height."

Residents race from their houses. As the dying bomber drops lower, shocked citizens glimpse Hermann Wilms's desperate eyes looking back through the Heinkel's thick glass nose as he flies to what seems a certain death.

The bomber pancakes into a field two miles outside town. This is the first German plane of the war shot down on English soil. The dying Heinkel slams into a tree, shearing a wing but just missing the cockpit. Pilot Wilms survives. He tries in vain to burn secret documents on board before the local constable takes him into custody.

Twenty-five-year-old Rudolf Leushake and twenty-three-year-old Johann Meyer will be buried in a joint grave at the German Military Cemetery at Cannock Chase. Hermann Wilms becomes a prisoner of war, praying for a successful German invasion and quick release. *Unteroffizier* Karl Missy, a loyal member of the Nazi Party, joins him, but only after having his leg amputated high above the knee.*

---

* The site of the Heinkel's crash is now a memorial. The North Riding County Council erected the monument in the early 1950s, near the junction of the A169 and A171 roads.

Flight Lieutenant Townsend visits Missy in the hospital. He brings a carton of cigarettes and a bag of oranges to the man whose leg he shot away.

At first, Townsend was jubilant about recording his first kill. The victory makes news all over Britain.

Yet the visit depresses him.

"Perhaps I should end up like him, with no legs, or burnt or disfigured, or pieced together to be buried in some strange cemetery, with other pilots saluting," Townsend fears, "as my broken remains were lowered into the earth."

.   .   .

ON FEBRUARY 14, 1940, the British declare that all merchant vessels in the North Sea are now armed.

On February 15, Nazi Germany classifies British merchant vessels—fishing boats, trawlers, freighters—as ships of war.

On February 22, attacking at an altitude of twenty thousand feet, Flight Lieutenant Peter Townsend shoots down his second German bomber.

"The effect of my guns was devastating," he describes the scene. "It tipped into a steep dive at a terrifying speed. Suddenly, both wings were wrenched off with fearful violence and the dismembered fuselage plummeted straight into the sea."

Once again, the struggle between humanity and necessities of war consumes Townsend.

"Only at that moment did I realize what I had done to the men inside.

"I felt utterly nauseated."

But as Townsend well knows, the Germans are coming.

The flight lieutenant sets aside sympathy.

"There was no time for remorse," Townsend states after shooting down yet another Luftwaffe aircraft, this time a Messerschmitt fighter.

"If it was him this time, it could be me the next."

Due to the extent of his wounds, Karl Missy will be repatriated to Germany in a prisoner of war exchange in October 1943.

13

DOWDING

Stuffy is hours away from forced retirement.

Saturday. Distinguished forty-two-year career comes to an abrupt end tomorrow. Nothing to do but clean out the office and turn over command to an as-yet-unnamed successor. It's a brisk 45 degrees outside, with not a hint of rain. The mansion is quieter now that the Filter Room and the Operations Room have been moved into a steel-and-concrete bunker for protection from bombings. Women and men now work side by side in this technological marvel nicknamed "the Hole," Women's Auxiliary Air Force plotters having overcome concerns about their ability to focus, handle pressure, and—perhaps the greatest issue of all—inspire physical desires from male filterers.

"The Filterers are working not only close to their WAAF Plotters but have constantly to lean over them and push past them. It so happens that many of these young women are extremely attractive," one wing commander in Operations argued against the sexual integration. "They cannot fail to make some claim, even if only subconsciously, on the men Filterers working with them."

Dowding brushed that aside after watching the WAAFs work, "positively amazed at the way in which the way the so-called weaker sex" performs under pressure.

Should war arrive soon—and it appears that way, the London papers now reporting Nazi troops massing on the borders of France and Denmark—Dowding will leave Fighter Command with no regrets. He has long grown weary of dealing with people lacking the high level of intelligence he demands of himself to understand complex technical issues like aerodynamics and RDF. The air marshal's aide, Flight Lieutenant Francis Wilkinson, calls this "the fundamental stupidity of too many people on the air staff." Dowding being Dowding, he does not remain silent when faced with ignorance. His droll written correspondence and withering verbal responses to inane individuals would get a less senior man booted from the military.

Fearing no man, Dowding has bashed on, regardless.

The air marshal has significantly strengthened Britain's air defense network but the headaches never end. Dowding leaves behind a series of unfinished tasks: fighter command needs more all-weather runways, many aircraft still lack bulletproof windscreens, and attempts to perfect an RDF unit small enough to be placed inside an airplane are ongoing.

Most troubling is lack of aircraft.

Fighter Command began the war with twenty-five squadrons of regular pilots and fourteen more auxiliary units. Stuffy Dowding estimates that adequate defense of Britain means the total number should be fifty-two operational fighter squadrons. This is an enormous deficit.

In France, the Fairey Battle and the Bristol Blenheim bombers have been supporting the British Expeditionary Force since September. These are complemented by the four squadrons of Hurricanes that have been there since September. A contingent of outdated Gloster Gladiator biplanes is being sent home.

Making matters worse, even though Hurricanes were sent to France last fall, France demands more. The French, overly reliant on ground forces instead of their *armée de l'air*, have begun pestering the RAF about sending more planes and pilots. Incredibly, after years to prepare, the French claim their air force will not be ready for war until the summer of 1940.

London newspapers are reporting that in the past twenty-four hours, RAF fighters have shot down at least six German planes. Dowding is glad for this success but wants his fighters back. He frets they will be lost fighting a doomed cause in Europe, pilots dying and Hurricanes crashed for no good reason. There will be no Fighter Command to defend Britain on the day of the Nazi attack.

"You may rely on me to resist to the utmost any pressure that may be exercised by the War Cabinet to send more fighters," Dowding is informed by his commanding officer, Chief of Air Staff Cyril Newall. Dowding is almost four years older and was promised that top job before politics got in the way. Newall, whose clipped mustache and tall, lean build closely mirror those of Dowding, once flew bombers. But he has been a firm advocate of increased Hurricane and Spitfire production, and shares Dowding's views on fighter defense of England. "I am not preparing to sell Fighter Command to the French. I am merely asking you to take the necessary steps to ensure that if we are really in danger of losing the war in France through lack of fighters (a situation I do not think is likely to arise), we shall not find ourselves unprepared."

To which a very stuffy Dowding replies, "The French difficulties are largely due to the pathetic inefficiency of their interception system. I have not been told what steps they are taking to set their house in order, even at this late date."

Newall proposes sending two additional Hurricane squadrons to France. Detaching Spitfires is out of the question. Because Spitfires are the better of the two planes, Dowding is adamant they must remain in Britain for national defense.

But this is no longer Air Marshal Hugh Dowding's problem. As of midnight tomorrow, he will cease to be AOC-in-C. There's a war about to rage, and it's not his anymore to win.

Then, as today's afternoon light begins to wane, another letter arrives from Chief of Air Staff Newall.

This is quite the surprise.

"It has been decided to ask you to continue in your present position until July 14th of this year," Newall writes. "I shall personally be very glad if you are willing to accept this extension, as I feel it would be undesirable for a change to take place at Fighter Command at this stage when we may be on the verge of intensified air activity."

Air Marshal Hugh Dowding is in no hurry to respond. He returns to his home, Montrose House in Stanmore, enjoys a quiet dinner, and sleeps on the offer. Life would be so much simpler if he retired. He's won snow skiing competitions and was once president of Britain's national ski club. That might be a way to pass the time—though right now all the best mountains in Europe are under Nazi control. His son, Derek, still flying Spitfires for 74 Squadron at Hornchurch, just got married. Those two pursuits are all-encompassing. The young couple would have little time to spend with an air marshal put out to pasture before the RAF is really put to the test.

The air marshal himself has no matrimonial prospects, though he is not averse to remarrying—a prospect that might arise once his days and nights are no longer consumed by saving England.

There's the rub: no one but Hugh Dowding and Winston Churchill seems to have any clue how to do so.

Dowding decides to stay on.

"I shall be glad to continue in my present command until July 14th of this year," he responds to Chief of Air Staff Newall.

Stuffy Dowding gets back to work.

14

THE AMERICAN

APRIL 12, 1940
MINSTER LOVELL, ENGLAND
DAY

That didn't take long.

Life is good in the Cotswolds for Billy Fiske, just named acting pilot officer on probation, Royal Air Force Volunteer Reserve. In less formal terms, the American has earned his RAF wings. Every instructor agrees that if there is such thing as a natural pilot, Fiske answers that description.

Acting pilot officer Billy Fiske

Picryl/UK Government Artistic Works

Like all student aviators, Fiske has divided his days these past seven months with time in the cockpit and in classes on the ground. But he does not live the monastic life of his peers. Fiske neither resides on base nor in the barracks. He sleeps each night with his British wife, Rose, in a small, rented home in Minster Lovell. The village is simple: a pitch, a river, a fifteenth-century manor home, a dovecote, an inn, a pub, and a road. No. 2 Flying Training School is four miles away in Brize Norton, where Fiske flies the antiquated Gloster Gladiator biplane.

Fiske's bold plan to fight for England is coming to fruition. War is surely coming. On April 2, Prime Minister Chamberlain warned Germany that the Royal Navy was prepared to fight in German waters, stating: "We have not yet reached the limit of our effective operations in waters close to the German bases." British vessels soon sank several German warships.

But the Nazis quickly gained the upper hand. Germany invaded Denmark and Norway three days ago, ending what many are calling the "Phoney War," as the British spell it.

Winston Churchill, much more dramatically, calls this lull the "sinister trance." During a speech before a packed House of Commons yesterday, Churchill foresaw the downfall of Adolf Hitler in the Norwegian invasions, calling it "as great a strategic and political error" as Napoléon's disastrous attack on Spain in 1808.*

The Nazis have been brilliant in their execution of these invasions, catching the British unaware despite ample warning of impending attack. London newspapers fill pages with articles about the next phase, a likely invasion of France. "The governments of Britain and France will find

---

* The Peninsular War in Spain and Portugal was an attempt by Napoléon to continue his Europe-wide trade blockade with Britain. Though initially successful, Napoléon was never able to break the will of the Spanish people. The term "guerrilla" came into use for the first time as irregular troops fought for Spain. The forty-four-year-old Napoléon was so weakened by this defeat that he was forced to unconditionally abdicate his throne as emperor of the French at the war's end in 1814.

their people ready for any call," reads today's *Daily Telegraph*, the tone more hopeful than realistic.

Right now it is Billy Fiske who is ready for any call. No one mentions his nationality. Despite his wealth, the American has a reputation among his fellow British fliers as "terribly nice and extraordinarily modest." Through his social contacts at White's, he is trying to arrange his longed-for posting to 601 Squadron, currently at RAF Tangmere on England's southern coast. The Millionaires' Squadron is currently switching over from the twin-engine Bristol Blenheims to Hurricanes, so it is likely Fiske's next stop is not 601, but a fighter training squadron.

That means his assignment to 601, should it come through, is months away.

On the other hand, what good are connections if they're not put to use? Acting Pilot Officer Fiske makes a few calls.

15

THE BOY

APRIL 1940

RAF LITTLE RISSINGTON

DAY

Come on, Mr. Wellum. This is not good enough. No good at all. You can do a lot better."

Flight Sergeant Eddy Lewis badgers his pupil from the back seat of the Harvard trainer. The British countryside flashes thousands of feet below. The Boy is days away from taking his wings test, and Lewis rides him hard. Even at this late point in the training, pilot candidates are washing out. Two friends flying the Avro Tutor were transferred for failure to perform: one sent to navigator training and the other to Equipment Branch. Another good friend crashed a Harvard and was killed. Now Sergeant Lewis is determined to see Wellum complete his training and sew that flying badge on the chest of his uniform.*

"I have so many bad habits and faults that I get annoyed with myself," Wellum frets. "Add the intense flying lectures and evening work and you've got yourself maximum pressure and a very busy time. No trips out to the local pub. The chips are down."

Wellum is not told the date or time of his wings test. Sergeant Lewis is

---

* The Royal Air Force Flying Badge, commonly referred to as "wings" for its shape, is worn above the left tunic pocket. The design consists of the letters "RAF" surrounded by a brown laurel wreath, topped by the St. Edward's Crown. The wings extending on either side are those of an eagle.

relentless in his search for perfection from his pupil, using repetition and bullying to rid Wellum of the most minute deficiencies. Tells him he's lazy. Says "Do it again" more times than Wellum can count. It is Lewis who will decide when the young pilot is ready for his wings test—and right now Wellum is not ready.

"Nothing slips by Eddy Lewis," the Boy grumbles. "He is meticulous."

There is nothing else to life right now. Only flying. Port and starboard. Rudder, stick, throttle. Straight and level.

War and women are abstract concepts, distant distractions that siphon precious mental energy from the rigorous process of earning wings. Every mistake can be fatal, like in the Harvard crash, when the student pilot took off before noticing that two key instruments were broken.

Winter is long over. The weather can't make up its mind about hot and cold, fluctuating from extreme highs to temperatures better suited to February. It's harder to fly on the hot days. Engine performance decreases as the temperature goes up. Engines like the cold.

Without warning, test flight day arrives. "Oh, by the way, you'll be taking your wings test this afternoon," the flight commander says casually as Wellum arrives at the flight line.

But that summons takes place first thing in the morning, giving Wellum all day to ruminate about what is to come. Way too much time. Even when he reports to his assigned aircraft just after 1500 hours, he spends five minutes starting the engine and sitting alone with his thoughts.

It's more than a year since Geoffrey Wellum passed the first flight interview in London. That hurdle, which once seemed so enormous, pales in comparison to what will occur next. No one ever talks about second chances when it comes to passing the wings flight. Wellum knows he will be in the sky for roughly one hour, tested on all manner of aviation, from rolls to spins to engine failure. He calms himself, in the Harvard's small cockpit, dressed in a green waterproof Sidcot flight suit. Helmet, gloves. Radio and oxygen connections attached. Gone are the days when this space and all its apparatus were a mystery. He knows very well that he can place a blindfold over his eyes and still know the precise name and location of every instrument on the control panel—just as Eddy Lewis predicted during those earliest days of flight school.

The examiner finally arrives. Without pleasantry, the seasoned pilot climbs into the rear seat and straps in. "OK, Wellum. All set?"

"Yes, thank you, sir."

"Right, then. Taxi out. Take off and climb on due west to eight thousand feet. Carry on in your own time."

Wellum calms himself. *This is the hour,* he thinks. *The whole future depends on it. My future. It's important.*

And what an hour it is. Whatever nerves Geoffrey Wellum has felt all day are replaced by confidence—almost overconfidence—as he capably responds to every challenge the examiner throws his way. Wellum silently thanks Eddy Lewis for driving him so hard. *I settle to the task of waging war on the wings test, and the gentleman in back. Everything he asks of me I find I can do without much trouble—and he throws the book at me.*

Wellum is finally instructed to land. The fateful hour is over. The examiner says nothing other than good-bye. But after Wellum shuts down the Harvard and walks back to the headquarters hut, the flight commander beckons him into his office.

"I understand you have done a good test, Wellum. Well done."

Geoffrey Wellum has passed.

Later, Wellum having also passed his classroom exams, his name is placed on the official list of new pilot officers. He breezes back to his quarters, feigning nonchalance. But the mantle of potential failure is gone. The relief of finally making it through flight school is overwhelming.

Later, the Boy stands before a mirror. The man staring back at him wears a pressed blue uniform with new pilot's wings. "I can see nothing but those wings. A real pilot and a badge on my tunic to prove it," he marvels.

"No one will ever take that badge away from me."

. . .

TIME TO LEAVE. Next leg in the journey is the Advanced Training Squadron. Geoffrey Wellum seeks out Flight Sergeant Eddy Lewis to say his good-byes. The instructor stands outside the flight tent, a wry look on his face.

"I just want to thank you for all you've done to help me," Wellum says, choosing his words carefully. Their relationship has always been that of a teacher to pupil, with no fraternizing outside the curriculum.

"That's all right. We've had our moments, of course, but we got there in the end."

The two make pleasant small talk for a moment.

"Thanks once again, Flight," Wellum says by way of leaving.

"Just one thing, Mr. Wellum, before you dash off and leave. Remember, you still have an awful lot to learn and a long way to go. The going is still liable to be tough."

More tests. That's what Lewis is saying.

Always, more tests.

16

CHURCHILL

Neville Chamberlain is in pain.

The British prime minister has never lacked for good health. A touch of gout now and then, but otherwise no complaints. Now something isn't quite right. Not a dull throb or a sharp wince. Just an upset stomach and extra stops in the men's room, making this long session of Parliament more inconvenient than it already feels. It's been hours since Chamberlain concluded a fifty-seven-minute defense of his war policies, and there are surely several more hours before today's—*tonight's*—debate winds up. Arguments will spill over until tomorrow. The prime minister's wife, Anne, dressed all in black, watches from the gallery.

In fact, Chamberlain is suffering from undiagnosed advanced bowel cancer. He will be dead in six months and two days. The funeral service will be held at Westminster Abbey, where his ashes will be interred. Its date will be kept secret to prevent Nazi bombing. Winston Churchill will serve as a pallbearer, then eulogize Chamberlain here in Parliament, solemnly intoning eloquent words about sincerity and "the verdict of history."

But that is all to come.

At stake right now is whether or not Neville Chamberlain has the stomach to fight Hitler. Many will refer to this session of Parliament as

Neville Chamberlain

Wikimedia Commons/Original image housed in the National Archives of Poland

the "Norway Debate." Officially, the Hansard will label today's rancorous discussion "Conduct of the War." But it is really about the "Conduct of Prime Minister Chamberlain." This is the day his government slips away for good.

It was midafternoon when Chamberlain entered the chamber to loud applause. Those cheers have died. The prime minister delivered today's opening remarks at a few minutes to four, and has been under attack ever since. Churchill sits at the prime minister's side. The Ambassadors Gallery is full.

Chamberlain's cancer twines with the pain of ridicule and public humiliation to make him look broken and defeated. Because he is. Norway is a disaster. Nazi Germany has inflicted "a certain loss of prestige" upon Britain, in Chamberlain's own words, which will be quoted tomorrow in the *Daily Telegraph*. Germany invaded Norway in April. In response, men from the British Expeditionary Force were landed near the northern city of Trondheim to support Norwegian resistance. But the Luftwaffe had to-tal control of the skies and subjected British troops to relentless pounding. After suffering more than one thousand casualties, Britain is admitting defeat and withdrawing its forces—a kind term for running away. Some are comparing the retreat to the World War I debacle at Gallipoli, where a once proud British Army slunk off to avoid annihilation by the Turks.

The subtext of today's parliamentary drama is whether or not the prime minister is capable of leading the nation in the next phase of this expanding conflict. Later tonight, his own secretary of war, Oliver Stanley, will admit in this chamber to the "greatest storm" bursting on the Western Front "which might be decisive for this country."

Indeed, tomorrow's headlines will tell of drama on the main European landmass: Dutch reserve troops being called up to military service and all leaves canceled, a sure indicator that German invasion of their nation is coming. The British troops withdrawn from Norway are en route by ship to defend France.

That greatest storm might burst any day.

Sir Roger Keyes, admiral of the fleet, wearing full military dress for dramatic effect, appears in Parliament to call the Norway debacle "a shocking story of ineptitude"—sure fodder for tomorrow's headlines. As prime minister, Chamberlain must take full blame.

Such attacks have piled up throughout the debate, not in scathing insult but in careful and continuous undertones of faint praise and planted doubt, like picking at a scab. "The atmosphere," Chips Channon will journal with great understatement, "was intense."

Hour by hour, the House turns against Neville Chamberlain. "In the first major effort of this war," rails Arthur Greenwood of the Labour Party, now serving as a member of the War Cabinet, "we have had to creep back to our lairs."

Adds Archibald Sinclair of the Liberals: "I do think we must face facts and not bury our heads in the sand."

Churchill himself might have spoken the same words, were it not for his loyalty to Chamberlain.

Sinclair, a gentleman pilot who flies for fun, fought with Winston Churchill on the Western Front near Flanders as a major in the Royal Scots Fusiliers. Sinclair was Lieutenant Colonel Churchill's second-in-command. This political interlude occurred when Churchill left the government in November 1915 and joined the army. He served in the trenches on the front lines for three months, often crawling into no-man's-land between the British and German lines on nighttime patrols. "He never fell when a shell went off," one fellow soldier remarked of Churchill's courage. "He never ducked when a bullet went past with its loud crack. He used to say, after watching me duck: 'It's no damn use ducking; the bullet has gone a long way past you by now.'"

Bonded by their time in the cold and mud of Belgium, Sinclair and Churchill remain good friends.

But on this night, beginning at 8:03, it is Leo Amery of Chamberlain's own Conservative Party who delivers stinging damnation. Chamberlain sits impassively as he endures Amery's words, later telling friends it was one of the most effective speeches he has ever heard, even though every syllable comes at his expense.

Amery is sixty-six, an ardent foe of appeasement and a self-styled authority on military preparedness. Born in British India. Former journalist, former first lord of the Admiralty, former secretary of state for the colonies. Noted mountain climber, bagging summits in the Swiss Alps, Germany, Austria, and Yugoslavia. Canada has even named a peak in his honor.*

To his great sadness, Amery will endure the disappointment of his elder son's increasingly pro-Nazi sympathies, the young man doomed to one day be hanged in Britain for treason.

In short, Leo Amery is a man of depth and distinction whose words carry great impact.

---

* Mount Amery is located in the Canadian Rockies, in Banff National Park. The peak was named in Amery's honor in 1928, a time when no climber had ever reached the summit. Leo Amery traveled to Canada the following summer and became the first man to climb his namesake mountain.

This statesman of robust health now deals a cruel blow to a fading politician and dying man.

"Somehow or other, we must get into the Government men who can match our enemies in fighting spirit, in daring, in resolution, and in thirst for victory."

Speaking in words borrowed from seventeenth-century British hero Oliver Cromwell, Leo Amery then demands Neville Chamberlain step down as prime minister.

"You have sat too long here for any good you have been doing. Depart, I say, and let us have done with you.

"In the name of God, *go!*"*

Chips Channon writes:

"Everywhere one heard whispers: 'What will Winston do?'"

---

* On January 19, 2022, Conservative member of Parliament David Davis directed this same withering quote at Prime Minister Boris Johnson. Ironically, Johnson had previously written a biography of Winston Churchill, in which he used the diaries of Leo Amery as a source. Yet Johnson would claim that he had never before heard the infamous Oliver Cromwell quote.

WAR

17

CHURCHILL

MAY 10, 1940
LONDON, ENGLAND
6 P.M.

Winston is off to see the king.

The first lord enjoys an exultant moment with Clementine at Admiralty House, both knowing that their lives are about to change forever. Then he is driven to Buckingham Palace. London plane trees form an archway down the length of the Mall. Londoners are out in force on this start to the weekend. Excitement, fear, confusion, and patriotic defiance sizzle through the city like electric current. Pedestrians walk with purpose toward Trafalgar Square, Green Park, Embankment, and Piccadilly. Lovers enjoy a warm dusk on the clipped grass of St. James's Park, with its stately lake right in the heart of the great city. Gulls, coots, grebes, and moorhens, oblivious to war, calmly float on the water and peck for food.

No spectators block the tall iron palace gates as Churchill's Daimler turns into the entry. It is as if Churchill is on a secret mission.

Which, in many ways, he is.

A secret mission that will impact world history for generations to come.

Churchill is driven into the courtyard, past the King's Guard. Red uniforms. Black bearskin hats. Black boots polished to a high shine. Churchill steps out of the limousine and is led immediately inside to the sovereign.

George VI is forty-four, a kind man in a tailored suit with a perfectly knotted tie and wavy brown hair parted on the left. The king stutters. Married with two young daughters. Good enough at tennis to compete but lose at Wimbledon. Like Churchill, he is a navy man, having served in World War I. Also like the first lord, the king is a pilot, and he transferred into the Royal Air Force upon its founding in 1918.

"His Majesty received me most graciously and bade me sit down," Churchill will write.

Palace walls a subtle shade of green. Oversized portraits with ornate, gilded wooden frames. Chairs of gilded beechwood and silk damask cushions. An ashtray never far from the king' s reach.

"I suppose you don't know why I've sent for you," begins the monarch.

"Sir, I simply couldn't imagine why," Churchill responds, coy smile on his lips.

The first lord knows why he has been summoned. King George VI is certain of that.

Both men are also aware Prime Minister Neville Chamberlain is soon to address the nation and state that he is stepping down. He came to the palace today, just after tea, to tender his resignation to the king.

Two men have been considered as the obvious successor: Churchill and Lord Halifax, the urbane and rail-thin secretary of state for foreign affairs. Chamberlain prefers the wealthy Halifax, who shares his enchantment with appeasement. Halifax privately believes Britain can survive only by making peace with Hitler.

Backroom discussions about a next prime minister have been going on since the Norway Debate. Chamberlain clung to power, trying to cobble together a new coalition, vacillating about quitting. Winston Churchill well knows of the parliamentary intrigue, having followed every moment closely through friends like Leo Amery, who played a role in the horse trading.

The prime minister offered longtime friend Halifax the job yesterday morning.

But Lord Halifax declined, stating that his membership in the House of Lords will make it impossible to form a true wartime coalition government in Commons. Lords can sit in the House for debate but cannot cast a vote. "He was not enthusiastic," King George will write of the response from Halifax, "as being in the Lords he could only act as a shadow or a ghost in Commons, where all the real work took place."*

King George VI suggests Chamberlain offer the job to "the only other person whom I could send for to form a government."

So Churchill, the second choice, gets the nod—and this royal invitation.

The timing could not be more coincidental. On this very day, Adolf Hitler has validated every fear Churchill has shared with the British people over the past decade. Nazi troops launched *Fall Gelb* (Case Yellow), the surprise invasion of France and the Low Countries. More than three million German troops have poured across those borders, supported by tanks and aircraft. British Expeditionary Forces, many freshly arrived from Norway, are now fighting in Belgium and the Netherlands.

The RAF is engaging the Luftwaffe and suffering horrible losses.

Western Europe is being bombed like Poland nine months ago. The London headlines are one terror after another.

"The Nazis attacked soon after dawn with wave after wave of Dorniers, Heinkels, and Junkers," reads one newspaper story.

"Scores of Nazi Troop Planes Land."

"Bombs Start Fire in the Heart of Brussels."

"Parachute Troops in Fake Uniforms Land in Holland."

"Waves of Hitler's Planes Attack Towns and Villages," screams the *Daily Herald* banner. Tales of British heroism are beginning to fill column inches, including the saga of a single Hurricane that took on five Dornier bombers before breaking off for want of ammunition.

Tonight's *Evening Standard* adds human-interest stories that relate

---

* The king is never allowed to enter the House of Commons. This dates to 1642, when King Charles I and a cadre of armed guards stepped into the House and attempted to arrest some of its members. No king or queen has been allowed inside since.

vignettes about brave Londoners who traveled to Europe to protect their business interests and returned alive. Others tell of British citizens now embarrassed by their German heritage. "Wartime Breakfasts Then and Now" talks about British food during the Crimean War—anything to find an angle.

Only a page six editorial hints at the need for a strong new prime minister: "A Government Now!" shouts the *Standard* headline. "Germany has staked all on an immediate grapple with the Allies in every theater of the war. Days and hours, even minutes, may be decisive. The blow is delivered when Britain, in effect, is without a government."

Which is exactly why Winston Churchill has come to see the king, a man he barely knows. The sovereign would have much preferred Halifax. Churchill is sixty-five, an age when most men retire. Stuffy Dowding is seven years younger, and the RAF is impatient for him to be gone. But politicians are subject to the same rules as authors and orchestra conductors, allowed to ply their trade as long as the public approves. Churchill has lived a long, full, famous, and often eccentric life. He has always lived by his own rules. Everything has prepared him for this very moment. It all seems so promising, but nothing is certain. The burden will be crushing. Serious Learned Men do not drink like otters, chomp all day on Cuban cigars, or sleep in pink silk pajamas. Yet Serious Learned Men have proven incapable of governing Great Britain. How can Churchill do better? Most likely, he could be on the verge of colossal failure. He has enemies. Nothing would make those people happier than his return to the wilderness.

John "Jock" Colville, assistant private secretary to Neville Chamberlain, will write that "there seems to be some inclination in Whitehall that Winston will be a complete failure and that Neville will return."

There seems no hope of Churchill's success, Colville will add, because the British establishment is "so dubious and so prepared to have its doubts justified."

The king sees otherwise.

"I want to ask you to form a government," the royal personification of England says.

Francis Drake. Horatio Nelson. R. J. Mitchell. Save our great island nation.

Churchill has one last chance to say no.

"I will certainly do so," Great Britain's new prime minister tells his king.

. . .

AMERICAN JOURNALIST EDWARD R. Murrow broadcasts the news back to the United States from a studio in the basement of BBC headquarters. Thirty-two years old but starting to look forty. Clothes smell of tobacco from his five dozen unfiltered Camel cigarettes a day. Black hair slicked back. Arrived in London three years ago for CBS News with his wife, the former Janet Brewster, herself a broadcaster. Great Britain is their beat. The couple have gotten to know more than a few of the nation's most powerful leaders. Murrow often attends sessions of the House of Commons. Unlike Ambassador Joseph P. Kennedy, the broadcaster has a deep fondness for the British people. So it is with the knowledge of an insider and the tone of an ally that he introduces America to the new prime minister.

"At nine o'clock tonight, a tired old man spoke to the nation from 10 Downing Street," Murrow says in reference to Neville Chamberlain. "He sat behind the great oval table in the Cabinet Room where so many fateful decisions have been taken during the three years he directed the policies of His Majesty's government. Neville Chamberlain announced his resignation.

"Winston Churchill, who has known more political offices than any living man, is now prime minister. He is a man without a party. For the last seven years, he has sat in the House of Commons, a rather alone bellicose figure, voicing unheeded warnings of the rising tide of German strength.

"Now, at the age of sixty-five, Winston Churchill—plump, bald, with massive round shoulders—is for the first time in his varied career [as] a journalist, historian, and politician, the Prime Minster of Great Britain."

. . .

THE EVENING STANDARD reveals the true mood of Winston Churchill's new constituents. It is Friday night as he assumes power. Pubs filled. War all the talk.

"The British people know now they are fighting for their existence," writes the *Standard*. "Either we awaken every energy in our being or this soil of England will be drenched by blood and unending tears."

The anonymous editorial writer adds: "Either we fight back as even Britons have never fought before or all our institutions, all the life that we love, will perish for generations from the earth."

.   .   .

MAY 13. MONDAY afternoon. 2:54 p.m. Winston Churchill rises to address Parliament for the first time as prime minister. He announces the formation of a War Cabinet. Asks for a week to affect the transition of power.

Six minutes into his speech, Churchill shifts the rhetoric from business to defiance.

"I have nothing to offer but blood, toil, tears, and sweat," states the prime minister. He is eager to be a wartime leader and shake his gadfly reputation once and for all.

"We have before us an ordeal of the most grievous kind. We have before us many, many long months of struggle and of suffering. You ask, what is our policy? I will say: It is to wage war, by sea, land and air, with all our might and with all the strength that God can give us; to wage war against a monstrous tyranny never surpassed in the dark, lamentable catalogue of human crime. That is our policy.

"You ask, what is our aim?"

Winston Churchill waits. The House watches, taking his temperature. He is a sharp departure from the calm deportment of Neville Chamberlain. Every word of this speech will be weighed for notes of worthiness, inspiration, and competence. Now is the time to be specific.

Then, in one stunning sentence, Churchill abolishes Britain's policy of appeasement toward Adolf Hitler's ruthless ambitions once and for all.

"I can answer in one word: it is victory."

18

HANDSOME RICHARD

Richard Hillary is eager to fight.

And knows the perfect aircraft in which to do the job.

The Below Average student has been training in Scotland for five months now. Germany surprised absolutely no one but the French by invading through the Ardennes Forest four days ago. Nothing phony about this very real war. Even as these young British pilots eagerly await their next assignment, German bombers are obliterating the Dutch city of Rotterdam. Centuries-old buildings flattened. Fires burning out of control. Almost nine hundred Dutch are dead and eighty thousand homeless. It is not hard to imagine Germany inflicting the same barbaric fate on London.

Yet while the carnage in Rotterdam is more than seven hundred miles away, the war visits RAF Kinloss often, with bomber crews using the base as a launching point for raids on German targets. The withdrawal of British ground forces has not halted aerial bombings on Norway and Germany. Hillary studies the faces of these Bomber Command pilots, navigators, and gunners as they return from each mission. They betray no expression of loss on the night five bombers don't come back—just acceptance, a few games of bridge, then planning the next night's run.

"The pilot is of a rare race of men who since time immemorial have been inarticulate; who, through their daily contact with death, have realized, often enough unconsciously, certain fundamental things," Hillary observes.

He likes to observe.

Not to pass judgment but for cues. The social animal constantly finds himself assessing the behavior of experienced fliers, planning to use this as his own code when finally assigned to an operational squadron. It is no different from studying the expected decorum for joining a social club back at Oxford. In these pilots, he discerns something unique, very much in line with his own thinking: "These men, who in their air must have their minds clear, their nerves controlled, and their concentration intense, ask on the ground only to be allowed to relax."

Hillary has grown used to the mundane sight of training aircraft and the warlike mien of bombers. So he is stunned to find his heart thrumming in the waning days of flight school when a new sort of plane lands at Kinloss. The sight takes away Hillary's breath. He is filled with a most unfamiliar emotion: ambition.

The object of his new infatuation was designed by R. J. Mitchell.

"One day a Spitfire Squadron dropped in. It was our first glimpse of the machine," Hillary describes the moment he falls in love. "The trim deceptive frailty of their lines fascinated us and we spent much of our spare time climbing onto their wings and inspecting the controls. . . .

"We were most anxious to fly single-seater fighters."

Hillary has earned his wings but does not make much of the moment, although it is a relief to be done. His focus is on leaving dreary Northern Scotland. The time on this flat coastal plain has been long and demanding. Winter has come and gone. Summer is six weeks away. Hillary is glad for his new skill as a pilot. He enjoyed the classroom discussions about aerial combat as much as the actual flying. As always, the social element is among his highest concerns, and he feels prepared to behave properly in the skies when finally assigned to a squadron.

But Hillary well knows the personality of a squadron is not defined by classroom discussion. Nor by how well its pilots fly. This character is chosen by their type of aircraft. The plane chooses the mission. And each mission molds the behavior of its pilots in ways that extend far beyond the cockpit.

So the mood is taut as the day arrives for the newly graduated pilots of Richard Hillary's flight school to receive their next assignment. "Postings," they're called. This list is everything. Postings determine how the new pilots will wage this war: bomber, fighter, anti-submarine, coastal patrol, reconnaissance, transport. Then the subsets: day bomber, torpedo bomber, night fighter; India, Burma, Gibraltar, Mediterranean, Singapore, and so on. Lifelong friends will be made in these squadrons. Girlfriends from the local villages might become wives. Future reunions, future children, future joys and sorrows—all born of today's postings.

Tragedies will also come from the list: being in the wrong plane on the wrong mission at the wrong time. Instant death. Widowed wife. Orphaned children. Bereft parents unbelieving that their son has died before them. Carnations and a tombstone—if squadron pilots are "lucky" enough to be shot down over land. No such memorial for those lost at sea.

On this dreary May morning, a simple line on this simple posted list stipulating that a young pilot fly a specific aircraft for a specific squadron will determine the course of his future just as surely as being born in Great Britain instead of Germany.

So it is unsurprising that, in Hillary's words: "We awaited our final postings with impatience." He has high hopes to be that lone man in a Spitfire, the chivalrous knight, the medieval jouster, locking eyes with his opponent as he opens fire.

"But their arrival was a bitter disappointment."

Only three members of Hillary's class draw fighters.

He is not among them.

Months flouting regulations, long hair, mediocre test scores, and flippant remarks about the ways of the Royal Air Force have not gone unnoticed. He worked just hard enough to scrape through flight school, even becoming a credible pilot, but arrogance comes with a punishment.

And that stiff penalty will be watching three other men—some he considers his social inferiors—fly single-seat fighters into combat. Richard

Hillary will instead learn how to provide close air support for the army. His coursework will consist of aerial photography and reconnaissance. There will be no more exciting lectures about dogfighting. He is to report to the No. 1 School of Army Co-operation at an airfield between Bath and London known as Old Sarum for training, beginning May 20. The course will last six weeks.

Hillary's new airplane will be the Lysander, a high-winged, fixed-landing-gear tail dragger. Seats four, plus a pilot. Lysanders are already in France supporting the British Expeditionary Force. They are neither quick nor nimble. Among their nicknames is the "flying coffin." The plane is such a lumbering beast that each flight requires fighter protection, as if the Lysander were a fully laden bomber.

If Hillary is lucky, he will be one of the daring pilots flying special-duty Lysanders loaded with secret agents into France in the dark of night, heart racing as he lands on improvised runways temporarily lit by the flashlights of partisans, drops off his passenger, then hurriedly takes off and flies home to England before the Nazis confirm his location and take him prisoner—or shoot him dead. For all its danger, the romance of such an assignment is a spectacular fit for Richard Hillary's dramatic personality.

Most likely, however, the former Trinity College student will be an artillery spotter.

Richard Hillary has told others in the past: "I shan't be sitting behind a long-range gun working out how to kill people sixty miles away."

Yet that's precisely what he will be doing.

The glorious chivalry of midair combat does not exist in a Lysander.

19

CHURCHILL

MAY 15, 1940
LONDON, ENGLAND
DAY

Winston has choices to make.

Ten Downing Street. Morning meeting of the War Cabinet. The "Old Man," as private staff have begun calling their new boss, sits with four handpicked men—Clement Attlee, Arthur Greenwood, Lord Halifax, and even Neville Chamberlain, whom Churchill has brought in as a show of respect and to maintain Conservative Party unity. The situation in Europe is changing rapidly, and these veteran politicians will meet several more times today—and every day for the foreseeable future.

At the very top of the agenda: France and fighters.

A desperate 7:30 phone call from Paris this morning brought news from French prime minister Paul Reynaud that his nation was lost. Speaking in English, Churchill's terrified counterpart told him, "We have been defeated."

When Churchill tried to calm Reynaud with reminders that the Wehrmacht could not have possibly made it all the way from Germany to Paris in five days and nights, the defeatist Frenchman corrected him: "We are beaten. We have lost the battle."

The prime minister adores adventure and travel. Tomorrow morning will bring both. To ease Reynaud's fears, the prime minister ended the call by promising to pay a visit. Churchill will squeeze into the narrow fuselage of a de Havilland Flamingo and fly to Paris at a cruising speed of 203 miles per hour. An RAF fighter escort will attempt to keep him safe from the Nazi planes that are now everywhere in the French sky.

These fighters will also see Churchill safely back to London, though the French sorely long for them to remain behind.

France covets British fighters—of this there is no disagreement among the assembled politicians around this table. Three days ago, May 12, the War Cabinet approved that four more squadrons be sent to France. Just twenty-four hours later, Stuffy Dowding was told to send thirty-two more individual aircraft to supplement that gift, so he had to pull Hurricanes in twos and threes from groups based in England.

Just one day later, Prime Minister Reynaud set a new standard for arrogant demands, requesting still more British planes. "If we are to win this battle, which might be decisive for the whole war, it is necessary to send at once at least ten more squadrons," he told Churchill.

And the French don't just want any aircraft. They could care less about the Fairey Battle and the Bristol Blenheim, which are getting clobbered by the Luftwaffe. What Prime Minister Reynaud covets are the very best: Hurricanes and Spitfires, the only aircraft capable of matching an Me 109 in combat.

And Winston Churchill is determined to give the French what they want.

He is committed to rescuing France. Yet somewhere in his obsessive daily study of the minutiae of this war, during which he spends hours poring over facts and maps, the new prime minister has made a mental mistake. Fighter Command has informed him that they require fifty-two squadrons to defend England.

Churchill has transposed this number in his head.

Twenty-five is the number he sees.

In fact, Fighter Command has just thirty-six squadrons. More than enough to spare a few in the mind of Winston Churchill and a desperate lack to the leader of Fighter Command.

. . .

STUFFY DOWDING IS furious.

Giving away ten more squadrons will ruin Britain's air defense network. Upon receiving the news at Bentley Priory, Dowding immediately sends word to Archibald Sinclair, longtime Churchill friend and newly appointed head of the Air Ministry, that he would like to address the War Cabinet as soon as possible.

Absurd. This is not done. Dowding has no business attending a War Cabinet meeting, let alone blessing those in attendance with his unwanted advice.

Yet, somewhat shockingly, this petition is immediately approved. Even Dowding is stunned. "It was a very unusual request," he will long remember. "I was very much surprised permission was granted."

The meeting will take place just hours after the morning's first cabinet meeting. Reynaud's frantic phone call is still a fresh memory to Winston Churchill. There is a large audience, some thirty military chiefs of staff and government ministers. The room is cigarettes, uniforms, pecking order. Dowding's direct superior, Chief of Air Staff Cyril Newall, is in attendance but keeps his distance as the head of Fighter Command takes a seat at the large conference table, six seats to the right of Churchill. Group Captain Elliot, the man who interviewed American Billy Fiske and admitted him to the RAF, is also a witness to this unusual moment.

Churchill leads the discussion. He is having a mood. Face hard and contrary. No jokes. No small talk. "Dowding, you know that this now puts us in a very precarious position with France," Churchill scolds.

Dowding replies with an utter lack of deference.

"I am well aware of the situation, Prime Minister, but my task at hand is for the air defense of this country and it is my belief that I cannot achieve this if half my aircraft are in France." The air marshal's inability to play politics has cost him dearly in the past and may well do so today. When given a chance to plead his case, he firmly states that if more fighters are taken from him, Fighter Command would be too weak to defend Britain.

But Dowding is not all pessimism.

"Provided no more fighters were removed," reports the Chief of Staff Committee minutes for tonight's meeting, "he was confident that the Navy and the Royal Air Force would be able to keep the Germans out of the country."

Dowding's words are succinct, his tone direct. He is not afraid of Winston Churchill, who appears to believe the head of Fighter Command is attempting to grandstand at the prime minister's expense before the assembled decision-makers. Nor does Dowding trust the new air minister, Sinclair, who has long been considered Churchill's toady.

The room grows more hostile with every passing argument from Downing. "He was factual and to the point," the minutes will report. "The professional airman stating expertly and concisely a case that had to be made. There was no room for rhetoric."

Yet no one wants to offend Churchill. Dowding is alone. In frustration, he suddenly pushes back his chair, stands, and walks toward the prime minister.

"I think some people thought I was going to shoot him," Dowding will state about what happens next. "I felt like it."

Others believe Dowding is about to resign.

The leader of Fighter Command pulls a piece of paper from his pocket. Prior to the meeting, he sketched a graph using red ink. He walks to Churchill and thrusts the paper at the prime minister. "This red line shows the wastage of Hurricanes in the last ten days. If the line goes on at the same rate for the next ten days, there won't be a single Hurricane left either in France or in England."

Churchill is dumbstruck.

"We are losing aircraft at a far quicker rate than we can produce them," continues Dowding. "We need more aircraft, and more pilots to fly them."

Group Captain Elliot will long remember how Dowding "put his case so ably and spoken with such sincerity that there was no room for further discussion."

"That did the trick," Dowding will recall, knowing he had won. "He never uttered another word."

The War Cabinet makes a decision: "No further fighter squadrons should for the present be sent to France."

Winston Churchill will inform Monsieur Reynaud in the morning.

. . .

BUT HUGH DOWDING is not convinced. He knows the desperate French will never relent. He believes Churchill might change his mind. "I knew that if this wastage, this great flood of Hurricane exports to France, was not checked, it would mean the loss of the war."

Back home at Montrose House, Hugh Dowding puts what remains of his career on the line. For his own peace of mind and the good of the nation, he must commit his arguments to paper.

SECRET

May 16, 1940

Sir,

I have the honour to refer to the very serious calls which have recently been made upon the Home Defence Fighter Units in an attempt to stem the German invasion on the Continent.

2. I hope and believe that our Armies may yet be victorious in France and Belgium, but we have to face the possibility that they may be defeated.

3. In this case I presume that there is no-one who will deny that England should fight on, even though the remainder of the Continent of Europe is dominated by the Germans.

4. For this purpose it is necessary to retain some minimum fighter strength in this country and I must request that the Air Council will inform me what they consider this minimum strength to be, in order that I may make my dispositions accordingly.

5. I would remind the Air Council that the last estimate which they made as to the force necessary to defend this country was 52 Squadrons, and my strength has now been reduced to the equivalent of 36 Squadrons.

6. Once a decision has been reached as to the limit on which the Air Council and the Cabinet are prepared to stake the existence of the country, it should be made clear to the Allied Commanders on the Continent that not a single aeroplane from Fighter Command beyond the limit will be sent across the Channel, no matter how desperate the situation may become.

7. It will, of course, be remembered that the estimate of 52 Squadrons was based on the assumption that the attack would come from the eastwards except in so far as the defences might be outflanked in flight. We have now to face the possibility that attacks may come from Spain or even from the North coast of France. The result is that our line is very much extended at the same time as our resources are reduced.

8. I must point out that within the last few days the equivalent of 10 Squadrons have been sent to France, that the Hurricane Squadrons remaining in this country are seriously depleted, and that the more Squadrons which are sent to France the higher will be the wastage and the more insistent the demands for reinforcements.

9. I must therefore request that as a matter of paramount urgency the Air Ministry will consider and decide what level of strength is to be left to the Fighter Command for the defences of this country, and will assure me that when this level has been reached, not one fighter will be sent across the Channel however urgent and insistent the appeals for help may be.

10. I believe that, if an adequate fighter force is kept in this country, if the fleet remains in being, and if Home Forces are suitably

organised to resist invasion, we should be able to carry on the war single handed for some time, if not indefinitely.

But, if the Home Defence Force is drained away in desperate attempts to remedy the situation in France, defeat in France will involve the final, complete and irremediable defeat of this country.

I have the honour to be,
Sir,
Your obedient Servant,
Air Chief Marshal,
Air Officer Commanding-in-Chief,
Fighter Command, Royal Air Force

. . .

DOWDING'S FEARS PROVE true. Prime Minister Churchill still believes twenty-five squadrons is Britain's safety margin. In Paris, the prime minister goes back on the War Cabinet decision and promises French leader Paul Reynaud six additional Hurricane squadrons. Ever so slowly, Great Britain's fighter defenses are being whittled to nothing.

20

CHURCHILL

MAY 19, 1940
CHARTWELL, ENGLAND
EVENING

Winston faith in the French is misplaced.

Now he will tell that to England. Churchill prepares to make his first national broadcast as prime minister. Clementine has pored over each draft of what he is about to say, and offered suggestions and corrections. She reminds the prime minister to speak in simple, ordinary terms, avoiding words the general public might not understand. He readily agrees.

Rather than broadcast from BBC headquarters, his country home, Chartwell, will serve as tonight's studio. This is his last chance to visit his beloved longtime estate before it is closed up for the winter. Everything about this manor says "Winston." A land once wandered by Saxons and Normans. Brick and beams dating back six centuries. His personal bedroom window puttied shut to keep out any pollen that might drift in from the Weald. Trees everywhere. Goldfish in a pond. Only one of his black swans has survived Churchill's long absence in London, the rest eaten by foxes. But one last man standing is cause for hope, no different from England preparing to fight on alone.

Churchill dresses casually, white shirt under a black jacket zipped all the way up to his thick neck. Two BBC microphones, his prepared text, and a green lamp rest on the small desk before him. British stage director

Tyrone Guthrie stands behind the prime minister, not to give comments but to direct Churchill's head toward the microphones. Decades of speaking in Parliament have gotten the prime minister in the habit of constantly rotating his head from left to right, making eye contact and addressing the entire House. Tonight, that would turn his mouth away from the microphones.

"I speak to you for the first time as prime minister in a solemn hour for the life of our country, of our empire, of our allies, and, above all, of the cause of freedom," Churchill begins. He paces his words, enunciating carefully. The lisp is faint. "Hour" and "our" lose the "r"—"ow-waa." Churchill is never folksy, but tonight he is friendly.

It's been a day. Clementine attended Trinity Sunday church services at St. Martin-in-the-Fields, only to walk out when the rector delivered a sermon preaching pacifism. President Franklin Roosevelt is refusing to loan Britain the fifty old destroyers Churchill has requested to shore up naval defenses. And news from France says the British Army is in retreat, their French allies surrendering in large numbers. French general Maurice Gamelin is already conceding a German victory. This comes just days after the surrender of Holland. Lord Gort, commander of the British Expeditionary Force, is almost demanding his troops be evacuated from France, requesting permission to fall back to a beach resort known as Dunkirk. The prime minister, fearing British troops would be pinned down and become easy fodder for German bombers, refuses to grant Gort's request.

Churchill tells his audience none of that. He delivers a brief summary of the German advances, then offers good news in the form of Royal Air Force success. "In the air—often at serious odds, often at odds hitherto thought overwhelming—we have been clawing down three or four to one of our enemies; and the relative balance of the British and German air forces is now considerably more favorable to us than at the beginning of the battle. In cutting down the German bombers, we are fighting our own battle as well as that of France. My confidence in our ability to fight it out to the finish with the German Air Force has been strengthened by the fierce encounters which have taken place and are taking place," the prime minister states in detail.

The speech follows the same pattern Churchill uses in Parliament, laying the foundation with hard facts. Now comes the matter that all in Britain are worried about and that must be addressed. Churchill enjoys playing upon these fears and even amplifying blunt honesty to keep his audience's attention.

"As soon as stability is reached on the Western Front," he speaks into the microphone. Churchill's cigar smolders in an ashtray. This first national address is too important for him to dilute its power by speaking with a stogie clamped into the corner of his mouth.

"The bulk of that hideous apparatus of aggression which gashed Holland into ruin and slavery in a few days will be turned upon us. I am sure I speak for all when I say we are ready to face it, to endure it, and to retaliate against it—to any extent that the unwritten laws of war permit. There will be many men and many women in this island who, when the ordeal comes upon them, as come it will, will feel comfort, and even a pride, that they are sharing the perils of our lads at the front—soldiers, sailors and airmen, God bless them."

There it is. The first glimmer of inspiration. Telling civilians that they will serve as de facto warriors on the bleak day Germany invades.

Winston Churchill has many enemies within Parliament and the highest levels of British establishment, but his nationwide popularity is soaring. The man who once divided England with his long-ago worries that war is coming now unites her people in a way that seemed impossible just last week. He uses that sentiment to shove aside fears of invasion, exhorting his audience to find a courage they never knew existed.

"Our task is not only to win the battle—but to win the war. After this battle in France abates its force, there will come the battle for our island—for all that Britain is, and all that Britain means. That will be the struggle. In that supreme emergency we shall not hesitate to take every step, even the most drastic, to call forth from our people the last ounce and the last inch of effort of which they are capable. The interests of property, the hours of labor, are nothing compared with the struggle of life and honor, for right and freedom, to which we have vowed ourselves."

Churchill continues: "Having received His Majesty's commission, I have formed an administration of men and women of every party and of almost every point of view."

Here Churchill speaks of his War Cabinet: himself from the Conservative Party, Clement Attlee from Labour, Halifax from the House of Lords, Arthur Greenwood from Labour, and the fallen former prime minister Chamberlain. Churchill has specifically requested that men of opposing political viewpoints serve in his cabinet. His goal in every way is a true national government.

"We have differed and quarreled in the past," the prime minister says of those men. "But now one bond unites us all—to wage war until victory is won, and never to surrender ourselves to servitude and shame, whatever the cost and the agony may be."

Churchill adds a few lines about the people already under the Nazi thumb losing hope "unless we conquer, as conquer we must, as conquer we shall."

Finally, the prime minister reminds his island nation that God is on their side.

"Today is Trinity Sunday. Centuries ago words were written to be a call and a spur to the faithful servants of Truth and Justice: 'Arm yourselves, and be ye men of valour, and be in readiness for the conflict; for it is better for us to perish in battle than to look upon the outrage of our nation and our altar. As the Will of God is in Heaven, even so let it be.'"*

Finishing his speech, the prime minister turns to his wife.

"Was that all right?" he asks Clementine.

---

* Trinity Sunday falls on the first Sunday after Pentecost, which is the fiftieth day after Easter. Trinity Sunday honors the Holy Trinity of the Christian faith: the Father, the Son, and the Holy Spirit.

. . .

MORE THAN ALL right.

Tonight's speech is not long. Ten and half minutes. Hardly enough time to unite a nation.

Amazingly, Winston Churchill has done just that.

British admiral Sir William Milbourne James, commander of the naval base in Portsmouth, is among those awed by what he has just heard.

"The hour has struck and the man has appeared."

21

THE VETERAN AND 85 SQUADRON

MAY 20, 1940
SUSSEX, ENGLAND
8 A.M.

The train for London clickety-clacks into the small country station. Monday morning. A short weekend of leave is finally over. Peter Townsend eagerly steps from the platform into the carriage. Stows his luggage. Finds a seat. Blue service dress uniform. The twenty-five-year-old pilot has been promoted to squadron leader. "Scraper" rings on his uniform sleeve denote the new rank. Four days since his last patrol with 43 Squadron. As always, the North Sea clawed at his senses during that final flight. He is still overwhelmed by the loss of good friend Tiger Folkes, crashed and lost forever in "the menacing tumultuous sea which had claimed indifferently both our own and the enemy's airmen," on April 16.[*]

First stop upon arriving in London will be the Air Ministry. From there it is on to France and command of 85 Squadron, unit code VY, which has been based in France since September 9, 1939. The 85 was one

---

[*] "Squadron leader" is equivalent to a major in the British Army. "Scraper" rings get their name from piston rings inside an engine. The slang term is a nod to the thin center sleeve stripes of the squadron leader service dress uniform, which some compare to a scraper's position inside a piston.

of Stuffy Dowding's original four Hurricane squadrons sent to help the French right after war was declared. Their time has been spent flying support for Bristol Blenheim and Fairey Battle bombers. The king paid a personal visit in December. But what began as an idyllic tour of duty has become the first major aerial test of the war. Since Germany attacked into France on May 10, the unit has seen some of the most ferocious fighting of any squadron in the Royal Air Force. Her exhausted men are ready to come home. It will be Townsend's job to lead the recovery process before a refreshed 85 is put back on the line.

The promotion came after being awarded the prestigious DFC—Distinguished Flying Cross—at the end of April. His courage and skill have not gone unnoticed: "Flight Lieutenant Peter Wooldridge Townsend (33178). In April, 1940, whilst on patrol over the North Sea, Flight Lieutenant Townsend intercepted and attacked an enemy aircraft at dusk and after a running fight shot it down. This is the third success obtained by this pilot and in each instance he has displayed qualities of leadership, skill and determination of the highest order, with little regard for his own safety," reads the citation.

Townsend is a passionate man, prone to the occasional impulsive whim. Yet he has no one special in his life right now. The pilot was recently entangled in a torrid romance with a "blue-eyed fair-skinned Danish goddess" named Bodil. The romance continued after she returned home to Copenhagen. At first, Townsend paid dearly for their love in the form of long-distance phone calls. But the breakup came soon after, a byproduct of war and separation, both of them aware that Townsend's devotion to the Royal Air Force leaves zero time for romance. So his short weekend leave was not spent in London pubs or in the arms of a lover, but in Sussex, at the home of his mother, Gladys.

Townsend is the fifth of seven children, born in faraway Rangoon, Burma, during his military father's service to the Crown. The pilot's life since the family's return to England has been transient in many respects: boarding schools, RAF Training College Cranwell, and the occasional stop at family residences in Whitchurch, Northam, and Bournemouth. He even lived with an aunt for a time while his parents returned to

Burma. Flight school was a shy child's salvation, a passion born of the day his father took him to an air show when the boy was just thirteen. Six years later, with Lieutenant Colonel Edward Townsend dead after a sudden illness, Peter Townsend suffered eczema on his skin from the combined stress of his new role as head of household and the danger of being a pilot. The only "palliative," in Townsend's estimation, has ironically been to fly as often as possible. It's been a long while since the last outbreak.

Life happens fast. It's just a dozen years since that air show. Now Townsend is not just an accomplished pilot in single-seat fighter aircraft, but a decorated hero about to become a squadron commander.

The Sussex air smells of new grass, tilled earth, serenity. Townsend has been struck by the bucolic charm, a countryside totally at peace—so far from the war, it is as if the fighting does not exist at all.

Only by day. At night, enemy planes probe Britain's southeast coast. Spotlights search the sky. The heavy thud of antiaircraft fire. From the far side of the Channel, ominous sounds of heavy shelling bursting in the sky like fireworks, visible all the way back in England. Winston Churchill's final words from last night's broadcast seem so horribly appropriate right now. They come from the Apocrypha's Book of Maccabees: "Arm yourselves and be ye men of valor, and be in readiness for the conflict, for it is better for us to perish in battle than to look upon the outrage of our nation."

Yesterday afternoon, in a moment of nostalgia, Squadron Leader Townsend walked alone across woodland and heath to where he could see the Channel. He stared wistfully out to sea.

France is out there somewhere. The 85 has been based near Lille of late, one of its many postings in France. Townsend wonders if he'll ever make it home again. A lot of good men haven't. RAF Hurricanes are holding their own against the Luftwaffe, but numbers are on Germany's side. Townsend hears rumors that 85's commander was shot down. Some say they've lost all but four of their Hurricanes.

And the German advantage is not just in the air. Yesterday in Paris, where citizens have long denied the threat of Nazi occupation, Trinity Sunday Mass was said at the Cathedral of Notre Dame to beseech the

Almighty for Allied victory. German forces now hold the center of France and are pushing hard for the Channel. The notoriously haughty Parisians are finally showing their fear.

It seems nothing can stop the Nazi onslaught.

.   .   .

THIS MORNING'S TRAIN stops frequently during the slow seventy-mile ride to London. Plenty of time to think. A few wispy clouds cast their shadows over the city. Short drizzle. Seventy degrees. Squadron Leader Townsend walks directly to the Air Ministry.

Instead of command orders, the pilot receives stunningly bad news from a heavyset flight lieutenant ten years older. Though junior in rank, the middle-aged officer pretends not to notice Townsend's scraper rings. "I'm sorry, my lad, there's chaos in France and we have lost 85 Squadron." The delivery is condescending. Townsend is offended and angry but maintains his outward calm.

A pilot without a command or an aircraft, Peter Townsend steps into the warm spring sunshine and does his best to enjoy London.

.   .   .

BUT 85 LIVES.

Even as a stunned Squadron Leader Townsend tries to fill his suddenly empty Monday, the pilots he is meant to command are improvising an exodus from Europe. The squadron has endured nine long months in France, but their toughest work has come since the German invasion. On that first morning, the 85 flew their first sortie at 4:15 and continued until past dark. Their Hurricanes have engaged the enemy in most dogged fashion every day since. These are the men of valor Churchill spoke about on the BBC last night. Men like Flight Officer D. H. Allen are an example of this commitment. On May 15, Allen was forced to bail out over Belgium, but immediately found a way back to the squadron, only to get shot down again on May 18. This time the flight officer was killed. He was twenty-two.

That heroism continued right up until the squadron's final moments in France. Squadron Commander M. F. Peacock, Pilot Officer R. W. Burton, and Pilot Officer R. W. Shrewsbury were all shot down and killed by ground fire while making one last attack on the German bomber base at Arras. Peacock had only just assumed command of the squadron earlier in the day, taking over for Squadron Commander O. W. Oliver, shot down over Belgium by an Me 109 on May 13.

Since May 10, the squadron has confirmed ninety enemy kills. Lost eleven pilots. Six more are missing. They have just three—not four—functioning Hurricanes to their name.

Time to get out of France.

Ground staff are rushing to Boulogne for evacuation by sea. They will endure a night of heavy German bombing before setting sail tomorrow.

Pilots without a plane have stayed behind at the squadron's base near Lille, awaiting cargo transport. Some are taking matters in their own hands, commandeering any aircraft that will fly. One pilot even crosses the Channel in a bright yellow Miles Master trainer.

Pilots of the three operational Hurricanes are flying home now, bringing nothing more than the clothes on their backs.

·   ·   ·

TOWNSEND IS INFORMED about this series of events.

"I arrived at Debden, Essex, to take command of the remnants of 85 Squadron," Townsend tells friends of the moment, going on to describe all that needs to happen next: The beleaguered men will need time to heal. New aircraft must be found. New pilots. Then dogfight training, live-fire drills. Townsend must build a squadron from scratch and have it fit and ready to fly as soon as humanly possible.

That is, if he has enough time.

Running low on fighters, pilots up and down the British coast exhausted, all of Fighter Command needs a pause to catch its breath. Attempts to save France have pushed the Royal Air Force to its breaking point. A sudden German thrust across the Channel right now will be disastrous.

The saga of 85 and Peter Townsend, the most legendary commander the squadron will ever know, has begun.

22

THE BOY

Geoffrey Wellum is new to 92.

Eighteen years and nine months old. One hundred sixty-eight hours of total flying time—just ninety-five of them solo. The Boy stands before his new commanding officer, a barrister turned pilot, now holding that flight log in his hands. To Wellum's eye, the man looks "pretty hefty" and "just plain ugly." It's right after lunch. The squadron commander is not pleased with Wellum's scant flying time.

"Where were you trained?"

"Number Six FTS Little Rissington, sir."

Wellum was rushed to the squadron prematurely, the loss of so many pilots in France cutting short his advanced training. He has never even so much as sat in a fighter. Now Wellum is expected to fly combat missions within the next few weeks.

"You are not of much use to the squadron. I pay little attention to an assessment made after a hundred-odd hours of flying."

"I appreciate that, sir."

"I'm bloody sure you don't."

Squadron Leader Roger Bushell is South African by birth. Twenty-eight. Dark haired, brooding. Fluent in French and German. Learned to fly with the Millionaires' 601 Squadron. Runs in the same St. Moritz circles as Billy Fiske, only as a skier instead of as a bobsledder. So good on snow that the Swiss named a black piste—most difficult—after him. Aggressive enough that a high-speed crash saw the sharpened edge of one ski slice open skin near his left eye. The scar makes that eye droop, thus Wellum's "ugly" description.

"You've never even seen a Spitfire, I gather," Bushell continues, "let alone flown one."

The 92 flies Spitfires. The transition from the Bristol Blenheim Mk IF began in March.

"I'd try very hard, sir," Wellum assures him.

A nonplussed Roger Bushell could not care less. The squadron was declared "operational" yesterday. Missions over France will begin any moment. Winston Churchill's agreement with French prime minister Paul Reynaud states that British fighters will fly from England to the French coast, scramble to engage the enemy, then return home to the safety of England each night. The 92 is one such squadron.

At this intense time in history, Bushell's veteran pilots need to be knocking down German fighters, not babysitting. Operational focus is the beachfront at Dunkirk, where several hundred thousand British and French soldiers are stranded for one last desperate stand against the Germans. Squadron Leader Bushell cannot waste a single aircraft on an untried pilot.

Yet Geoffrey Wellum is now a member of 92 and thus the commanding officer's problem. Somehow, the teenager must learn to fly the Spitfire.

The squadron leader has no choice: Wellum will have to teach himself.

"We have the best aeroplane in the service," Bushell tells Wellum, "or in the world, for that matter, and if you break one there will be merry hell to pay."

. . .

I AM A new boy, a bit of an outsider, Wellum thinks of his first days in the squadron. He is awed by the veteran fighter pilots with whom he shares meals and pints in the mess but feels a noticeable distance. They are heroic in his eyes, cocksure grown men with the swagger and confidence of individuals who have been tried and proven in the air many times over.

Theirs is a bond molded by enemy fire and hours flying together, each pilot accepting the others' strengths and weaknesses. *They are a team that formed the squadron and worked up together . . . little notice is taken of me.*

But that team is soon fractured over Dunkirk. The squadron loses five men on a single mission—"four of whom I'd met the night before in the officer's mess," Wellum is shocked to learn. The glory of being a pilot is instantly replaced by thoughts of dying. *Hold on a minute. This is bloody dangerous!*

Two days after Wellum's taut conference with his new commander, Squadron Leader Bushell is shot down over Dunkirk and taken prisoner. Geoffrey Wellum will never see him again.

Squadron losses mount. Pilots returning after long days over Dunkirk bear lined and weary faces, the strain of combat visible to the untried young pilot. Even if he learns to fly the Spitfire, he foresees another obstacle in his near future.*

Every untried warrior knows this great fear.

This test is still to come, he ruminates. *I must confess it worries me.*

Will I have what it takes to prove myself as the rest of them have done or shall I be a coward?

.   .   .

WELLUM APPROACHES A Spitfire for the first time.

All alone.

No back seat instructor chiding him. Wellum knows this is an opportunity hundreds of other pilots have sought, only to be denied. He carries his parachute and wears his helmet, attached oxygen masks dangling next

---

* Roger Bushell will remain a prisoner of war the rest of his life—though not for lack of trying. Feeling that escape is incumbent on any POW, he will break out of several German prison camps. Bushell will earn lasting fame as the mastermind of the famous "Great Escape" from Stalag Luft III, near the town of Sagan in Lower Silesia. After being recaptured once again, Bushell was among fifty prisoners machine-gunned by the Gestapo during a rest stop on their way back to prison. This was done on orders from Adolf Hitler. Roger Bushell died on March 29, 1944, at the age of thirty-three. Like those of the other executed prisoners, his body was cremated by the Germans and his ashes returned to the prison camp.

to his face. As he takes the final steps toward the plane with the "DL-K" on its fuselage, he now sees that the sleek machine looks "almost delicate."

Two ground crew help him strap in. On the left side, the Spitfire features a small half door that folds down from the top of the cockpit. Wellum pulls it shut and begins his instrument checks.

First time running the Spitfire checklist.

The Merlin rumbles to life, puffing flame and black smoke until it settles into rhythm.

The aircraft has become alive with feeling, Wellum becomes aware, the sensation of becoming one with the plane flooding his entire being. *It is transformed and seems to have a certain impatience to get on with the job and get into the air, its natural element.*

The Boy turns into the wind and takes off.

23

DEERE

ovely day, sir. Sun will soon be shining."

Flight Lieutenant Alan Deere wakens to the cheery voice of Roach, his batman. Rain dripping on the bedroom window. Darkest before the dawn outside. Spitfire pilot Deere is twenty-two, New Zealand born. Square jawed, square-shouldered, and square-cut, regulation-length red hair. A born leader.*

And exhausted.

The physical and emotional stress of nonstop combat makes it an act of will to get out of bed so early. Deere's 54 Squadron has been flying across the Channel several times a day to France. Their mission is to protect the besieged British troops stranded on the beach at Dunkirk, penned in on three sides by the German Army. The ocean is their only escape. Operation Dynamo, the naval evacuation of all those defeated soldiers, began two days ago. Deere flies air cover, attacking Luftwaffe aircraft strafing and bombing the defenseless soldiers.

---

* A batman was an airman or soldier serving as a personal servant for a commissioned officer. The term originates from the French noun for "pack saddle"—*bât*—first used in a military era when such a servant would be responsible for preparing an officer's horse each day.

Alan "Al" Deere in a Spitfire

Air Force Museum of New Zealand/Creative Commons BY-NC

One week ago, Flight Lieutenant Alan Deere hadn't shot down a single enemy plane.

He made "ace"—five kills—two days ago. Yesterday, Deere bagged one more.

But this morning is the last of it. One more dawn patrol. With 54 down to just eight serviceable fighters, the squadron is being withdrawn from action for a rest.

. . .

A SPOT OF tea in the officers' mess, then predawn takeoff. Low cloud cover. Rain pelting Deere's Spitfire's canopy. Altitude a low thousand feet over the Channel to stay beneath the clouds. A New Zealand "Kiwi" logo is affixed to the fuselage near the cockpit. The morning is still more dark than daylight. Deere flicks his eyes right and left, watching that his wingtips don't get too close to the other aircraft as they assemble in formation. Flying toward the sliver of morning on the horizon, 54 vectors directly across the Strait of Dover. Four minutes after leaving the white cliffs behind, the squadron passes over the French coast halfway between the embattled garrisons of Calais and Dunkirk. In that instant, Deere spies a

Do 17 headed in the opposite direction, skimming the wave tops. Instructing four other pilots to follow him, Deere breaks off and attacks.

The German bomber's aircrew is not expecting enemy aircraft at this early hour. Deere closes to within five hundred yards before being seen. As the Dornier's gunner opens fire, its pilot turns the plane back for land. Flight Lieutenant Deere switches off the safety and shoots to kill from three hundred yards—an almost perfect distance. From this range, each bullet fired from the eight Browning machine guns will converge as one on the target. He sees flame as the damaged Dornier's left engine is destroyed. A thin line of black smoke.

Flight Lieutenant Deere flies closer for one last shot.

Before he can press the firing button, it is the New Zealander whose plane is hit. He hears the dull pounding of bullets hitting his engine, like a hammer striking an anvil. The header tank is punctured. Coolant sprays into the cockpit, coating Deere in a fine mist. White smoke makes it impossible to see out the front windscreen. With no other choice, Deere aims for the French coast, searching for a place to land.

Black smoke from the burning engine makes it even harder to get a bearing. The beaches below are flat and long, like landing strips made of fine, hard-packed sand. Dunkirk is one of the biggest, more than six long miles of coastline. It's several hundred yards from the surf to the dunes fronting the coastal city's buildings. The Royal Navy, utilizing nearly a thousand civilian and military ships of all types and sizes, is now attempting to ferry more than 380,000 defeated British and French soldiers off that long beach and back home to England.

On May 24, the führer ordered his panzer divisions to hold back from completing the conquest of Dunkirk, opening a small window of opportunity for something as implausible as this British evacuation. The Luftwaffe, however, is free to attack at will. Dunkirk is intended to be a scene of slaughter, these hundreds of thousands of helpless men butchered from the air by Hermann Goering's Luftwaffe.

Stranded British troops fill those sands in clusters great and small. Some still carry weapons. Many more are no longer armed. They are leaving behind 90,000 rifles, 120,000 vehicles, and 7,000 tons of ammunition. A great stone jetty thrusts out into the sea from the city's inner harbor; it is lined with men waiting to board a large navy rescue destroyer docked alongside. Smaller British civilian ships—trawlers, sailboats, fishing boats—bob in the swells offshore. Soldiers wade into the surf, heads barely above water as they struggle to reach these vessels and pull themselves on board for the dangerous voyage home through a sea thick with mines, under a sky ruled by the Luftwaffe.

This is the deflated residue of the great British fighting force that attempted to stop the surprise Nazi invasion of Western Europe. If they are destroyed, few professional soldiers will be ready to defend England when the German landing force steps ashore. But these men are not thinking that far ahead. They are terrified of being taken prisoner, traumatized by the constant Luftwaffe strafing and bombing, and desperate to go home. The eighteen days of fighting and retreat that trapped them on Dunkirk are in the past, one debacle after another. They are furious about their desperate plight but don't blame their generals or the French.

The toothless British Expeditionary Force directs their rage at the RAF.

When the only aircraft they see overhead are German, these men in British Army khaki are certain the Royal Air Force has deserted them.

Flight Lieutenant Alan Deere looks down and sees the masses at Dunkirk, but is still too high to land. The beach seems to be on fire. He glides above the coast, slowly losing altitude, broken engine no longer functioning. Sliding open his canopy for a better view, he chooses a narrow Belgian beach miles north of the British position. Deere crabs in to land at the water's edge. His wheels touch down in the white spume and wet sand, sending a geyser of salt water up over the canopy. The sudden jolt from landing on the soft surface throws him forward in the cockpit; he strikes his head on the windscreen and jerks his shoulders hard against his safety harness. Blood pours from a gash over Deere's left eye as he climbs from the cockpit and drops down from the left wing onto the sand. Burning the Spitfire would be the right thing to do now, preventing it from falling into German hands.

No need. The Spitfire, personalized with an emblem of Deere's home nation, bursts into flames just moments after he pushes himself up and out of the cockpit. Fire consumes the instrument panel and melts the fuselage. Sand and oil mingle with the blood on his face as the New Zealander stands and wonders about his options.

The time is 5 a.m. Flight Lieutenant Alan Deere watches the Kiwi logo burn. He's somewhere in German-held territory between Dunkirk and Ostend.

And determined to get back to 54.

"*Anglais?*" asks a soldier coming out of nowhere and pointing a rifle at Deere.

"*Oui,*" the pilot replies. He is unsure whether or not the man is German.

To Deere's great relief, the soldier lowers his gun and beckons him to follow.

· · ·

THINGS HAPPEN FAST for Al Deere. He is delivered to the town of Oost-Duinkerke, five miles from the British lines, where a young Belgian girl dresses the cut over his eye. As a gesture of thanks, he gifts her his yellow Mae West life jacket with "Flying Officer Deere" stenciled in red paint on the front.*

The downed pilot begins walking toward Dunkirk. The roads swarm with refugees. A horde. A herd. Families from Belgium and the Netherlands trudge slowly south, many destined for the perceived safety of Paris. Others hope to get as far away as Spain. Most walk, pulling wagons and pushing prams loaded with belongings. Water is scarce. Food is closely guarded. Privacy is nonexistent. Exhausted children ask to be carried. Jews wonder if rumors coming out of Poland about Nazi treatment of their people is true. Some drive cars, hoping to get as far from the action as possible before the inevitable moment they run out of gas and

---

* The kapok flotation vest was nicknamed a "Mae West" because of its comparison to the buxom Hollywood star when fully inflated.

abandon the vehicle forever. Stukas and Messerschmitts circle ominously overhead, too focused on the troops at Dunkirk to waste their ammunition on innocent men, women, and children—for now.

The New Zealander joins in, jumping aboard a bus crawling through the fray. When the inevitable traffic jam brings the bus to a halt, the pilot steals a bicycle parked outside a small store. He pedals toward Dunkirk. A chance encounter with three British soldiers leads to a ride into the embattled waterfront town—and also a sudden awareness that BBC reports of an organized retreat is propaganda. There is nothing organized about this chaos. Throughout this last week of flying, Al Deere had been under the impression that the escape he was witnessing from the skies was part of a well-executed plan. But now he learns the truth that absolutely no one is in charge. It's every man for himself.

Finally the pilot arrives in Dunkirk with the three young men in khaki. The total destruction is sickening. Fuel dumps are being burned to keep them out of German hands, sending thick black columns of smoke into the air. The pilot chokes on the greasy smell. British trucks, tanks, and personnel carriers are abandoned in the streets, many even driven off the road into the deep canals threading through the city. Buildings gape with holes from artillery shells. Phone wires dangle uselessly from toppled poles. A Spitfire flies low overhead as a British machine-gun unit opens fire, mistakenly believing that all aircraft over Dunkirk must be German.

Deere meets a naval officer who tells him about the destroyer soon to arrive in port. He promises the aviator there will be room.

So the Spitfire pilot waits. The same rain that dripped on his windows at 3:30 this morning now pelts the fine French sand. Troops huddle on the beach in the mist. The Luftwaffe can't fly in this soup, a blessing that speeds the evacuation process, the ships able to dock and load without threat from above. British soldiers wait patiently in line for their turn to board a vessel—any vessel—despite the dire situation.

But the weather clears during the hours-long wait for the destroyer. The drone of German fighters and bombers drowns out the evacuation sounds of waves, shipboard loudspeakers, and bawled orders. Al Deere hides behind a rock, understanding from ground level what an enemy bombing attack looks and feels like. British machine gunners firing from the dunes don't knock down a single plane, but it seems to Deere that the Heinkels, Dorniers, and Stukas don't miss anything. He witnesses one line of patient British soldiers decimated as a German bomb turns their queue into a single deep sand crater littered with arms and legs and bloody bits of uniform fabric. Deere feels the concussion in his solar plexus and ears. It is suddenly very hard to hear.

The destroyer arrives. But there is no room for Deere, despite the promise. Then another big gray ship slides alongside the jetty. This time, the flight lieutenant pushes his way on board. Uniform in shambles, face a mess, Deere doesn't look at all like a pilot. But he pulls rank, picking a fight with an army major intent on keeping him off the boat. Even after he finally secures a berth and strides up the gangway, the battle is not over. Sullen British officers in the destroyer's wardroom berate him about Germany's control of the skies. These navy and army men insist the Royal Air Force has done absolutely fuck all to save them. Deere absorbs the abuse. He knows their world is sea level. They cannot see the battle taking place five miles in the air. Thick ground fog makes that impossible. Nor have they seen the RAF in days—and yet these desperate men see and hear the Luftwaffe around the clock.

A German aircraft suddenly attacks. The wrath of these army and navy officers only increases when the destroyer's guns open fire on the assailant—words to the effect that if the Royal Navy wants the job done right, they need to do it themselves. Relief comes in the form of an order demanding that Deere make his way to the bridge to assist with aircraft identification. The captain doesn't want to mistakenly shoot down a British plane as his vessel finally draws near to England.

Safely arrived in Dover, Deere pushes his way off the ship. He avoids the lines of soldiers being treated to hot tea and snacks on the dock. Uniform filthy and face still a bloody mess, he immediately finds the train station and steps on board a coach bound for Charing Cross Station in

London. The pilot takes a first-class seat though he has no money. A railway guard tries to kick him off, but a kindly brigadier general intervenes, much to Deere's relief.

Shortly before midnight, a filthy and exhausted Flight Lieutenant Al Deere returns home to RAF Hornchurch. "At 11:15 p.m. I walked into the officers' mess which I had left just nineteen hours previously. It was deserted except for three officers chatting in front of the fire in the reading room."

"Good gracious, you've made it," one pilot exclaims as if Deere's return were nothing out of the ordinary. "I said you would."

24

MURROW

"This . . . is London," CBS news reporter Edward R. Murrow greets his American listeners with his trademark opening line. Second broadcast of this warm, dry Sunday. The first was at 8 a.m., a report on the Dunkirk situation. The journalist had harsh words about Hitler's next moves. Sharp criticism of how the British military "gilded defeat with glory" after the retreat from France. Cynical tone. Defiantly pro-Britain. Now Murrow shifts from analysis of what happened to questions about what might come next.

If any one man is responsible for keeping the people of the United States abreast of the war in Europe, and how it might affect their lives, it is this chain-smoking reporter with the quintessentially American life history: a childhood in a North Carolina log cabin, a marriage to a woman directly descended from a *Mayflower* passenger, and a rags-to-riches rise to self-made success in the exciting world of broadcast journalism.

"Yesterday, I spent several hours at what may be tonight or next week Britain's first line of defense: an airfield on the southeast coast. The German bases aren't more than ten minutes' flying time away—across that ditch that has protected Britain and conditioned the thinking of British-ers for centuries.

"I talked with pilots as they came back from Dunkirk. They stripped

Edward R. Murrow
*Wikimedia Commons/Originally published
in* Billboard *magazine, May 3, 1944*

off their light jackets, glanced at a few bullet holes in wings or fuselage, and as their ground crews swarmed over the aircraft, refueling motors and guns, we sat on the ground and talked. Out in the middle of the field, the wreckage of a plane was being cleared up. It had crashed the night before. The pilot had been shot in the head, but managed to get back to his field. The Royal Air Force prides itself on never walking out on a plane until it falls apart."

Murrow is amazed at how young these pilots are. He's only thirty-two, but they're a decade younger. The conversation becomes a calm analysis of German planes and tactics. The newsman expects to hear boasting and bravado like in the movies. But instead, "there were no nerves, no profanity, and no heroics. There was no swagger about those boys in wrinkled and stained uniforms."

Death enters the conversation. This morning's sortie brought down six German planes at the loss of two British fighters. The pilots tell Murrow about the odds against them, which always seem to be two to one. As the young men return to their aircraft for another sortie, a fellow pilot is driven out to the airstrip in a local family's station wagon. Murrow guesses the boy to be about twenty. He speaks too loud. His uniform is torn. The young pilot asks if someone can fly him back to his unit. He was shot down over Dunkirk this morning, landed in the ocean, swam to the beach, and caught a ride back to England on one of the last ships leaving the French coast.

"His voice sounds like that," one of the pilots informs Murrow, "because he can't hear himself. You get that way after you've been bombed for a few hours."

. . .

ON THE SAME afternoon, sixty miles away at Bentley Priory, Air Marshal Hugh Dowding wishes he could be like Edward R. Murrow, visiting his men at their bases to speak in person. The air battle over France has led him to feel an unexpected and profound awe for his fighter pilots, and he very much wants them to know this.

Dowding does not have the immediacy and reach of a radio broadcast to share this emotion, letting his men hear his voice as he says what's on his mind. Instead, he sits at his desk to write a very un-Stuffy letter to his "chicks," as he has nicknamed his pilots. Dowding knows he has a reputation for being cranky and argumentative. The emotion in his words reveals a side of him they've never seen before.

"My dear fighter boys," Dowding begins. "I don't send out many congratulatory letters or signals, but I feel that I must take this occasion, when the intensive fighting in Northern France is for the time being over, to tell you how proud I am of you and the way in which you've fought since this 'blitzkrieg' started.

"I wish I could have spent my time visiting you and hearing your accounts of the fighting, but I have occupied myself working for you in other ways."

The letter shifts from the battle in France, which he never championed, to the aerial combat that will soon take place over Britain. His air crews are already exhausted from long hours in the cockpit, the strain of combat, and ever-present moments of loss as good friends perish.

Air Marshal Dowding's worst fears have been proven correct: Fighter

Command lost 229 aircraft over Dunkirk—all replaceable in time, yet staggering nonetheless, the equivalent of almost twenty squadrons. Of greater concern is the loss of 128 pilots, many of them veteran flight and section leaders. It will take at least a year to train replacements.

A year England does not have.

The German attack is coming. Adolf Hitler issued War Directive No. 13 one week ago, formally authorizing an invasion. "The Luftwaffe is authorized to attack the English homeland in the fullest manner," the führer proclaimed.

Dowding can only pray this does not happen tomorrow. He needs months to get his broken planes fixed and battered men restored. Six weeks is the minimum. Of course, Fighter Command will still be heavily outnumbered. But perhaps, given just a little more time, Dowding can outsmart Luftwaffe counterpart Hermann Goering.

Air Marshal Dowding is more than up for the contest. He well knows that the English Channel is a violent body of water from fall through spring: enormous swells, raging winds, bitter-cold seas. Amphibious invasion during these months is impossible. So Dowding's plan is simple: hold off the Germans until summer ends. He's once again due to retire any day now, but this will give his successor six to nine months to build a brand-new Fighter Command.

. . .

IT CERTAINLY WON'T be easy.

So as he prepares to say good-bye next month, Dowding steels his pilots with a few last words.

This is just the beginning, Dowding tells them. The stakes are being raised even higher. Great Britain's very future is in their hands. He will do his job as their leader, but Fighter Command is nothing without its pilots. They just have to hang on.

"I want you to know that my thoughts are always with you, and that it is you and your fighting spirit that will crack the morale of the German Air Force and preserve our country in the trials which yet lie ahead.

"Good luck to you."

Air Marshal Dowding signs the document with his typical bold signature. He then orders the letter circulated to every pilot in Fighter Command.

On June 17, Stuffy Dowding addresses a jaunty letter to Prime Minister Churchill. "Well! It is now England against Germany," the air marshal exclaims.

Then, speaking of the Luftwaffe, Dowding adds:

"I don't envy them their job."

25

CHURCHILL

JUNE 4, 1940
LONDON, ENGLAND
3:35 P.M.

Winston voice sounds defiant.

Three weeks in office. One calamity after the other. As he has promised, it's now time to tell that story.

On May 24, after Adolf Hitler issued his Directive No. 13, Lord Halifax argued for peace with the führer, leading to a series of War Cabinet meetings from May 26 through May 28 that not only pitted his lordship against Churchill, but threatened the prime minister's hold on power. With British troops on the verge of being captured by the hundreds of thousands at Dunkirk, Halifax's belief that Britain could never defeat Nazi Germany seemed plausible.

Yet the prime minister prevailed, reining in his War Cabinet by reminding them that "peace" with Hitler is a kind word for "surrender"— and surrender is forever. Hitler must never reign over Great Britain, and German troops must never march in formation through the streets of London.

Lord Halifax, his defeatist stance at odds with Churchill's determination to win at all costs, lost the room. He had no choice but to resign.

Then came the miracle at Dunkirk. Those hundreds of thousands of fighting Brits, and more than a few French, spirited across the Channel to safety. The nation rejoices. Dunkirk is the first good news in months.

Yet Churchill well knows wars are not won with retreats. And this war is far from over.

Britain's army has returned home to fight another day, but the battle for France significantly weakened Britain's air defenses. Blame can be placed at the feet of Winston Churchill.

There are also suggestions in some circles that Churchill is complacent. No matter that he drives himself and his staff so hard that Clementine reminds him to be less of a grump. Still, his critics claim he is unfit. No better than Neville Chamberlain.

Thus, some very candid words to his brothers and sisters in Parliament are needed right this instant.

One week ago, as it appeared the entire British Army would be lost, Churchill promised this chamber he would deliver this painful address today. He keeps his word, holding nothing back.

"War Situation" is the topic, sounding very much like the same Norway Debate that got Chamberlain eased from office. But Dunkirk was not at all like Norway.

It is not a secret to Winston that his speeches are England's currency of hope. Whether broadcast on the BBC or delivered in the House of Commons, then printed in newspapers, his carefully chosen words give him a direct connection to the British people. Nobody can tell the prime minister what to say or turn off his microphone. All newspapers in Britain are limited in size because of a newsprint shortage but that doesn't stop readers from squinting a little more closely to read the latest diatribe or confession or message of salvation. The *Daily Mirror, Daily Express*, and *Daily Mail* reach a combined five million citizens. The national Sunday paper *News of the World* has a circulation of almost four million. *Radio Times* magazine is surging past three million readers.

And those are just a fraction of Britain's many newspapers. The broadsheets are so vital to daily life that British intelligence will begin recruiting code breakers through the *Daily Telegraph*—specially invited individuals who can do their Sunday crossword puzzles in less than twelve minutes are considered suitable applicants.

So Churchill knows words matter. The dilemma this afternoon in Parliament is delivering very bad news in a way that makes the people of Britain want to fight back, not seek peace.

The House of Commons clearly agrees.

"The attitude of the House was worthy of all praise," writes the *Guardian*. "As Mr. Churchill unfolded the position, its spirits rose instead of drooped."

. . .

CHURCHILL TALKS ABOUT the Royal Navy's heroism and that of the small-craft owners who motored through mine-laden waters to rescue perfect strangers in the name of Britannia.

Then the RAF. Churchill's fondness for Fighter Command has grown since his first run-in with Stuffy Dowding.

"Meanwhile, the Royal Air Force, which had already been intervening in the battle, so far as its range would allow, from home bases, now used part of its main metropolitan fighter strength, and struck at the German bombers, and at the fighters which in large numbers protected them. This struggle was protracted and fierce. Suddenly the scene has cleared, the crash and thunder has for the moment—but only for the moment—died away. A miracle of deliverance, achieved by valour, by perseverance, by perfect discipline, by faultless service, by resource, by skill, by unconquerable fidelity, is manifest to us all. The enemy was hurled back by the retreating British and French troops. He was so roughly handled that he did not harry their departure seriously. The Royal Air Force engaged the main strength of the German Air Force, and inflicted upon them losses of at least four to one."

Churchill adds: "All of our types—the Hurricane, the Spitfire, and the new Defiant—and all our pilots have been vindicated as superior to what they have at present to face."*

A moment. A pause. Let that sink in. There's more, statistics about the heavy guns and tanks left behind in Dunkirk—virtually all the British Army possesses.

But the talk, as it must, inevitably turns to what's next. Nazi Germany is assembling all manner of boats in Channel ports for invasion. These

---

* The Boulton Paul Defiant was a British two-seat interceptor aircraft that was lackluster in daylight but found great success as a night fighter.

are not just traditional naval craft, but also barges and cargo ships, anything to transport a marauding force from one side to the other.

"Turning once again, and this time more generally, to the question of invasion, I would observe that there has never been a period in all these long centuries of which we boast when an absolute guarantee against invasion, still less against serious raids, could have been given to our people," Churchill clarifies.

"Even though large tracts of Europe and many old and famous states have fallen or may fall into the grip of the Gestapo and all the odious apparatus of Nazi rule, we shall not flag or fail.

"We shall go on to the end."

Here Churchill begins to paraphrase Rudyard Kipling, a most British nuance for all those catching the reference.

"We shall fight in France.

"We shall fight on the seas and oceans.

"We shall fight with growing confidence and growing strength in the air.

"We shall defend our island, whatever the cost may be.

"We shall fight on the beaches.

"We shall fight on the landing grounds.

"We shall fight in the fields and in the streets.

"We shall fight in the hills.

"We shall never surrender."*

.   .   .

THE HOUSE OF Commons erupts in thunderous applause and cheering. Today's speech is a smash. The message is sent. A new appreciation for his policies sweeps England. Churchill is instantly far from losing his job.

"After this," writes the *Guardian*, "no one is going to accuse Mr. Churchill or his government of complacency."

---

* The House of Commons was not wired for recording in 1940. Churchill was too busy to rerecord his speech for the BBC at the time but later taped it from Chartwell in 1949. This is the recording heard by the public to this day.

26

HANDSOME RICHARD

The Rumor is everywhere.

Time to learn next assignments. Twenty new graduates of No. 1 School of Army Co-operation gather to hear their new squadrons. Crisp spring day. Airstrip smelling of freshly mowed green grass. Long row of vintage World War I hangars. Old Sarum has been home for six weeks but it's time to begin aviation's next chapter.

Richard Hillary is now proficient in the Lysander. He is about to transition from student aviator to full-fledged Royal Air Force operational pilot. Everyone is on a wartime footing. It has been weeks since Hillary and his fellow students have been allowed to travel more than thirty minutes from base. Officers carry sidearms. It's not over yet, but Nazi troops are days away from marching into Paris. Great Britain stands alone against Adolf Hitler. It's time to fight back.

"It could actually happen," Hillary realizes with a jolt, confronting the very real possibility of German invasion. "England's green and pleasant land might at any moment wake to the noise of thundering tanks, to the sight of an army dropping from the skies—and to the realization that it was too late."

Yet not even that profound and world-changing threat matters more this very minute than the Rumor.

The Rumor says this: Air Ministry has had a change of plans. Fighter

Command needs more pilots to replace men lost over France. Not every new graduate of the No. 1 School will be defending England in a Lysander.

Some will be sent to . . .

. . . fighters. Maybe even Spitfires.

Twenty nervous pilots wait for the chief instructor to read the list of new postings. Only then will they know if the Rumor is true.

.   .   .

RICHARD HILLARY GOT his first taste of war three weeks ago—a second-hand one at that—after driving two hours west with friends to Bristol. One last outing before all leaves were canceled. It was known that Dunkirk survivors had been off-loaded back onto British soil at the port straddling the River Avon. A curious Hillary, observer to the core, wanted to see these men in the flesh.

He is immediately disappointed.

The aspiring pilots walk into a sweaty barroom filled with men in soiled khaki uniforms. These infantry survivors are exhausted, stinking of body odor, angry, and looking for a scapegoat. A group of British pilots seems like the perfect target. "Before we could even get a drink we were involved in half a dozen arguments over the whereabouts of our aircraft over Dunkirk."

Hillary knew better than to give his tongue free reign. A fistfight would have turned into a melee. The dozens of angry soldiers filling the pub, with dozens more outside, were all eager to make someone pay for their near-death experiences. Hillary's small band of pilot trainees would have been no match.

Richard Hillary knows pilots who died in France. He also hears stories of Lysanders flying without fighter escort to drop supplies on surrounded garrisons—suicide missions to save their brothers-in-arms. Dunkirk wasn't the only place where British soldiers were stranded. Calais, just across from the cliffs of Dover, was cut off. St.-Valery-en-Caux. Boulogne. If the battle for France somehow lasts much longer, Hillary might be one of the Lysander pilots risking his life to push back the German threat.

But Hillary and his classmates could make no such claims that night in Bristol. They got drunk, then almost got themselves killed, rolling their car in a high-speed crash on the moonlight drive back to Old Sarum.

Hillary always seems to find good luck, and that night was no exception. No one in the car was even scratched.

. . .

Now, AS THE chief instructor rises to address the graduating class of the No. 1 School, Richard Hillary hopes for more luck. Stuffy Dowding has lost hundreds of his precious Spitfires and Hurricanes. Skilled pilots have been killed or taken prisoner. Everyone standing here today knows that someone will have to take his place. Hillary hopes to make the cut. He also hopes two good friends earn fighters. Colin Pinckney and Peter Pease share his Oxford background. All three pilots were originally posted to Lysanders and the No. 1 School. They enjoy a tight bond that they have labeled the "triangle of friendship."

The chief instructor addresses the assembled group. He confirms the Rumor about Fighter Command. Names will be drawn from a hat. Fifteen men will go to fighters. Five men will remain with the army and fly Lysanders.

A Westland Lysander

Picryl/Original image housed at the Imperial War Museums

The lucky fifteen will travel immediately to fighter training.

One by one, the young pilots reach into the hat and draw. Each man prays to see "fighters" written on his folded slip of paper.

Richard Hillary takes his turn.

Handsome Richard will not fly Lysanders after all. Nor will Pinckney and Pease from the triangle of friendship. The Rumor has proven a god-send for the three comrades.

Yet the instant he reads the word "fighters," Richard Hillary's mind is already ten steps in front of him. He knows he might end up a Hurricane pilot, but more than anything, he longs to strap into a Spitfire. "It was what I had most wanted through all the long dreary months of training. If I could fly a Spitfire, it would be worth it."

For that to happen, Richard Hillary must prove himself quickly. The fighter course at No. 5 Operational Training Unit at Aston Down is just two weeks long. The flying will be intense, under the guidance of pilots who survived the Battle of France. Hillary will learn the latest tactics and dogfight against men who know all the tricks.

Then he will travel straight to a combat squadron.

. . .

"Do you feel as dead as you should?" asks one instructor pilot after embarrassing Richard Hillary in a fake dogfight. For forty minutes in the air, Hillary could do nothing correctly. He'd be bobbing in the Channel if this had been an actual combat mission.

"On one occasion I went up against Kilmartin," Hillary tells the story. This is a barroom tale, best told to other pilots over a large beer, "flying" his hands one in front of the other like airplanes in a dogfight. "We climbed to 10,000 feet and he intimated he would get on my tail. He succeeded. In frenzied eagerness, I hurled my machine about the sky. Never, I felt, had such things been done to a plane. They must inevitably dislodge him. But a quick glance in my mirror showed that he was quietly behind me like a patient nursemaid following a too boisterous charge."

Flight Lieutenant John Ignatius "Killy" Kilmartin is Irish, a man with movie-star looks, brown hair just a shade too long for regulations, and a perfectly aquiline nose. So handsome, he's almost pretty. Direct gaze.

Father died when he was nine. Twenty-six. Former jockey. Fourteen confirmed victories during the Battle of France.

When Hillary agrees that he feels very dead indeed, Kilmartin lets him down easy. "I meant you to. Now I'll give you some tips for next time."

And so it is that Richard Hillary learns small maneuvers to help him stay alive: half rolls, turning inside the enemy, controlled spins, how to escape a dogfight by pretending his aircraft has been hit. There is an immediacy to this calm tutelage. Hillary is just weeks away from the real duels he has long romanticized. None of those fantasies involved the smell of glycol or oil or acrid cordite or his own stale sweat—the functional aromas of aerial combat. "The reek of an aircraft," as a fellow RAF pilot describes it.

J. I. Kilmartin will never see Hillary again after his pupil is assigned to a squadron, but in the two short weeks of their acquaintance, the older pilot leaves a deep impression. Kilmartin's life-or-death instructions will forever shape how Hillary dogfights.

Richard Hillary soaks up every lesson Kilmartin offers. This is no time to put on airs, even for one of the long-haired boys.

"All this and more he impressed upon me," Hillary finishes the story, referring to those valuable lessons. "And I did my best to carry it out on subsequent flights. These were one sided."

Here Richard Hillary pauses, making his fellow pilots wait for the punchline.

"But then, I never flew with him again."

On July 4, 1940, Richard Hillary is assigned to the 603 Squadron, based at RAF Montrose near Edinburgh, Scotland.

The 603 flies Spitfires.

A dream come true—and yet this sudden immersion into war feels all too real. Gone are the romantic visions and gallant dissertations about combat postulated as a self-absorbed college student.

"I was about to achieve my ambition and felt nothing," Hillary admits, confused by the sudden change of emotion. "I was numb, neither exhilarated nor scared."

27

AMBASSADOR KENNEDY

Joe Kennedy writes in his diary.

It's a longtime habit. The ambassador is fanatical about the written word—notes to family, journal entries, a firm eye on the minutiae of posterity. Someone, someday, some biographer will need these missives. He rattles around the big official residence alone with staff, having sent his family home to America for safety. Fourteen Prince's Gate is a mile walk across Hyde Park, past the Serpentine and the Connaught, where self-proclaimed French leader Charles de Gaulle is soon to spend his nights, to the American embassy on Grosvenor Square.

The ambassador writes of tonight's visit to 10 Downing, one mile in a more southeasterly direction through posh London neighborhoods, an appointment that was pushed back, then canceled. "I expressed my resentment at this because I felt it was personal," Kennedy fumes in his journal. The ambassador is aware that the prime minister and Randolph had a row at dinner the previous week. Churchill's son has proven a terrible husband to a pregnant Pamela, who confides freely to Clementine that her son is a wastrel with little interest anymore in making love. Randolph also snores and passes wind with great frequency. Winston Churchill left the table after bitterly informing his newly wed, drunk, and problem-gambler offspring that he had a "poisonous tongue."

That unsavory moment still very much on Churchill's mind, he found time for Kennedy at seven thirty this evening. The ambassador ran into Neville Chamberlain and Air Minister Archie Sinclair on his way into the Cabinet Room. Chamberlain took a moment to reach out to the American, and reminded Kennedy that the United States would have a great impact on British morale if it entered the war in some small way. And that morale sorely needs a boost: The Germans crossed the Seine today, finally driving toward Paris.

But Chamberlain and Kennedy both know President Franklin Roosevelt's priority right now is getting reelected in November, not declaring war.

Churchill offers Kennedy a drink. The ambassador declines. The man reputed to have made his fortune running bootleg liquor into America during prohibition reminds the prime minister that he does not touch alcohol. Milk is his drink of choice.

"I asked him about help for France," Kennedy now writes in his diary of what happened next. He prefers to record the sequence of events while they are still clear in his head. Kennedy will write a long and thoughtful analysis later. He records the moment when Churchill refers to Italian leader Mussolini as a "jackal of all things good and fair. Hitler was a gentleman compared to him"—a diplomatic sop to Kennedy and his pro-Nazi leanings.

"America will come in when they see England bombed," the prime minister adds with a candor he can never display in public. "How about those destroyers? We need them badly."

Joe Kennedy knows better than to take the bait.

Churchill adds: "Hitler has not won this war until he conquers us. Nothing else matters. And he isn't going to do that."

"We'll hold out until after your election and then expect you'll come in."

"I'll fight them from Canada," Churchill assures the American ambassador, alluding to fleeing England and fighting Germany from some other corner of the Commonwealth. "I'll never give up the fleet."

· · ·

"MY VIEW OF the situation this a.m.," Kennedy writes at the top of a brand-new diary entry the following morning. "I am of the opinion that outside of some air defense, the real defense of England will be with courage and not with arms."

He writes of the sympathy American people will feel toward Britain once they read of towns "bombed and destroyed. They will rise up and want war." He fears that just one "incident," such as a surprise attack on an American military base by a foreign power, will immediately drag the United States into the conflict. Kennedy's aversion to his nation's involvement grows with every passing day. He has become fond of a quote attributed to the fallen French leader Maxime Weygand that "England will be invaded in a few weeks' time and will have its neck wrung by Hitler like a chicken."

So Kennedy wonders if it is the British who will initiate an "incident."

"Desperate people will do desperate things," the ambassador concludes to no one but himself. "The point of all this is the fact that the preparedness for carrying on a war from here on is pitiful and we should know this in the light of any action we in America might see fit to take.

"A course of action that involves us in any respect"—the night is late as Kennedy continues in his journal; he is looking forward to his glass of cold milk before bed—"presupposes the Allies have much to fight with except courage is, as far as England goes, I think fallacious."*

---

* Future US president John F. Kennedy titled his Harvard thesis "Why England Slept," a poke at Winston Churchill's 1938 book *While England Slept*. Both reference Great Britain's lack of prewar readiness in light of Nazi Germany's arms buildup. However, JFK's original title was *Appeasement at Munich*. The title change was the idea of *New York Times* columnist and family friend Arthur Krock. In a letter to his father, delivered to London as France was falling, JFK asked if Prime Minister Churchill would mind the critical title. There is no record of Churchill being consulted by either John Kennedy or his ambassador father. *Why England Slept* was published in 1940 and sold more than eighty thousand copies in Britain and America.

28

CHURCHILL

Paris has fallen.

Nazi troops marched into the City of Lights four days ago. The column of victorious German soldiers stretched for miles. An enormous swastika flies from the Eiffel Tower. German troops wander the grand boulevards, lounging in cafes, snapping photographs like tourists, marching in goose-step formation, and turning Paris into a German-speaking Nazi city. French prime minister Paul Reynaud has resigned and fled into exile.

Almost two million French soldiers are laying down their arms, including many rescued at Dunkirk who chose to return home and fight. The cease-fire began yesterday at 12:40 p.m.

In Berlin, men and women cry tears of joy at this amazing news. Traffic is at a standstill as complete strangers hug one another in streets during delirious impromptu celebrations. German radio plays triumphal patriotic songs. "Germany, Germany above all, above all in the world," citizens sing along to the Fatherland's national anthem, "Deutschlandlied." "German women, German loyalty, German wine, and German song."

Taking Paris is nothing new to the Germans. They did so in 1871 during the Franco-Prussian War, laying siege to the city for so long that Parisians ate the animals in the zoo. And Germany almost captured the City of Lights in the First World War.

But German troops have never goose-stepped into London.

Imagine the celebration when that day comes.

. . .

WINSTON CHURCHILL DOES not have much to fight with.

Only courage and an air force.

So no surprise that he is weary.

Tuesday afternoon in London. Weather warm and dry—an otherwise beautiful day for a walk along the Thames. Winston Churchill meets with Charles de Gaulle of France for an hour, the tall general now exiled to England. De Gaulle will address the French people on the BBC tonight. After the meeting at 10 Downing, Churchill came here to the House of Commons to deliver today's speech.

Another tedious title: "War Situation." Another group of journalists in the gallery ready to record every word for tonight's deadline. Another packed chamber desperately needing the prime minister's theatrics.

A more mundane politician might see today as drudgery. A necessary evil. Delivering a message about the war situation is no man's idea of a rhetorical triumph, yet Winston Churchill is quite sure it must be just that.

By all appearances, Adolf Hitler is delaying his invasion of Great Britain to seek a negotiated peace. There is little Churchill can say in today's speech to deny the cold truth that there is no other nation in the world caught in Nazi Germany's crosshairs but Britain. America shows no signs of galloping to the rescue. Nevertheless, Churchill speaks for thirty-six minutes, laying out the arguments for British victory as if he were speaking to a room of generals and admirals. Military strengths and weaknesses. Tactics. Blah, blah, blah.

In a BBC studio three miles from here, Edward R. Murrow labors over tonight's radio address. In another recording studio in the same building, the nasal, self-important General Charles de Gaulle is telling the French people that *their* fight is beginning—when, in fact, it is an audacious myth contrived from his own forceful personality.

Winston Churchill might soon share the fate of de Gaulle: cast into exile (he will have no choice, for the Nazis will surely kill him when they conquer), the head of a government without a nation of its own, he might be delivering these inspirational addresses in a small, cramped Canadian recording studio to a faraway audience forbidden by Nazi Germany to own radios, let alone secretly listen to them in attics and root cellars late at night.

People in France are being shot for just tuning their radios to hear the little-known de Gaulle. Lord knows what they'll do to Britons rallying for Winston Churchill, a man who has gloriously defied Adolf Hitler by name.

So for Churchill, his destiny and that of his nation come back to the one group of people in the whole world who might save his life: the Royal Air Force. The days of the navy saving England are over. The Royal Navy will be defenseless against even a lone dive-bomber if the RAF no longer controls the skies.

"The great question is: Can we break Hitler's air weapon?" Churchill asks.

"Now, of course, it is a very great pity that we have not got an air force at least equal to that of the most powerful enemy within striking distance of these shores. But we have a very powerful air force, which has proved itself far superior in quality, both in men and in many types of machine, to what we have met so far in the numerous fierce air battles which have been fought."

Churchill's talk about the "most powerful" enemy is based on pure statistics. The Luftwaffe now has an estimated 4,074 available aircraft. Of these, 1,107 are single-seat Me 109 fighters, 357 two-seat Me 110 fighters, 1,380 medium bombers, 428 dive-bombers, 569 reconnaissance, and 233 coastal aircraft.

Great Britain has held her own. But she is overwhelmed by the German numbers. The RAF's 1,963 defenders number 754 single-seat Hurricane and Spitfire fighters, 149 two-seat fighters, 560 bombers, and 500 coastal aircraft.

Churchill talks like a lecturer, thinking specifically of Air Marshal Hugh Dowding and his demand that as few British aircraft as possible be sacrificed over the French coast: "During the great battle in France, we gave very powerful and continuous aid to the French Army both by fighters and bombers, but in spite of every kind of pressure we never would allow the entire metropolitan strength of the air force, in fighters, to be consumed. This decision was painful, but it was also right, because the fortunes of the battle in France could not have been decisively affected, even if we had thrown in our entire fighter force."

The prime minister continues. He will wrap up with the perversely optimistic comment that this could be Britain's "finest hour."

Yet Winston Churchill's greater message is that of warning, tucked in a typed line at the top of that same paragraph.

"The Battle of France is over. I expect that the Battle of Britain is about to begin."

BATTLE OF
BRITAIN

29

DOWDING AND THE VETERAN

The Battle for Britain began yesterday.

Showers over the Channel and all of England. Eleven days since June 30, when Luftwaffe commander Goering ordered his staff to find a way to pull Fighter Command into combat. *Kanalkampf*, as the Germans are calling this first wave of attacks, was deemed the best choice. Their focus is closing the English Channel to all shipping. British naval convoys are the target. Stuffy Dowding's fighter boys have no choice but to sally forth and offer protection.

This is the toe-to-toe battle the whole world has been waiting for.

Yet just the opening rounds of the great bout that is sure to come.

Thankfully for England, Stuffy Dowding got his breather. In the six long weeks since Adolf Hitler issued Directive No. 13, Fighter Command is rested, refitted, and ready. So, as the Dowding System warns of incoming German attackers, his chicks eagerly storm into the skies.

Reprieve also came from the prime minister himself. No less than Winston Churchill yesterday rebuked thoughts of getting rid of the air marshal during this time of crisis, writing Secretary of State for Air Archibald Sinclair that Dowding is "one of the very best men you have got . . . in fact, he has my full confidence."

Hugh Dowding's only real friend in the world is Lieutenant General "Tim" Pile, in charge of Fighter Command's searchlight and antiaircraft defenses. The Irish-born Pile calls Dowding "a difficult man, a self-opinionated man, a most determined man, and a man who knew more than anybody about all aspects of aerial warfare." The two senior officers meet in Dowding's office every morning at 10 a.m., where the air marshal paces while delivering lengthy monologues about his many opinions and frustrations.

It now appears that Stuffy Dowding has a new friend in Winston Churchill.

Hugh Dowding's official retirement date is pushed back to October.

. . .

"100 NAZI PLANES Attack," reads the headline in this morning's *Daily Herald*. "The Most Furious Air Battle Britain Has Yet Seen Raged for More Than an Hour over the Channel Yesterday."

But those Luftwaffe raids are only over water. German bombers are currently forbidden by the Luftwaffe to attack the British mainland during daylight. Solitary fighters are allowed to joyride if they have the gas, making short reconnaissance probes for future reference. At the direction of Stuffy Dowding, these lone Messerschmitts fly unbothered. Their limited fuel range means these *freijagd* excursions—"free hunt"—in search of random targets will be too short for a dogfight. Better to leave the Nazis alone than lose a precious Spitfire or Hurricane when there are still far from enough.

Messerschmitt Me109
American Heritage Museum/Original image housed at the National Archives

Adolf Hitler's two-to-one advantage in aircraft makes everyone nervous.

Counting airplanes in the sky is a tricky business under the best of circumstance and much harder with what pilots call "ground clouds"—known to the rest of the world as fog. So the "100 Nazi Planes" is off the mark. In fact, the true number is forty Messerschmitt Me 109 fighters escorting two dozen Me 110 twin-engine bombers and Dorniers to attack a British convoy code-named "Bread" crossing through the Channel pinch at Dover. Hurricanes from 32, 56, and 111 Squadrons were scrambled, as well as Spitfires from 74 Squadron. Fourteen German aircraft shot down. Two British planes also lost. The 466-ton Dutch steamer *Bill S* was sunk.*

. . .

No such fireworks at 85 Squadron's forward airfield. East coast of England. Peter Townsend and his pilots now loll on cots in their dispersal tent next to the flight line. Yesterday was rough, six hours in the air flying convoy protection. No combat, but Townsend fell asleep exhausted in his clothes all the same.

Sleep is precious. A full night's rest is rare. Those assigned to morning readiness—given only five minutes' notice before launch—have been up for an hour. Warm summer drizzle. Low fog. Ground crews start up the Hurricanes of Yellow section, revving engines for immediate launch: wheel chocks in place, parking brake engaged, engine pushing more than 1,200 revolutions per minute, radiator fully open. The process gets pilots into the air three precious minutes faster.

Sleeping in the tent is another means of a quick takeoff. The typical dispersal hut on many of these frontline bases is a brick structure with a potbellied stove and chairs for lounging. But those buildings are often too far from the aircraft, like here at Martlesham Heath. The tent offers no running water nor toilet facilities, only constant clouds of dust and very

---

* Scholars of the Battle of Britain still dispute actual losses of men and aircraft in each day's fighting. Aircraft claimed down often survived and flew back to base, making such numbers difficult to track.

often blankets that have long gone unwashed. And conversation can be impossible as engines are being warmed. Yet when the bell rings, each man is just steps from his bird.

Now Townsend confirms Yellow is ready. Flying boots, pants, a light sweater. Flight helmet and gloves waiting in his cockpit.

Townsend took command of 85 seven weeks ago. The squadron has been operational for a week. His new unit is normally based in Debden, at a quaint two-runway base between Abbot's Farm and Peverel's Wood in Essex. Three hangars and a tower. Been open only two years. Martlesham Heath is much the same, just seventy miles closer to France—and the Luftwaffe. Moving closer to the Channel increases Dowding System efficiency.

The upside is that British aircraft now intercept incoming attacks much sooner, all the more reason for pilots to sleep in tents as close as possible to their fighters. Some squadrons sleep underneath their planes, parachutes serving as pillows. The most fretful—and exhausted—pilots doze in their cockpits.

The downside is that these forward bases are extremely vulnerable to sudden German bomber raids. Strangely, the Luftwaffe doesn't seem to fully grasp that concept.

Not yet.

Attacks on RAF bases are rare.

On the opposite side of the Channel, the Luftwaffe has taken up residence in air bases from which French and British planes were once launched during the Battle of France. *Luftflotte* 2 is a fighter-and-bomber command headquartered in Belgium, commanded by Field Marshal "Smiling Albert" Kesselring. The Me 109s launch from Pas-de-Calais, just across from the white cliffs of Dover. Because this is the narrowest point in the Channel, the fighters have more time to escort bombers before their fuel runs low. *Luftflotte* 2 controls the northernmost reaches of the Channel.

To the south, *Luftflotte* 3 is under the command of Field Marshal Hugo Sperrie, who enjoys an office in plush Paris while his fighters and bombers launch from Normandy and Brittany. This puts them just across the water from Portsmouth and Deal.

Martlesham Heath's location north of London means an attack will likely come from *Luftflotte* 2. Townsend gazes toward his waiting Hurricane. The pilot feels a deep personal connection to VY-K. The letters are painted on its fuselage—squadron code of VY followed by the individual identifier K. It is a feeling no different from the sentiment a man might have for a beloved horse, the perfect way the plane reacts to his commands. "K had been my 'kite' since I came to 85," is his explanation. "A pilot has a feeling of belonging to his aircraft, and when I had been strapped into the cockpit of my Hurricane, I felt we became an integral whole."

. . .

YESTERDAY'S FIGHTING HAS every pilot on edge. If the Battle of Britain has truly begun, as many are saying, 85 can expect to see waves of German bombers searching for targets over the Channel, escorted by fighter protection. The Ju-87 Stuka dive-bomber, so effective during the Spanish Civil War and then the bombing of Wieluń and Warsaw, is now the least of the RAF's worries. Too slow and far from agile, Stukas are no match for Spitfires and Hurricanes.

And yet, given protection, a Stuka can sink a battleship.

The Heinkel He 111, Junkers Ju-88, and Dornier Do 17Z and 215 models have just enough speed and defensive firepower to make them far more deadly threats. All four outclass the Hawker Fury biplane, which the RAF was flying just one year ago. If not for the switch to Spitfires and Hurricanes, German bombers would rule the British skies with the same impunity as zeppelins from the last war.

In terms of comparison between the four German planes and their British bomber counterparts, there are many. But it is undisputed that the twin-engine Ju-88 is currently the best bomber on either side of the war.

The Heinkel lumbers through the skies, but is highly armored and carries double the bombload of a Dornier. When painted black, making it almost impossible to find on a moonless night, the Heinkel is

Twin-engine Ju-88   *Picryl/Wikimedia Commons*

Germany's ideal stealth attacker of major cities. By day, when the plane has nowhere to hide, its glazed glass bubble nose is already a familiar view in the gunsights of Commander Townsend and more than a few other British pilots. By night, London has no defense other than the searchlights and antiaircraft batteries on the ground. The RAF is worthless when it comes to night fighting.

Heinkel He 111
Wikimedia Commons/Original image housed in the German Federal Archives

Because of its long, narrow fuselage, the Dornier has been given the nickname "flying pencil." Lacking the speed of a Ju-88 and the bomb capacity of the Heinkel, the 17 and 215 versions of the Dornier are best used for reconnaissance. To bomber crews, selection to Dorniers instead of to the Ju-88s is like kissing their sisters. For British fighter pilots, getting shot down by the flying pencil is among the highest forms of embarrassment.

Dornier Do 17

*Spieth/Wikimedia Commons/Original photo housed
in the German Federal Archives*

. . .

THE PHONE RINGS. Sector Operations. "One aircraft only. Scramble and call controller when airborne."

Commander Townsend takes the assignment. "None was worth his keep," he believes about squadron commanders, "unless he could do any job he expected of his pilots, and tackle the most dangerous ones himself."

Townsend climbs into VY-K. Waves for his ground crew to remove the chocks. Releases brakes. Teases the throttle to begin his takeoff roll over the bumpy grass, then climbs east, out over the Channel. The pilot's uneasy relation with the ocean continues. He's been based near rough coastal waters the past eight months, "flying convoy patrols in all weathers and in all seas." There are times when Townsend wonders if he's pushing his luck. As the controller guides him up through thick gray clouds, he makes a comfortable mental note of the yellow Mae West draped around his neck and torso. He ruminates about the lack of a dinghy to keep him out of the cold, hypothermia-inducing waters below, should he bail out over the dreaded Channel, and reminds himself to self-inflate the vest through the tube near his neck, should the need for flotation arise.

That tube is life. There's no other way to state it.

Then he sees the Dornier. It's a 17, originally built back in 1934 for flying airmail. Slow, lumbering, stable. Hard to tell if it's dropping bombs or performing reconnaissance. Four-man crew. Armed with two MG-15 machine guns capable of firing a thousand rounds per minute. Yet of all the four main Luftwaffe bomber types, the Dornier 17 is the lightest armed. Though alone in the sky, with no wingman to protect his flank, Peter Townsend is confident this will be nothing more than a brisk few minutes of adrenaline before breakfast.

Eight thousand feet. The German bomber and its crew are hidden in the darkening mist, flying straight back home to their base in Arras, France. Clouds are sanctuary to lone bombers. Unbeknownst to the RAF pilot, these German airmen are celebrating the successful bombing of British shipping at the mouth of the Thames. The crew sings "Goodbye, Johnny" over their intercom as their triumphant dig at the enemy.

Townsend goes for the kill. "I wheeled my Hurricane around, craning my neck backwards, my eyes riveted on the Dornier.

"It must not escape."

Rain pelts Townsend's windscreen. He flies closer to the German aircraft, diving in and out of the clouds to stay hidden. The pilot draws within a few hundred yards. Visibility is so bad, he slides open his canopy and pokes his head out to one side for a better view. Amazingly, despite the propeller and the rain and wind blasting his cheeks, it works. He's still too far away to open fire. Ideally, Townsend would like to get within two hundred fifty yards—the distance that Stuffy Dowding has decreed as perfect range for bullets from his eight machine guns to converge on a target as one powerful mass.

Townsend switches the gun button to active.

His thumb hovers over the tit as VY-K draws nearer the unsuspecting Dornier. The sky grows black from thunderclouds.

That's when illuminated tracer bullets streak towards his head. The cry of *"Achtung, Jaeger!"* has resounded throughout the flying pencil and the battle has begun. As the Dornier gunner zeroes in on Townsend, the

British pilot finally pushes hard on the tit. "Pieces of metal and other fragments were flying everywhere," Dornier radio operator Werner Borner will later remember of the German bomber absorbing Townsend's first deadly accurate shots.

The Dornier rear gunner takes a bullet to the skull. Flight mechanic hit in the throat, blood spurting everywhere. Radio operator Borner reloads the MG-15 and opens fire once again. Townsend's Hurricane now fires at point-blank range. The German is near enough to memorize the British pilot's lean, goggled face, like a condemned man remembering every detail of his executioner. German tracer bullets and Browning .303 ammunition pass in the sky, hurtling in opposite directions.

Townend's aim is precise, practiced. The pilot is in total control of his aircraft and guns. Borner will live long enough to remember the carnage inside the Dornier: "blood covered faces, the smell of cordite, all windows shot up. There were hits everywhere in the wings, in the fuselage, and in the engine."

One shot is so clean, Townsend knocks the MG-15 smack out of his opponent's grip.

But Radio Operator Werner Borner fires one lucky shot of his own.

Townsend's cockpit explodes in orange flames. The engine immediately shuts down. Without power, his only hope is to glide through the low rain clouds and search for a place to land.

Incredibly, the Dornier dives back into the darkening mist for a successful escape to Arras. A doomed Peter Townsend turns his focus to ditching in the English Channel. There is no hope for survival. Seven miles from England. Twenty from France. Townsend was captain of the swim team at Haileybury, but this is ridiculous.

He calls the ground controller, calmly informing the Dowding System of his position and that he will soon be bailing out. The intimate partnership with VY-K is at an end. The sea, that enemy he has feared so long, awaits his arrival. He can't help but think of the cruel morning Tiger Folkes disappeared.

The fighter pilot takes his time preparing to slide back the canopy and jump into the sky he thought he knew so well until this very minute. He studies the Channel waters for a vessel.

Any vessel.

A punt will do just fine.

Nothing.

Then a speck, like a small toy boat in a very large bathtub—or enormous watery grave.

Townsend glides toward the speck.

Philosophical thoughts about death and reasons for living. A desperate desire to properly execute an emergency egress. Townsend reaches to his chest for the rip cord handle and clutches it in a death grip. He rolls the Hurricane and lets gravity pull him out, diving headfirst.

Townsend watches VY-K fly on without him.

The pilot counts aloud to three. Upside down and falling fast, Townsend yanks on the rip cord.

A very long, quiet moment.

Then, an enormous wave of relief as the parachute jerks him upright. Silk blossoms. Extreme and sudden pressure. A boa constrictor choking his thighs and chest. But swinging in the air on this traumatic day feels like life itself.

As the parachute slows his fall, Townsend watches VY-K plunging vertically toward the water. She slams into the Channel violently. A towering white geyser of water erupts at the point of impact. It subsides. Townsend searches the waves for his trusted Hurricane, but VY-K is consumed by the sea. Not so much as a shattered wing floats on the surface.

Seconds later, the English Channel swallows Peter Townsend, too.

The water is green. Townsend presses the quick release on his parachute harness just before he gets wet. He sinks hard beneath the swells. Townsend fights back to the surface and takes a deep breath before grabbing hold of that beautiful, lifesaving, gorgeous breathing tube, which is suddenly as essential to his existence as VY-K was until moments ago. He breathes in hard, a deep and desperate gulp of air before inflating his Mae West.

But Townsend gags instead, filling his airway and the tube with mouthfuls of cold, salty ocean. His heavy flying boots feel like anchors, pulling the pilot under as he struggles for air. In desperation, Townsend kicks them off. Finally grabbing a breath, he swims toward his flying helmet, bobbing one hundred yards away. The water is very cold, but constant movement staves off hypothermia.

Townsend's landing has not gone unnoticed. The minesweeper *Cape Finisterre* is the speck—and just one half mile away. Ironically, it bears the same name as an iconic German ocean liner. Five sailors lower a boat and motor to Townsend. Rescue, however, is not assured.

"Blimey," the group's leader tells his crew, "if it ain't a fucking Hun."

Townsend, treading water, answers in a crisp, furious British accent.

"I'm not. I'm a fucking Englishman."

. . .

IT IS THE tradition of the sea to ply shipwrecked mariners with strong liquor. So it is that Squadron Leader Peter Townsend is returned to his squadron later that morning, a little worse for rum.

"You got shot down by a Dornier?" jokes Flight Lieutenant "Hammy" Hamilton. Twenty-two. Canadian. Big smile. Dark brown hair and Peter Pan eyes. Joined 85 two weeks after Townsend. Hammy loves Townsend like a brother, but this humiliation will long live in 85 history.

Ten hours later, rum just a fume in the back of his throat, Commander Townsend straps in to a brand-new Hurricane and goes hunting.

30

THE AMERICAN

Billy Fiske is a Hurricane pilot.

Yet he almost got sent back to America.

Newest member of the 601 Squadron, aka the "Millionaires' Mob." Not a group known for following rules. Red silk linings in their flight tunics, red socks, fond of playing polo on the most expensive and newest motorcycles. The rest of the RAF wears black ties, but the 601 insists on dark blue. "Black is so morbid" is their belief. "We'll only wear it for funerals."

An ideal group for the irreverent, speed-loving Fiske. He knows better than to grandstand, and his playboy image is well known, so he does his best to be polite and respectful. In no time, he and Rose will be among those from White's club invited to race his Bentley to the Cornwall home of Willie Rhodes-Moorhouse. The visits offer a weekend of golf, tennis, and backgammon. "Spratting" with hooks for sand eels and wading into rock pools in search of crabs and lobster are also part of these popular society getaways. The guest list runs to a dozen names or more, all well-connected couples.

Fiske and Rose arrived at this forward base on the southern coast two days ago. Tangmere has been expanded by the RAF in preparation for war; local houses and a hotel have even been demolished in the process. Billy and Rose rent a nearby home, just like at their last posting in the Cotswolds; then they settle in for whatever war might bring.

Now, after months of politicking, it is time to fly a Hawker fucking Hurricane.

. . .

"July 14," he notes in his flight log. Fiske writes with a black pen, in neat block letters. Under "Aircraft" he writes "Hurricane." Under "Pilot" he writes "Self." When asked to name which sort of flight, "Solo."

Almost time to fight.

Despite friendships with squadron members through White's social club, Fiske must still prove himself as a pilot before he can fly Hurricanes in combat. The training curve is steep. Fiske is expected to fly the plane and familiarize himself with it every day. On these flights, "Solo" will hopefully be replaced by "Sector Recce," "Sea Firing," "Night Test," "Off," "Dusk Landings," and myriad other exercises.

If all goes well, the wealthy, well-intended American will fly his first operational sortie on July 20.

One week from now.

That's it. Billy Fiske has seven days to master one of the most dangerous flying machines in the world.

It helps that, as with everything else in life he has conquered, Fiske is an amazing aviator, and other members of 601 see that immediately. Flight Lieutenant Archibald "Archie" Hope, a Scottish aristocrat who has flown with the 601 since 1935, soon calls Fiske "a natural as a fighter pilot.

"He picked [it] up so fast it wasn't true."

In the weeks to come, Hope will expand that praise, calling Fiske "unquestionably . . . the best pilot I've ever known."

High compliments from a war-hardened observer. In time, Sir Archibald Hope will become a fighter ace, recording five victories. He is already a Battle of France veteran; his plane was crippled over the Channel by a pair of Me 110s on May 27. Though five miles out to sea, Hope evaded the Germans and aimed for France, coaxing his Hurricane to a landing on a flat French beach. After setting fire to his aircraft, lest it fall into

German hands, Hope made his way on foot to Dunkirk, spent a night sleeping with the thousands of stranded soldiers on the bare dunes, then returned to England on board HMS *Wakeful*, all the while clutching his parachute, like all thrifty RAF fliers.

Silk, just like Hurricanes and Spitfires, is in short supply.

. . .

DESPITE SQUADRON LEADER Hope's endorsement, politics may keep Billy Fiske out of the cockpit.

Great Britain needs the United States' help to win this war, yet for the US government to support struggling Britain, the nation must first win the hearts and minds of the American public. A nonintervention group known as the America First Committee is now being formed. It will soon have 850,000 members. An ebb tide of fear, pacifism, and isolationism fills Americans with hard memories of the last war to defend England. Isolationists like Ambassador Kennedy and American hero Charles Lindbergh stoke that head-in-the-sand mentality.

"Germany now has the means of destroying London, Paris, and Prague if she wishes to do so," Lindbergh wrote to Kennedy after touring Nazi bases in October 1938. "England and France together have not enough war planes for effective defense or counterattack."

Changing that public belief will take great convincing.

The British Foreign Office goes one step further. "We are only likely to win this war if we obtain the wholehearted cooperation of the United States," states Thomas North Whitehead, a British-born Harvard professor on leave to contribute to the war effort. "The only way to make our power for offensive vivid to Americans is 1) to attack as often and as dramatically as possible and 2) let the Americans see us doing it through their own countrymen."

Countrymen such as Edward R. Murrow broadcasting every day from London.

And Billy Fiske.

Fiske could be the new American hero, a brave flier who might counter the pro-Nazi beliefs of the aging pilot Lindbergh, a man who came very close to moving to Berlin two years ago. "The Germans are losing a few more planes than the English, because they are attacking," Lindbergh has rationalized in his journal about the surprising British aerial success so far against the Luftwaffe. "The English save every man who jumps from his plane over England, while all the Germans who jump are naturally put in concentration camps," Lindbergh writes, unaware of the difference between German internment camps, where torture and death are common, and Britain's prisoner of war camps, where prisoners are given food, shelter, and medical care as they sit out the war.

Conditions are still not ideal for captured German airmen: meager rations, manual labor for enlisted men—but not officers—and utter boredom. Escape from a camp is possible, but there is no way off the island. Many Luftwaffe fliers feel shame for being shot down and taken prisoner, but the extreme mental and physical brutality inflicted upon concentration camp inmates is not among their worries.

Taking up Fiske's cause, the British ambassador to the United States, Lord Lothian, wishes to send "one or two fighter aces" on a tour of the United States. The ambassador well knows of Billy Fiske's nationality. He has formally requested that the RAF send the American on leave to return home and speak with "influential senators, editors, and others."

At stake is the ongoing attempt by Prime Minister Winston Churchill to purchase fifty aging destroyers from the United States—anything to prevent invasion by sea. Yet if the aerial Battle of Britain is lost—as many Americans believe it soon will be—the deal makes no sense and violates US neutrality.

And like it or not, the war has already reached American shores. At the World's Fair in New York City, which began in 1939 and will continue through 1940, Great Britain has already modified its pavilion to show life during wartime, including screenings of war documentaries. There are plans to take this popular exhibition on a tour of the United States when the fair ends.

Nazi sympathizers have taken notice.

On July 4, a mysterious suitcase was discovered in the British pavilion.

Two members of the New York Police Department bomb squad were killed when it exploded.

. . .

THE AIR MINISTRY has the final say about Billy Fiske's future.

They do not see Billy Fiske as a hero. He's never seen combat. Gallant young British men are flying to their deaths every day. Nationality does not make him special. Lord Lothian's request is denied. The matter will be revived if, and when, the American shows his worth in combat. Other young pilots have traveled to England from the United States. There are rumors that these men might be formed into an all-American "Eagle" squadron. Billy Fiske's name is already being floated around as a possible group commander.

Until then, Fiske will remain with 601, learning to fly the Hurricane.

. . .

"OPERATIONAL TAKE-OFF," FISKE writes in his flight journal on July 20. He has just eleven hours in a Hurricane when he launches into the air on his first combat mission. No enemy engagement, just an otherwise routine patrol to protect British shipping in the Channel.

Then, on the opposite page, in excited cursive: "My first patrol . . . Cherbourg!"

And that is just the start. Billy Fiske has achieved his ambition of flying fighters in the defense of Great Britain.

. . .

ON JULY 16, Adolf Hitler issues War Directive No. 16: Preparations for Operation Sea Lion, the amphibious assault on England. The führer does not take these proclamations lightly, handing them down mostly for important events like the invasion of Poland, the invasions of France and the Low Countries, and his upcoming and still top secret planned invasion of the Soviet Union.

So his words carry immediate weight and authority. Generals and admirals know to give Hitler's directives the utmost priority. And Operation Sea Lion will be much more than just an invasion. Nazi Germany will enact a complete change of British culture. London, Liverpool,

Newcastle, and Glasgow are among the cities soon to be designated German headquarters. George VI will be removed from the throne, replaced by his pro-Nazi brother, Edward VIII, who abdicated in 1936. Winston Churchill's birthplace at Blenheim Palace will become Hitler's personal refuge, along with the seaside resort at Blackpool, which he also sees as a place of rest and relaxation for war-weary German troops. The führer even forbids the Luftwaffe from bombing Blackpool for just this reason.

In addition, a "Black Book" naming prominent British thinkers and intellectuals is being compiled. After the Germans complete a successful invasion, these men and women will be rounded up and shot. All British men between eighteen and forty-five will also be arrested, then deported to the continent to serve as slave labor. Perhaps most chilling of all is that British Jews will be located and murdered by the same *Einsatzgruppen* units now machine-gunning men, women, and children in Eastern Europe.

And, of course, Winston Churchill will be executed.

. . .

THE TOPIC OF Hitler's directive reads: "On preparations for a landing operation against England.

Luftwaffe commander Hermann Goering

Wikimedia Commons/Original image housed at Harvard Law School Library, Harvard University

"Since England, in spite of her hopeless military situation, shows no signs of being ready to come to an understanding, I have decided to prepare a landing operation against England and, if necessary, to carry it out.

"The aim of this operation will be to eliminate the English homeland as a base for the prosecution of the war against Germany and, if necessary, to occupy it completely."

The German Navy responds to the führer by stating they will be ready in two months. They will have a small window of opportunity before autumn and winter weather renders the Channel too turbulent. This means landing troops on British beachheads no later than the end of September.

Luftwaffe commander Hermann Goering has no problem with the schedule.

"The RAF will be destroyed in time for Operation Sea Lion to be launched by September 15," he assures the führer.

31

MURROW

JULY 14, 1940
LONDON, ENGLAND
11 P.M.

Edward R. Murrow tells America what invasion will be like.

By parroting Winston Churchill.

The prime minister has just spoken to Britain on the BBC. The words are stirring in a way that makes Murrow think hard about what will soon happen to this island nation. Churchill's studio was just upstairs from the basement, where Murrow now broadcasts. The two men know each other. Clementine is friends with Janet. As one who makes his living on the power of the spoken word, Murrow has great admiration for Winston Churchill.

Such admiration that the American takes the unprecedented step of using the prime minister's own words to open tonight's broadcast. Murrow's unique observations are always his own, spoken from his singular point of view. But he cannot do better than what he just heard. Churchill's words are honest and dire, an extension of those wilderness jeremiads. Only now, with two-thirds of Great Britain having tuned in for the prime minister's "War of the Unknown Warriors" address, there is little disbelief about what Churchill predicts.

"We await undismayed the impending assault. Perhaps it will come tonight. Perhaps it will come next week. Perhaps it will never come," Churchill told his people. "Be the ordeal be short or long or both, we shall seek no terms, we shall tolerate no parley, we may show no mercy—we shall ask for none."

Murrow adds his interpretation: "In those words, Prime Minister Winston Churchill summed up the position of Britain tonight, and his listeners in British homes everywhere—in public houses, in barracks, and on the high seas—that so long as he's leader of this country, those words represent for them completely the fears and hopes of this Empire."

Murrow continues, describing the valor of British fighter pilots and the strong anti-German sentiment he experiences wherever he travels. But his point has been made. The Democratic National Convention opens tomorrow in Chicago. President Franklin Roosevelt seeks nomination for his third term in office. America needs to know that from the point of view of the citizens of this beleaguered island, they are in desperate need of any and all help. A pro-Britain man like Roosevelt deserves America's support.

"Good night and good luck."

32

AMBASSADOR KENNEDY

D ear Bobby," begins Ambassador Joseph Kennedy's letter to his fourteen-year-old son. Robert Francis Kennedy is the seventh of nine Kennedy offspring. The teenager is known to have, among other traits like dogged determination and a deeply competitive chip on his shoulder, such an avid interest in philately that President Roosevelt once sent stamps for his collection. So Bobby's sudden lack of interest in the postal system has his father in a cynical mood.

"Well, it was finally nice hearing from you. I was really quite surprised that all during the spring I didn't hear how you were getting along at school. But I suppose you were so busy you didn't get around to writing," the ambassador scolds his son.

Ambassador Kennedy is aware that his anti-British sentiment is known at the highest levels of the American administration, all the way up to Franklin Roosevelt. He knows that three weeks ago, the president sent an envoy to spy on him. "Wild Bill" Donovan is soon to return to America and report his findings. Yet Kennedy is unrepentant. He possesses the kind of wealth that allows him to speak his mind. And though the very role of an ambassador demands diplomacy, Kennedy has no problem making quiet comments to friends about the Luftwaffe putting the RAF "out of commission" and defeatist words like "England will go down fighting—unfortunately, I am one who does not believe that it is going to do the slightest bit of good."

The ambassador is no less truthful with his teenage son.

"As far as things are concerned over here, we are expecting that Hitler will really go to work and bomb the whole place this week. It seems to me it is entirely to his advantage to finish the war off quickly," Kennedy writes Bobby.

.   .   .

FOUR DAYS AGO. Kroll Opera House in Berlin. Adolf Hitler delivers a thundering speech to the Reichstag. A night of promotion for Hitler's top officers and fiery rhetoric. Enormous swastikas on the wall. An eagle clutching a swastika decorates the curtain as the führer speaks from the stage. Politicians, industrialists, and officers roaring their approval as one, right arms thrust straight out in vigorous Nazi salutes. This is not just a speech but a history lesson. Hitler walks the audience through this war and the last and the future of his great Third Reich.

This is the prompt for Ambassador Kennedy's predictions to Bobby.

Hitler rails for an hour, voice rising, falling, cajoling, booming. He saves the subject of Britain for the end. Germany is the peacemaker, the rational adult. Britain is the petulant child.

"Mr. Churchill has repeated the declaration that he wants war," Hitler points out.

"Up to now I have given little by way of response. This is not intended to signal, however, that this is the only response possible or that it shall remain this way."

Hitler speaks of the bombings of London and other British cities to come, as if he has no power to stop the devastation: "I am fully aware that with our response, which one day will come, will also come the nameless suffering and misfortune of many men. Naturally, this does not apply to Mr. Churchill himself since by then he will surely be secure in Canada, where the money and the children of the most distinguished of war profiteers have already been brought. But there will be great tragedy for millions of other men."

Impotence is replaced by threat: "Mr. Churchill should make an exception and place trust in me when as a prophet I now proclaim: A great world empire will be destroyed. A world empire which I never had the ambition to destroy or as much as harm. Alas, I am fully aware that the continuation of this war will end only in the complete shattering of one of the two warring parties. Mr. Churchill may believe this to be Germany.

"I know it to be England."

Now the führer throws out an olive branch.

"In this hour I feel compelled, standing before my conscience, to direct yet another appeal to reason in England. I believe I can do this as I am not asking for something as the vanquished, but rather, as the victor, I am speaking in the name of reason."

Adolf Hitler directs his final words to Winston Churchill, giving Britain one last chance to quit: "I see no compelling reason which could force the continuation of this war."

Joseph Kennedy agrees with Hitler's every word.

· · ·

"I AM INCLINED to believe he will try to finish this war off quickly," Kennedy writes to young Bobby. "Whether he can or not depends on the strength of his air force. The English people have been led to believe that England is a fortress . . . on top of that, they have been led to believe that their air force can take care of any attacks that Hitler might make."

Kennedy continues, placing himself in the mindset of Hitler. "If he can beat the air force, the navy and the army will not be of great value to England.

"So we are like the fellow in the theater waiting for the curtain to go up.

"We should know very soon."

33

THE VETERAN

Peter Townsend waits for the weather to lift.

There won't be a German attack today. Not a patch of blue sky in sight.

Torrential rain. Runways underwater. Low-lying buildings flooded. All flight operations canceled. A welcome break from the boredom of routine daily patrols over the Channel. The pilots of 85 have been professional in the air, but mishaps have marred Squadron Leader Townsend's peace of mind. And on this gray day, waiting to see what the Luftwaffe has planned for the Royal Air Force, he has plenty of time to think about them.

Three Hurricanes of "B" flight shot down a Heinkel on July 12, one day after Townsend was forced to bail out. But Flight Sergeant Leonard Jowitt was lost in that battle, crashing into the ocean, never to be found. Twenty-nine-year-old Jowitt had risen through the ranks from fitter to pilot after joining the RAF in 1928. Jowitt was known for being quick with a joke; one enduring squadron photo shows him standing before a Hurricane with his head shaved—his penalty for losing a bet. The flight sergeant flew over France with the 85, shooting down an He 111 on May 15, before the squadron's evacuation home to England.

"A Hurricane was seen to crash into the sea between 0835 and 0840 hours," the official squadron version of Jowitt's disappearance reads. "There was no parachute descent from the aircraft."

Mourning Squadron Leader Townsend personally signs the battle casualty report.

Jowett had flown with 85 for almost two years and was well known by all. His loss leaves a deep emotional hole in the unit. But every loss is jarring. Pilot Officer John Bickerdike, a twenty-one-year-old New Zealander who joined 85 just two days after Townsend took command, crashed in an aerobatics exercise on July 22. This preventable loss had nothing to do with war.

The rain keeps pouring down.

"No one could be sure of the error they committed—one moment they were flying with the sense that training had instilled in them, the next moment they had fallen helpless to earth," Townsend rationalizes.

"Our responsibilities as squadron commanders often weighed on us heavily," he adds with understatement, reflecting on the burden of not just everyday leadership, but of sending young men to their deaths.

The floodwaters continue to rise.

Townsend feels responsible for the two deaths. He has even been called before Commanding Air Officer Leigh-Mallory at 12 Group for a firm reminder that such losses must never happen again. But as the rain falls, those tragedies only add to the heightened sensation that the difference between life and death is very fine, indeed.

Peter Townsend is always polite to his pilots, even when being firm. This is common throughout Fighter Command. Death is a constant. Every conversation could be the last. No sense making those final words mean or belittling. Yet so much of being a squadron commander is out of his grasp. This deeply frustrates Townsend. New pilots need to become capable veterans. He can admonish them for faults and teach by example, using "experience and authority" to bring these boys into line. But in the end, their fate is in their own hands, just as his own mortality rests upon decisions he makes each moment in the sky.

In the end, the only answer is to fly well. "A single-seater fighter pilot in his cockpit, be he sergeant or squadron leader, was eventually master of his own fate," Townsend writes. "No one sat beside him to help."

The airfield is closed for two more days.

.   .   .

ON AUGUST 3, 85's squadron diarist writes: "Another day of convoy patrols and no E/A to liven things up."

E/A. Enemy aircraft.

Little does the diarist know, but this is the calm between storms. During the month of July, RAF victories amount to 180 German aircraft to
just 70 British planes.

The Luftwaffe can afford this battle of attrition.

The RAF cannot.

34

MURROW

T his is London," booms the voice of Edward R. Murrow. America knows his signature opening line so well, it's becoming a national catchphrase.

Sunday. The CBS newsman has spent the weekend traveling around coastal England. Today is a holiday, a time when Britons normally flock to the shore. After three years of living in London, Murrow knows how those crowds like to pack the beach resorts. But he now tells his American listeners that English beaches are tourist ghost towns populated only by soldiers, sailors, and pilots. He was bored spending his days hanging around the official media hotel, waiting for the air raid sirens to sound so they could finally watch some action. In the meantime, a roller rink across the street offers cheap entertainment: watching off-duty service-men fall down.

"The food was good, plentiful, and cheap," says Murrow, painting a word picture for the radio audience. His words are not extemporaneous. Like Winston Churchill, he prefers to type his carefully crafted scripts in advance, a Camel dangling from the corner of his mouth.

"In the evening the lounge was crowded with Navy, Army, and Air Force officers. The Army still favors the close-clipped mustache, black brier pipe, wrist watch on the left wrist, and identity disc attached by a silver chain to the right wrist. Pink gin remains a favorite drink of the navy, but the army and air force give preference to beer, or scotch and soda."

At the sound of sirens, Murrow and his fellow journalists drive pell-mell to the white cliffs of Dover to watch for incoming enemy aircraft. He sees France across the water.

"A screen of British fighters came roaring out over the Channel and swept down in front of us and back again. The antiaircraft gunners stripped the canvas jackets from their guns and the observers wearing headphones swung their big sound detectors. But it soon became clear that the action was to our left, out of sight. Sometimes when the Germans come over above the clouds it is possible to hear the whisper of high-flying aircraft and the growl of fighters diving with full throttle, interspersed with the bursts of machine gun fire.

"But nothing can be seen."

The weekend is a time of light action, despite Adolf Hitler's directive. Fog and low clouds down to 3,500 feet. The high point comes when the British steamship *Highlander* shoots down two Heinkel bombers as it comes under attack. A Spitfire flown by Sergeant J. P. Walsh crashes during a training exercise, killing the pilot.

In peace, those would be headlines. In war, they are statistics.

"Driving back from those three uneventful days on the coast, we passed through the usual number of barricades and roadblocks, much strengthened and improved since I last traveled that road a month ago," Murrow says, lips almost pressed into the microphone. "Occasionally one saw children playing in the sandbank barricades covering bridges and crossroads. People who live in that county of Kent, one of the most beautiful counties in England, tell me there isn't much talk of the war down there."

What they gossip about is the coming harvest of this year's hops and oat crops. Fruit needs preserving for the winter. For the citizens of England living near the Channel, where aerial attack is a daily happening, one does not get excited about air raid sirens anymore. It's just another normal day now.

Road signs no longer point the way back to London. No helpful markers show the name of a town or village. This is to confuse the Wehrmacht should that day of invasion ever arrive. But Murrow tells his listeners that the English capital will not be hard to find. "London's balloon barrage is a valuable landmark. Miles away one can see those balloons against the evening sky, looking like flyspecks on a dirty windowpane. You just drive toward the balloons and you are in London."

A dramatic pause. The newsman knows these quiet summer days will soon be replaced by more fighting. The E/A will resume soon enough. And in numbers never before seen over England. The German Army might very well be on the verge of using those balloons as a signpost.

"Good night and good luck."

Life for a well-known, pro-British broadcaster could get very difficult if Nazi Germany should take the British capital. Or a bomb might fall at random on top of his flat. His sign-off is as much for his own benefit as that of his listeners.

Edward R. Murrow may have been born and raised in America, but right now he is very much a Londoner.

35

THE VETERAN

Peter Townsend hears singing.

In German.

A familiar tune but he can't remember the name. Thick dawn clouds. Smooth summer seas far below. German rescue planes skim the waves, searching for downed pilots. Townsend chases a flying pencil as he tries to figure out that song.

"September in the Rain." That's it. The James Melton version. Only now it's *"Regnerischer September"*: *"Braune Blätter, fallen wirbelnd nieder, denke an en September im Regen."* Townsend is impressed. Thinks the singing is "catchy."

Between verses, a distant German pilot speaks over the radio to his *schwärme* mates, in a tone implying he is giving orders. A mystified Townsend keeps searching for the elusive Dornier, even as he continues listening to the German frequency and wondering where that song is coming from.

Then all is revealed.

Townsend spies twenty Me 110s circling like a murder of crows. The singing continues, telling the squadron leader that he has not been seen. Simple math suggests Townsend should cut and run.*

---

* A Luftwaffe *staffel* was composed of nine to twelve aircraft, much like a British squadron. Each *staffel* was divided into three *schwärme*, made up of four to six aircraft. Three or four *staffel* formed a *gruppe*.

But the Hurricane pilot has little fear of this version of the Messer-schmitt.

The Me 110 is not technically a fighter. Nor do its twin engines make it a bomber. But Luftwaffe leader Hermann Goering has made them a crucial part of his plan for elite "destroyer wings" known as *Kampf-zerstörer*. The 110s are flown by the very best German fighter pilots, handpicked from single-seat Me 109 units. The greatest asset of this fighter-destroyer is its firepower, with four MG 17 machine guns and two 20mm MG FF cannon. The crew features two men, the one in the rear manning a machine gun. The canopy juts atop the aircraft like a greenhouse, depriving the plane of essential aerodynamics but also providing that backward-facing gunner a complete view of the field of fire.

But the Me 110 is a heavy beast. The twelve-cylinder engines in each wing make it difficult to maneuver. Pilots complain about the enormous physical strength required to pull it out of a dive. Dogfighting is almost impossible because the 110 turns with all the agility of a drunken haus-frau. And yet, with its top speed of 350 miles per hour matching that of a Hurricane, the Me 110 is far from a clumsy bomber.

A confident Squadron Leader Townsend attacks the *schwärme*.

Sun at his back, he dives.

Townsend picks on a lone lost sheep first, attacking straight on. His Hurricane shakes as he enters the bomber's slipstream, then he fires at the very last second. No joy. The shots miss. Pulling hard on the spade grip, he climbs back above the enemy planes, only to encounter another Ger-man diving on his position.

But there's something different about this new opponent.

Something to be feared.

To Townsend's trained eye, his new attacker is surely a veteran of con-siderable skill. Perhaps the man doing the singing. In just seconds, they turn to face each other and begin to joust. They race fearlessly toward a head-on collision, the German firing the whole time. Townsend con-serves his own ammunition, already running low. He remains calm as red German tracer bullets whiz toward his canopy. Neither pilot dares flinch—turning or diving to avoid collision exposes their belly and wings to an easy kill shot.

Both knights miss.

Townsend's aircraft shudders from turbulence as the larger plane comes within inches of slamming nose first into his Hurricane.

In the split second after the Me 110 zooms past, Townsend makes a quick mental checklist of the sounds he did not hear: *no* thud of cannon shells impacting his wings, *no* screeching of metal as his propeller was bent by impact with the fighter-bomber's armored fuselage, *no* explosion.

A reassured Peter Townsend hides in a cloud.

But the battle is far from over. Townsend radios for help as he twists his head left and right, then cranes his neck skyward in search of his opponent. The Messerschmitt's twin cannon inflict a far greater punch than his eight Brownings. These scare Townsend more than he would like to admit. Help arrives in the form of a lone Spitfire materializing from the clouds, squadron unknown, guns blazing at the German plane until his bullets run out.

The helpful Spitfire disappears back into the clouds.

This might be a good time to get back to base.

After one more pass against a lone Me 110, Townsend turns for England. He's low on fuel and doesn't want to risk eternity in the drink. It's a source of contention with British pilots that the Germans have life rafts, bright dye canisters for easy aerial observation, and those lone rescue planes patrolling up and down the Channel. As Townsend is personally aware, the Royal Air Force depends on luck and God's grace when a pilot splashes into the Channel. Eighteen British rescue boats are responsible for the entire English coast, hardly enough to account for every downed pilot.

If the Dowding System has one keen failure, it is this.

Safety on this morning means landing back at Martlesham Heath. A place to rest and relax before the next sortie. Yet that respite will be fleeting. British intelligence reports confirm that the Germans are planning an aerial assault unlike anything seen so far in the Battle of Britain. What that means, Townsend has absolutely no idea.

.   .   .

"WITHIN A SHORT period you will wipe the British air force from the sky," *Reichsmarschall* Hermann Goering states in a message to Luftwaffe 2 and 3.

"Heil Hitler."

36

DOWDING

The German battle plan is changing. Air Marshal Hugh Dowding knows in an instant that the Channel war is over. RAF bases are now the Luftwaffe's primary targets. This is the day Dowding has long feared. No other tactic could successfully spell a quick end for Fighter Command.

"It's obvious that they are trying to knock out our radar and communications," he says to no one in particular. His two fractious underlings, Air Vice Marshals Keith Park and Trafford Leigh-Mallory, stand with him on the mezzanine level of the underground command post. The burly, mustached Leigh-Mallory of 12 Group advocates a "Big Wing" theory of defense, claiming that up to five squadrons flying together in formation are more effective than the single-squadron defense preferred by Dowding. Yet while a greater show of force, the Big Wing takes time to gather at altitude and has less operational flexibility.

Park from 11 Group, the squadrons most responsible for defending the southern approaches to England, flew in massive Big Wing formations during the Battle of France and found them ineffective. Keith Park believes smaller formations are more adept in getting off the ground and attacking quickly, not wasting precious minutes waiting for squadrons of planes to assemble.

Stuffy Dowding agrees with Park.

For now, at least, the great rivalry between Leigh-Mallory and Park simmers.

Below them, the giant map table bristles with activity. Dowding has traveled from Bentley Priory here to the home of 11 Group to watch today's developments.

Dowding's calmness belies the terror felt near the enormous Chain Home stations along the coast. It's not just the 360-foot-tall latticework towers that are buckling from the blasts of 500-kilogram bombs. The impacts hurl spires of dirt hundreds of feet in the air. Concrete shelters where airmen and WAAFs direct information back to Fighter Command are disintegrated, the people inside buried in rubble. Phone lines have been shredded.

Perhaps the worst of it is that these men and women knew the attacks were coming. They watched as the enemy drew closer on their radar screens, then looked up as the bombers began their long dives on the targets at 300 miles per hour. WAAF member Audrey Brown at the Ventnor tower will remember, "Almost straightaway everything went dark and the radar went off the air. We lay down on the floor but there was nothing more we could do."

Stuffy Dowding continues watching the busy map table. The activity only increases. He knows emergency-standby systems will be operating soon, diesel generators providing power. Mobile reserve units will be rushed to replace fallen towers. Most Chain Home stations will be back on line within hours. Ventnor will require three days.

But the air marshal soon realizes the towers are just the first phase of today's massive attack. Chain Home radar stations at Dover, Rye, and Pevensey have been temporarily knocked out. The map shows German bombers attacking RAF Lympne, on the southern coast. The Luftwaffe clearly knows that the British have no way of seeing their bomber crews approaching from a distance.

At 12:45 RAF Manston is attacked by eighteen Dorniers that drop 150 bombs.

Much has changed since May for Air Marshal Dowding. He has

become a close friend of Winston Churchill's over the summer, invited to spend weekends at Chequers. One month ago, when the chief of the Air Ministry sought to enforce the July retirement mandate on Dowding, even as the air war with Germany grew heated, the prime minister personally wrote his longtime friend and suggested he might like to see Dowding promoted to an even higher position in the Royal Air Force. For Archibald Sinclair, who has a strong aversion to Stuffy Dowding's impertinent behavior, this rang as a political threat. Yet he backed down, ensuring that for the duration of the Battle of Britain, Air Marshal Hugh Dowding had no worries about retirement or political intrigue—though what might happen afterward is anyone's guess.

And it was Churchill, two weeks ago, who relayed to Dowding intercepted German intelligence telling of the forthcoming Eagle Day attack, with its hundreds of Luftwaffe sorties and focus on radar and airfields—which appears to be occurring at this very minute.

Adlertag is Hermann Goering's most daring attempt to crush Fighter Command. "Our missions must consist of more bombers, bigger formations, more escorts that will fly with greater skills than they have done before," he told his top commanders during a meeting at his German hunting lodge, Carinhall. By sending more bombers, Goering hoped to lure more British fighters into the air. But the weather did not cooperate at first. Then a ridge of high pressure pushed away the morning clouds and gave the massive Luftwaffe formations the sunshine they needed to do their worst. Dowding knew all along that German raids on convoys in the Channel would not decide the air war. But he very much sees the German wisdom in destroying British fighters on the ground and taking away the virtual eyes that allow Fighter Command to see Luftwaffe bombers forming up eighty miles away.

For this reason, Stuffy Dowding considers that now, not July 10, is the true first day of the Battle of Britain. He even issues an order of the day to that effect.

"The Battle of Britain is about to begin. Members of the Royal Air Force, the fate of generations is in your hands."

.   .   .

THREE DAYS LATER, August 15, the battle escalates. Luftwaffe leader Hermann Goering issues a clear directive stating the next course of action: "Until further orders, operations are to be directed exclusively against the enemy Air Force, including the targets of the enemy aircraft industry allocated to the different *Luftflotten*. Shipping targets, and particularly large naval vessels, are only to be attacked where circumstances are especially propitious. For the moment, other targets should be ignored. We must concentrate our efforts on the destruction of the enemy Air Forces."

37

THE AMERICAN

Billy Fiske is hunting Stukas.

Friday. Second flight of the day. Hermann Goering's mighty on-slaught continues. Fiske flies at the controls of a Hurricane. Yesterday, the American wrote in his logbook about flying into a swarm of forty Me 109s, shooting down two, and damaging two more. He now has four kills to his credit. "Terrific fight," he wrote of his first victory last week. Unlike the terse flight descriptions from his first day in a Hurricane, the yellow lined columns of his flight log are now filled with vivid exhortations. "Terrified but fun. Had to lead the sqdn in. Willie's engine failed!"

The Luftwaffe shows no sign of backing down. Today will be another ferocious day of fighting. It is just after 1 p.m. as the 601 and 43 Squadrons are scrambled. Fighter Command orders them to intercept an incoming Stuka formation coming across the Channel east of the Isle of Wight. The German target appears to be the Tangmere Aerodrome, home to both squadrons.

Stukas have stopped dive-bombing the RDF towers, per direct orders from Goering, who feels they accomplish nothing. Goering's directive of August 15 showed little knowledge of the damage German bombs were inflicting on Chain Home stations: "It is doubtful if there is any point in continuing the attacks on radar sites, in view of the fact that not one of those attacked has so far been put out of operation."

This is an enormous mistake. However, attacks on RAF bases continue. Two Ju-88s will launch a successful bomb run on Brize Norton, near Oxford, this afternoon. Forty-six of Stuffy Dowding's precious fighter aircraft, fully fueled and waiting in hangars, will be destroyed.

There's a noticeable change in other German tactics, too. Fighters now fly alongside bombers, rather than above and ready to pounce. For the past month, the RAF strategy has been to send Spitfires up to high elevations to battle Messerschmitts, keeping Hurricanes down low to take out German bombers. On this day, Spitfires and Hurricanes are both commanded to focus on bombers.

Fighter Command orders Fiske's flight to Angels 12. Extremely urgent. A formation of Stukas is nearing the home of 601.

The climb lasts just over three minutes. In the time it takes to get off the ground and gain altitude, the first wave of Stukas is already diving toward Tangmere, screaming down almost vertically. The Hurricanes of 601 split up, one group chasing the Ju-87s that have dropped their bombs and are fleeing out to sea over Pagham Harbor. The other formation engages individual Stukas before they can heel over into their bombing dives.

Passengers on the Portsmouth–South Coast railway look out their windows and are shocked to see the enemy bombers high above tipping down into vertical descent. There's nothing they can do but watch and pray the train is not a target.

At Tangmere, the unmistakable sight of the gull wings and wail of the banshee siren can be seen and heard by base personnel as the Stukas prepare to drop their payloads. Screams, panic, everybody running in a wild search for shelter. Local villagers also gaze up at the sight, enthralled and terrified but watching nonetheless, wary of bombs that might miss the aerodrome and fall on their homes.

Back during the September 1939 Blitzkrieg of Poland (Blitzkrieg being the German term for "lighting war"), the Luftwaffe owned the skies. Stukas relied on this air supremacy to drop their bombloads without fear. But the Ju-87's top speed is 230 miles per hour, more than 100 less than a Spitfire. That speed decreases to 150 miles per hour when dive-bombing, "due to the speed reducing effect of the externally suspended bomb load," in the words of one German pilot.*

Showing the defenselessness of the dive-bomber, Stuka pilots no longer fly missions unescorted. Three fighter groups now fly to protect each Stuka *gruppe.*

Yet even though the plane is slow and inefficient, the Stuka's bombsight is still deadly accurate. Tangmere's hangars, dispersal hut, base hospital, and officers' mess are hit. The station commander's pet parrot survives, but forever after will relive the horror by imitating the sounds of diving Stukas.

"The once immaculate grass was littered with personal belongings which had been blasted from the wing which had received a direct hit. Shirts, towels, socks, and a portable gramophone—a little private world for all to see," Squadron Leader Sandy Johnstone of 602 will recall. "Rubble was everywhere and all three hangars had been wrecked."

The bombings last fifteen minutes. But as the Stukas turn for home, the 601 exacts revenge. Eight of the slow German dive-bombers are blasted from the sky, trailing smoke as they fall into the Channel in the same vertical descent for which they are so infamous—only this time their noses do not pull up at the last minute, banshee sirens wailing right up to impact.

But one Stuka rear gunner gets lucky. A single 7.92mm bullet from a Rheinmetall MG-15 machine gun penetrates Billy Fiske's fuel tank. His engine sputters to a stop. There are no flames—yet. The American courageously chooses not to bail out. He glides the Hurricane back to Tangmere. Wheels up, he executes a very capable belly landing. Fiske's Hurricane comes to a stop against the airfield's western boundary fence.

Then the flames begin. Still trapped inside the cockpit, Fiske is burned on his hands and legs. His pants are on fire. Ground crew members

---

* That pilot is Adolf Galland, one of Germany's top aces. Galland flew the Me 109 in the Battle of France and the Battle of Britain, earning ninety-six aerial victories. Galland survived the war and later died in Oberwinter, Germany, on February 9, 1996, at the age of eighty-three.

Corporal G. W. Jones and Aircraftman 2nd Class G. C. Faulkner race to the plane in an ambulance and lift Fiske from the cockpit.

But driving to the Hurricane, jumping out of the vehicle, climbing up onto the wings, and reaching inside the flaming cockpit take precious moments. All the while, Billy Fiske burns.

"I taxied up to [Fiske's Hurricane] and got out," remembers Flight Commander Archie Hope. "There were two ambulancemen there. They had got Billy Fiske out of the cockpit. They didn't know how to take off his parachute so I showed them. Billy was burnt about the hands and ankles. I told him, 'Don't worry. You'll be alright.'"

Jones and Faulkner extinguish the flames then drive the American to the base's medical facility.

But those Stuka bombs from moments ago have destroyed the small clinic. Medical Officer Courtney Wiley is incapacitated, having just endured portions of a chimney falling on top of him. Eardrums punctured from the percussion blast. As Jones and Faulkner approach carrying Fiske on a stretcher, the medical officer communicates in sign language, telling them to drive him to the local hospital in Chichester. The pilot is horribly burned from the waist down. Wiley administers morphine to ease the American's pain, but privately thinks Fiske is a dead man.

The Olympic gold medalist proves Wiley wrong. After surgery, as Hope will recall, "Billy was sitting up in bed, perky as hell," at Royal West Sussex Hospital, making jokes with Squadron Adjutant Tom Waterlow. The 601 squadron is informed that their new American friend will be just fine.

That jovial conversation, so typical of Billy Fiske's debonair personality, is misleading. His body's reaction to the traumatic event has severely impacted his lungs, blood vessels, and kidneys. Fiske's burns are septic. Fiske's blood pressure is falling rapidly. Fiske's heart and brain are not receiving enough oxygen.

The morning after his final flight, Billy Fiske passes away.

"The next thing we heard he was dead," dazed Commander Archie Hope will recount.

"Died of shock."

Billy Fiske was twenty-nine years old.

38

MURROW

Edward R. Murrow is not much older than Billy Fiske.

"There is something unreal about this air war over Britain. Much of it you can't see, but the aircraft are up in the clouds, out of sight. Even when the Germans come down to dive-bomb an airfield, it's all over in an incredibly short time," he tells the CBS audience.

"You just see a bomber slanting down toward his target—three or four little black things that look like marbles fall out, and it seems like a long time for those bombs to hit the ground."

Yesterday, starting at ten in the morning, German planes attacked British coastal targets all the way north to Scotland. August 15 was hellacious. The Luftwaffe launches aircraft from Norway, Denmark, France, and the Netherlands. It is a day when the birds are singing and a light breeze crosses the British countryside. The Germans approach with the heavy drone of an impending storm, bombers flying low across the Channel, heard but unseen. Large and dark, the attackers give citizens on the ground a fright as they pass over in deafening formation, seeking out British bases on which to drop their payloads.

Up and down the coast, these intruders make themselves known, hundreds of Luftwaffe bombers and fighters taxing the RAF to the limit. The dogfights are not over the Channel, as they were before. Now the aerial dueling is right above the British countryside. Entire families stand in the sun to watch. The whine of falling bombs and staccato chatter of machine guns from high overhead echoes through the countryside. Flaming aircraft fall out of the sky, trailing smoke as they drop straight down onto the landscape. Pilots from both sides of the conflict dangle beneath their parachutes, descending slowly to earth. Shrapnel from destroyed aircraft showers down on all those spectators, an insidious and unexpected threat.

On August 15 in Bentley Priory, an uncomfortable Stuffy Dowding studies the map table with Prime Minister Winston Churchill at his side. The air marshal has calculated the alteration of Luftwaffe tactics and made adjustments of his own. Today will show whether his decisions are right or disastrous.

The map table is busy. Bulbs are lit up and down the great board. One hundred German bombers with fighter escort approach the northern coast near Tyneside, where RAF forces are spare. Another eight hundred Luftwaffe aircraft approach down south. This stretches the aerial front lines to the length of five hundred miles. It will be impossible for the RAF to defend it all.

Winston Churchill and Stuffy Dowding watch helplessly as every single available British fighter engages in combat.

This is not a time of panic for the air marshal, who husbands his small bands of fighters with calm dispatch. Under his command, RAF fighters take off, fight, land, refuel, and return to the sky with a precision born of five weeks of constant battle—and years of planning the Dowding System. Despite the presence of the prime minister, Dowding does not attempt some sudden, bold coup de grâce. He stays the course rather than try to impress Churchill with grand theatrics, and has one small wing at a time doing its job. Fighter Command's role is the defense of Britain, not offense. Few pilots make the mistake of peeling off alone to chase German opponents back to France.

Take off, fight, land, refuel, and return to the sky. All day long, to the point of exhaustion.

. . .

THE GERMANS ARE also attacking Northern England on this day. There is every confidence on the part of Nazi Germany that these bombings will be an uncontested triumph.

But Stuffy Dowding knows something the Luftwaffe does not: Northern England has a secret air force.

The North is where Dowding sends weary squadrons for rest and recovery. Most go reluctantly. They are allowed to sleep late and shake off the trauma of weeks on edge. Yet they must still be ready to fight at a moment's notice, should the need arise. "The pilots respectfully represented that they were not at all tired," an amazed Winston Churchill will write, Dowding having shared with him the reluctance of pilots to be sent away for this period of enforced rest.

"Now came an unexpected consolation."

German bomber pilots are stunned as seven Hurricane squadrons meet them over the North Sea. Thirty Heinkels are shot down. Just two British pilots are injured, and survive the battle.

This has been the ultimate test of the Dowding System. As a relieved prime minister watches the light bulbs flicker off, he is thankful once again for the steel of Stuffy. Churchill now has nothing but respect for this anachronistic genius.

"August 15 was the largest air battle of this period of the war," Churchill will write in his memoirs.

"The foresight of Air Marshal Dowding in his direction of Fighter Command deserves high praise, but even more remarkable has been the restraint and the exact measurement of formidable stresses," Churchill adds.

"We must regard the generalship here shown as an example of genius in the art of war."

. . .

A TURN OF phrase comes to Churchill as he bids farewell to Dowding and Fighter Command. The words make him want to cry. "Don't speak to me, I have never been so moved," Churchill tells his top aide, Major General Hastings Ismay.

The emotion does not immediately fade.

Churchill says the words once more, then again as he steps into the car, letting the emotional phrasing roll off his lips and committing them to memory.

Someway, somehow, he will find a way to share these deeply heartfelt words with England.

. . .

FIGHTING CONTINUES INTO the evening. The RAF loses thirty-four fighters in the air and another sixteen destroyed on the ground. Fifteen British pilots are dead, missing, or taken prisoner. The Luftwaffe suffers fifty-five downed planes.

"I stood at a hotel window and watched the Germans bomb the naval base in Portland," Ed Murrow tells his audience. The journalist toured the same facility one day before. "The naval officers, including admirals, had been kind and courteous. But as I stood and watched huge columns of smoke and fire leap into the air, I thought some of those officers and men would no longer be of this world."

To Murrow's amazement, his return to London is slowed by the arrival of the king. On this day when the Luftwaffe wishes to deliver a stunning death blow to England and the Royal Air Force, the sovereign has traveled to the most impacted regions to show his support.

Driven by rumors of His Majesty coming through their villages, adults and young children line the roads in each village. Police block every intersection, ensuring that the sovereign can pass through without stopping. There is little in the way of security. The king's motorcade travels at a leisurely pace, in no hurry to return to London.

But even though air raid sirens wail as Murrow finally makes his own return to the capital, life goes on as usual. Football stadiums are filled. Greyhound tracks do brisk business. Pedestrians walk down Piccadilly and Oxford Street without a trace of fear, though they know all too well that German aircraft might soon pass low overhead. Murrow notes that these citizens walk as if the nearest bomber targets are hundreds of miles away—like there's absoutely nothing to worry about.

In Germany, as Hermann Goering is apprised of today's huge losses in

Luftwaffe aircraft, he swears to launch the same massive raids tomorrow—weather permitting.

Edward R. Murrow tells America that the British people are ready.

Yet he also warns that this may not be enough to halt the German threat.

"I have come to the conclusion that bombs that fall some distance away seem very unreal," Murrow informs his listeners as he prepares to sign off.

"One thing I do know: that is, that the bombs that drop close to you are real enough.

39

THE AMERICAN

The awareness of death is real enough.

The churchyard of St. Mary and St. Blaise, on the site of a church that has existed since before the Norman Conquest. Stone, flying buttresses. Tall trees—English oak, beech, Scots pine—and uncut green grass swaying in a light breeze. A long procession down Church Lane: two vicars in black stoles and white surpluses, columns of RAF airmen slow-marching in formation, a lorry pulling the lily-covered caisson. Central Band of the Royal Air Force playing mournful funeral marches—trombones, a French horn, trumpets, a tuba, a saxophone.

Black ties.

This is Billy Fiske's funeral.

Dressed all in black with a hat low over her eyes, a devastated Rose Fiske follows her husband's casket on the short walk from church to cemetery. Villagers have been buried here for almost a thousand years. Amid the gravestones, six Royal Air Force pallbearers take the coffin from their shoulders and place it on lowering straps over the grave. Fiske's fellow pilots from 601 are flying and cannot be here today. Ground crew represents the squadron.

America's Stars and Stripes and the British Union Jack are draped atop the casket. Billy's peaked cap bearing the RAF logo rests there, too.

The American's coffin is lowered into the earth. Rose stands close, never looking away.

The funeral of Billy Fiske   *Courtesy of British Pathé*

The guard of honor fires a three-salvo salute.

In London, Winston Churchill prepares a special speech devoted to brave men just like Billy Fiske.

Rose returns to their rented cottage.

Alone.

40

CHURCHILL

AUGUST 20, 1940
LONDON, ENGLAND
3:52 P.M.

Winston also stands alone.

House of Commons. Billy Fiske's burial in Sussex ended just hours ago. Churchill knows about the American's death. The loss of Billy Fiske is hardly the "incident" he was hoping for. The prime minister comes straight from his meal at Buckingham Palace with the king, their friendship growing through their regular practice of Tuesday lunch. George chain-smokes. Churchill drinks champagne from a bottle kept in an ice bucket at arm's reach. No servants allowed. No minutes are kept either, but Fiske's death has surely come up—Churchill will see to it that a memorial to the American finds its way into one of London's hallowed cathedrals. And the ongoing lack of confidence from American ambassador Joseph Kennedy is certainly worth a mention. He recently wrote to Franklin Roosevelt that the British demise is "inevitable." This man is no friend to the Court of St. James.

But that's just nuance to a royal lunch. Right now the prime minister—an accomplished landscape painter—will speak in broader brushstrokes. Today's discussion is simply titled "War Situation."

And yet he also has a few words for Mr. Kennedy.

This is a terrible month for Britain. The worst in centuries, dating back before Nelson and Wellington and Napoléon and Waterloo to the Spanish Armada sweeping up the Channel, England doomed. It was luck and weather that saved the nation then.

Only Fighter Command and Winston Churchill can save Britain now. The House is full. The session comes to order.

"Almost a year has passed since the war began," Churchill tells Commons, "and it is natural for us, I think, to pause on our journey at this milestone and survey the dark, wide field."

Today's speech is more than five thousand words long. He will talk for almost an hour. Yet every sentence has been carefully typed at the same methodical pace he uses on the BBC. These words need to be heard and digested by all who hear them.

"If it is a case of the whole nation fighting and suffering together, that ought to suit us, because we are the most united of all the nations, because we entered the war upon the national will and with our eyes open, and because we have been nurtured in freedom and individual responsibility and are the products, not of totalitarian uniformity but of tolerance and variety."

Churchill continues. It's hard to imagine another world leader in history whose first four months on the job have been so trying. Yet this is not a time for the downcast moods his private staff endures. England is in trouble. Hermann Goering's relentless attacks on RAF bases are a success. As the Battle of Britain becomes a war of attrition, there is no possible way Stuffy Dowding's pilots can win if these losses continue.

On August 18, which many are calling "the Hardest Day," an unprecedented number of British aircraft was destroyed or damaged. Aircrew are being killed and wounded like at no other point in the battle—so many that to avoid drowning, British pilots no longer fly over the Channel. Bomber pilots are being transferred to fighters to fill the losses. Major RAF bases at Biggin Hill, Kenley, Manston, Hawkinge, Lymphne, Hornchurch, Debden, and North Weald have been devastated. The Luftwaffe is increasing the number of fighter escorts, making it harder for Spitfire and Hurricane pilots to shoot down bombers before they reach their targets, and ensuring that this destruction of vital air bases will continue.

.   .   .

THE BLACK DOG of depression has no place in this chamber.

Parliament has seen the best and worst of the prime minister through his long decades of service. Now, because of his refusal to give in to fear, a hopeful mood fills the House, a positive wind, as the listening audience hangs on Churchill's every uplifting word.

"If all these qualities are turned, as they are being turned, to the arts of war, we may be able to show the enemy quite a lot of things that they have not thought of yet. Since the Germans drove the Jews out and lowered their technical standards, our science is definitely ahead of theirs. Our geographical position, the command of the sea, and the friendship of the United States enable us to draw resources from the whole world and to manufacture weapons of war of every kind, but especially of the superfine kinds, on a scale hitherto practiced only by Nazi Germany," he tells Parliament.

Churchill goes on to speak about Britain standing alone, calling Europe "captive peoples." He talks about Hitler starving the people of Europe, robbing their bountiful harvest to provide for the Nazi war effort: "Fats are used to make explosives. Potatoes make the alcohol for motor spirit. The plastic materials now so largely used in the construction of aircraft are made of milk," the prime minister says to educate his audience. He adds that the Germans are using these commodities to "bomb our women and children."

This is not the Winston Churchill who yearns to be right. Many who know him well speak of his fondness for forcing upon them his many points of view on topics wide and small. But now he is a teacher and friend redefining Britain's foe so that one and all who hear his voice realize he is speaking about nothing less than total evil.

"The great air battle which has been in progress over this island for the last few weeks has recently attained a high intensity. It is too soon to attempt to assign limits either to its scale or to its duration. We must certainly expect that greater efforts will be made by the enemy than any he has so far put forth. Hostile airfields are still being developed in France and the Low Countries, and the movement of squadrons and material for attacking us is still proceeding," states Churchill, a hidden reminder that the Germans are more—not less—of a threat than four months ago.

"The gratitude of every home in our island, in our empire, and indeed throughout the world, except in the abodes of the guilty, goes out to the British airmen who, undaunted by odds, unwearied in their constant challenge and mortal danger, are turning the tide of the world war by their prowess and by their devotion."

Then Winston Churchill shares with his nation that turn of phrase, which made him so emotional when leaving Fighter Command and Stuffy Dowding five days ago—words about the small, brave bands of Spitfire and Hurricane pilots who fight each day to save England. Words that led him to say he had never been so moved.

"Never in the field of human conflict," Churchill thunders in bold, clear tones. The House is dead silent. Those special words resonate through the packed chamber like inarguable truth.

"Was so much, owed by so many, to so few."

. . .

AND FINALLY, a few words for Ambassador Kennedy, the man trying to warn away President Roosevelt from friendship with the English.

"The principle of association of interests for common purposes between Great Britain and the United States had developed even before the war," Churchill states. Some in this chamber have accused the prime minister of not being truly British because of his American mother. Now that connection with the former colony is a benefit. He aims these words across the Atlantic. Churchill speaks a language Americans understand. "Undoubtedly this process means that these two great organizations of the English-speaking democracies, the British Empire and the United States, will have to be somewhat mixed up together in some of their affairs for mutual and general advantage."

Churchill closes with a vivid comparison to America, letting Ambassador Kennedy know nothing will stop him from securing that vital alliance.

"For my own part, looking out upon the future, I do not view the process with any misgivings. I could not stop it if I wished; no one can stop it. Like the Mississippi, it just keeps rolling along. Let it roll. Let it roll on full flood, inexorable, irresistible, benignant, to broader lands and better days."

· · ·

IT IS FOUR forty when Churchill finishes. Work to do at 10 Downing. The prime minister departs while the House is still in session. But he leaves behind a series of friends and enemies committed to giving their lives for Britain—and Winston Churchill.

"The speech of the Prime Minister is apt to turn the rest of the debate into an anticlimax. He has spoken for a united nation, and he has spoken in the name of free men in every country in the world," gushes new Labour opposition leader Hastings Lees-Smith.

Sir Percy Harris, the sixty-four-year-old chief whip, is even more effusive: "I wish to pay a tribute to the magnificent speech of the Prime Minister. I should like to see it translated into the languages of those countries now under the heel of the Nazi Government, and scattered broadcast, to give inspiration and hope because of the words uttered by the Prime Minister in the British House of Commons. Nothing would give more heart to those people in these difficult times. I should assure the Prime Minister, if he were here, that not only the House of Commons, but the country as a whole, stands four-square behind him."

It is not just Churchill's speeches that now bolster England. There is also the hard work of government, obsessive devotion to detail, the Dowding System, the Churchill-appointed minister of aircraft production, Lord Beaverbrook, in charge of manufacturing and fixing aircraft at an amazing rate.

And, of course, the Few.

But as these hardened, occasionally ruthless Parliamentarians now explain quite publicly to their peers in the House of Commons, the words of Winston Churchill are the thin floss holding their nation together. Not Chamberlain's appeasement. Not the surrender of Lord Halifax. Those attitudes are long gone. Even now, in the hardest moments of the Battle of Britain, nothing matters but what Winston Churchill says.

And that means victory.

Sir Percy is keen in his praise for Churchill: "No Prime Minister has had greater responsibilities or more difficult problems to solve than he."

41

MURROW

AUGUST 24, 1940
LONDON, ENGLAND
11 P.M.

This ... is Trafalgar Square.

"The sound that you hear right now is the sound of the air raid sirens."

No studio tonight. Edward R. Murrow broadcasts on this Saturday evening from the steps of St. Martin-in-the-Fields—two hundred years old, neoclassical design. A waning gibbous moon rides in the sky. Murrow calls this special outdoor episode "London After Dark." The reporter is standing in the open, taking in the sights and smells of a city under fire.

"A searchlight just burst into action off in the distance, one single beam sweeping the sky above me now," Murrow describes the scene.

Londoners in ones and twos on their way home from theaters and cinemas remain calm as they step quickly past the CBS reporter, eager to be safely inside the nearest shelter before the bombs fall. No one shows fear. Their intended bunker is the stone crypt beneath St. Martin's. Two stories underground. Buttressed ceiling of stone. Among those buried within is a seventeenth-century member of Parliament who went by the nickname the "Cavalier Colonel," but was more frequently known as Winston Churchill. The current prime minister is a direct descendant.

Edward R. Murrow is in the way. "I must move this cable now just a bit so that people can walk in," he explains to his audience in a most courteous tone.

A history lesson wherever Murrow looks. Across the street is a 169-foot-tall granite Corinthian column rising above the heart of Central London. St. Martin's is also supported by Corinthian columns, bringing a symmetry to this open space.

On top of the granite is an eighteen-foot-tall sandstone statue of Admiral Horatio Nelson, hero of Trafalgar. One-armed, one-eyed, killed by a sniper's bullet just before the moment of victory. The square on which Nelson's Column rises is named for the site of that great victory. Londoners hold this structure so dear that Adolf Hitler plans to steal it as a show of power, and relocate the iconic monument to Berlin when his army conquers London.*

Murrow stares up at the admiral, finding his silhouette in the darkness. "I can just see just straightaway in front of me Lord Nelson on top of that big column."

Suddenly, Nelson is brilliantly illuminated. "Another searchlight just square behind Nelson's statue," says Murrow, sounding surprised at the burst of strong light.

The broadcast journalist takes a pause, letting the sounds of nighttime London under siege tell the story. The sirens roar louder and more numerous. This is not a drill. German bombers are attacking Central London for the first time. Citizens have long been used to white fighter aircraft contrails during daytime and even the chatter of machine-gun fire. They've heard the whine as a stick of bombs falls on the nearby docklands. But not bombs dropping right on top of them. This moment has been feared since the declaration of war almost one year ago.

But this German attack is not part of the Nazi plan. Adolf Hitler has

---

* The phrase "to turn a blind eye" is attributed to Nelson. The admiral lost sight in his right eye early in his naval career when a cannon shot sprayed stone and sand into his face at the 1794 Battle of Calvi. In 1801, at the Battle of Copenhagen, signal flags raised by cautious Admiral Sir Hyde Parker ordered British ships to cease attacking. Disagreeing with the order, Nelson raised his spyglass to the blind eye and told his crew he could not see the flags. Nelson continued the attack and won the day. The eye would eventually mend on its own after more than a decade of blindness.

London Blitz damage

Wikimedia Commons/Original photo housed at the NLFDR National Records Administration

personally decreed that "London is not to be bombed." These pilots are lost and off course. They drop their loads before turning for home, but instead of aiming for military oil storage tanks beyond the city limits, they hit Bethnel Green, Hackney, West Ham, and other sections of residential London. Fires blaze through the East End.

Murrow broadcasts in the midst of it all. A man stops casually to light a cigarette, showing the fearless spirit the newsman hopes to capture for the American people. A red double-decker bus motors past, headlights dark but interior windows lit up in a way that reminds Murrow of "a ship passing in the night and you just see the portholes." He describes cars waiting patiently at a red light. As more men and women walk quickly toward the crypt, their Saturday night interrupted, he places his microphone close to the sidewalk so the audience can hear the sound of footsteps in the dark, "like ghosts shod with steel shoes."

A bomb falls on Oxford Street, just a mile away in the West End. The financial district is hit. Shattered window glass litters sidewalks in large sharp piles. One hundred Londoners will die tonight. Three hundred more will be injured.

More searchlights, their beams reflecting off the bottoms of clouds. Air raid wardens prowl the streets. Londoners remark to one another that the deafening screams of falling bombs is louder than the explosions. The ground shaking as each device lands and explodes. The sound of windows shattering from the percussive force, every pane of glass within blocks of a blast. Searchlights and flames turning the sky into a pink glow. Craters in the earth. Destroyed buildings toppling to earth long after a blast, bricks and wood and pipes breaking away from one another with a mighty crackle, followed by a sound like fabric tearing.

Murrow's listeners hear his tone of awe for what Londoners are enduring and for how strongly they are holding up. But there is no trace of fear in his voice. There is no way of telling his viewers—for the CBS reporter has no way of knowing—that Winston Churchill is so furious that he will retaliate by sending RAF bombers over Berlin tomorrow night.

Which, in turn, will enrage the führer. Hitler will up the ante, in monstrous ways London cannot conceive right now. Embarrassed that British bombs are falling on Berlin, he will launch on London the same bomber attacks that he did on Poland to start the war.

In German, it's called *Blitzkrieg*.

Londoners will give it a cheeky nickname of their own: the "Blitz."

"Good night," Murrow says, wrapping up with his trademark sign-off. The saying is something he borrowed from the people of London, who often say it to one another as a message of courage.

"And good luck."

42

HANDSOME RICHARD

More good luck for Richard Hillary.

The flight officer just shot down his first German plane.

Three days ago, he was grouse hunting in a Scottish bog during a wet, miserable weekend on leave. Then came the emergency message that 603 was on the move. Luftwaffe attacks on Southern England are increasing. London is being bombed. Hillary and his squadron mates, eager to join the action, fled immediately.

Now, less than two hours after his first victory, it is time to do battle again. Ten Spitfires from 603 Squadron take off, form up at low altitude, then continue climbing. They launch out of this satellite airfield on the Essex coast rather than from their normal posting at RAF Hornchurch near London for closer proximity to enemy attacks.

Life in Scotland was intense, but relatively plush. In the South, daily sorties to the point of exhaustion are the new routine. Four squadrons stand ready at Hornchurch. Pilots assigned to the early watch sleep in the dispersal huts, rising at four thirty. Breakfast, delivered from the mess tent, consists of eggs, bacon, and beans. By 5 a.m., Spitfire engines are revving, warming up in case of a morning attack. It is not uncommon that a predawn German assault forces the squadron to scramble before pilots have a chance to eat. "Some didn't even live to enjoy breakfast," one pilot will sadly reflect.

Hillary fusses about the cockpit while gaining altitude, adjusting his gunsight and turning on the heaters that will keep his instruments from freezing five miles above the earth. He lowers his seat, cinches his harness, and finds that sweet spot between too tight and just right as he tightens the parachute straps around his groin.

Hillary breathes easily through his oxygen mask as the formation passes twenty-five thousand feet. His gloveless hands wreathe the circular spade grip. The sun is setting behind him, so keeping his goggles pushed back up on his helmet does not present a problem. Southeast England sprawls below him. The squadron has orders to patrol right here and not to be drawn into a gun battle far out over the Channel.

The morning was quiet, with low clouds and showers. German activity was at a minimum. Exhausted aircrews enjoyed the chance to doze as they awaited the order to scramble, which did not come until afternoon. Hillary's first sortie wasn't until three hours ago. Nine planes from 603 were "bounced"—attacked—by two formations of Messerschmitts. Richard's kill was a gift, the Luftwaffe pilot accidentally flying into his gunsights while trying to evade Section Leader Brian Carbury. Hillary immediately twisted the safety knob on his gun button. Hastily fired a four-second burst into the German fighter. The Me 109 burst into flames and dove toward the sea.

The necessary murder of a fellow human being elates Hillary, even as he seeks justification for what he has just done.

"I had a feeling of the essential rightness of it all. He was dead and I was alive. It could easily have been the other way around," Hillary now understands. "The fighter pilot's emotions are those of a duelist—cool, precise, impersonal. He is privileged to kill well."

Now, at six fifty in the evening on this second sortie, Richard Hillary looks for his next victim. The Luftwaffe soon makes itself known. Reads the squadron's intelligence report: "At 27,000 feet over Manston, they saw about twenty-four Me109s in line astern, weaving over their heads. The Me109s made no attempt to attack, so 603 climbed and attacked. A dogfight ensued."

Hillary gets only one clear shot: a short burst that feels aggressive but hits nothing. He comes close to getting killed. Bullets strike his fuselage behind the cockpit but succeed only in destroying his radio. The bullet-proof plate aft his headrest spares him.

In the tangle and confusion, Hillary evades the Germans but completely separates himself from 603. When the killing and missed shots and whirling through space are over and the adrenaline whoosh dies down, a very lost Richard Hillary is alone in the sky. He prays to the horizon in his own agnostic way, beseeching the heavens to reveal distant specks ahead that might turn out to be fellow members of 603 (salvation), Luftwaffe killers (certain death), or maybe just sunspots (a reminder that night has not fallen, and with it the impossible task of discerning land from water in blackout conditions).

No matter what, the pilot is on his own. And Richard Hillary is not only a very long way from home—he has no way to call for help.

Altitude is Hillary's ally. He pulls back on the stick.

Miraculously, on this weary summer day, salvation appears in precise Fighter Command formation. Silhouettes of what appear to be British aircraft can be seen in the distance. This friendly miracle crosses the sky in line astern, emerging from a waning altocumulus cloud formation, their trim and welcoming RAF fighter profile and sharp three-plane formation beckoning the pilot with the broken radio to follow them home. Their aircraft bear the fuselage code VY.

"I climbed up in search of friendly Spitfires but instead found a squadron of Hurricanes flying around the sky," the relieved and very lost young fighter pilot jokes.

"So I joined on."

43

THE VETERAN

Squadron Leader Peter Townsend is bone-tired.

The Hurricane pilot scrambles for the fourth time today. He's not complaining. He's also not done. Six sorties is the new normal in these waning days of August as Hitler throws everything at Britain. Even now, despite overcast morning conditions, the Essex coast and 85 have just enough nice weather to encourage Luftwaffe probes. Townsend and his pilots are being pushed to their operational limit. The sun sets in ninety minutes, a red ball at Townsend's back as he climbs to Angels 18. Coastal haze but otherwise blue skies.

This window between August 24 and September 6 will later become known as "the critical period" by the RAF and the more telling "desperate days" by others for the endless waves of German sorties. The Luftwaffe averages one thousand airplanes in the sky over England each day. Production of new Hurricanes and Spitfires is falling behind the number of losses. Civilians from the Hawker and Supermarine factories have come to help RAF maintenance teams work overnight to restore damaged planes to flight status.

Experienced pilots are even more difficult to replace than fighters. Every loss is a tragedy in and of itself, but even more so in the cold calculus of pragmatic military strategy. If too many pilots die, Germany wins. It's as simple as that.

"In the fighting between August 24 and September 6," Winston Churchill will later admit, "the scales had tilted against Fighter Command."

Peter Townsend had a victory on the last sortie: an Me 109 fighter that attacked first. But the German pilot made a fatal error, exposing the bottom of his fuselage in full view of Townsend's gunsights. This is no less a call to action than a lover baring her breasts.

Townsend opens fire from two hundred yards and keeps closing. "I had him," the RAF pilot states without remorse. "The Me 109 staggered like a pheasant shot on the wing. A high piece flew off, maybe the hood. A plume of white smoke trailed. I had a split-second impression of the pilot, seemingly inert during those last dramatic moments. Then, the aircraft stalled and dived to earth."

Shooting his fellow man used to bother Townsend, who once considered himself a pacifist. Now it is kill or be killed. He lands soon after, spending just enough time back at base for his ground crew to perform their postflight ritual of preparing the Hurricane for the next battle. She is rearmed and refueled. The bowser's nozzle, as the gas pump is known, pours rich American gasoline into the two tanks located in the wing root. The third tank, located in the fuselage between engine and cockpit, is also topped off. Just months ago, British and German planes were both utilizing 87 octane fuel. But Stuffy Dowding, citing research showing the performance benefits of 100 octane, demanded that his fighters use the new aviation fuel that some are calling "avgas."

Stuffy calls it BAM 100.*

---

* "BAM" stands for British Air Ministry. The discovery of high octane is credited to Eugene Houdry, a French engineer who moved to America and worked for the Sun Oil Company. He invented a process that turned thick oil sludge into high-grade gasoline. The discovery was announced by Sun vice president Arthur E. Pew at the Stevens Hotel in Chicago on November 18, 1938, during an annual convention for the American Petroleum Institute. The Germans paid little attention to this discovery, but American scientists working at the direction of the British Air Ministry adapted the new fuel to work specifically within a Merlin engine. The Germans did not discover this secret until September 1940.

The British purchase the fuel from the Americans on a cash-and-carry basis. Isolationist US politicians demand that Britain pay up front for any items that might be used for war, in this way maintaining an anti-war stance while also turning a profit. President Franklin Roosevelt's intention is to help the British and the French. Technically, this offer is open to all nations. The Axis powers of Germany, Italy, and Japan can take advantage of it. But they lack the hard currency to do so.*

The first shipment of BAM 100 arrived in England in June 1939. Ever since, Stuffy Dowding has been stockpiling new loads of this top secret fuel, ferried across the Atlantic in any available merchant vessel the Air Ministry can procure.

BAM 100 increases the horsepower of a Merlin engine from 1,000 to 1,300—as opposed to the 1,140 of a Messerschmitt's Daimler-Benz power plant. Top speed increases 34 miles per hour. BAM 100 allows British fighters to climb faster and higher to gain tactical superiority, as well as making the Spitfire and Hurricane more maneuverable. Not used during the battle for France due to lack of supplies on the European continent, this fuel now has German pilots confused, wondering what sort of miracle engine the British have installed to rocket fighter airspeeds to such an amazing new level.

"Oil checked. Radio checked, retuned. Oxygen bottle changed. Windscreen cleaned. Five minutes and the Hurricane is ready to go. A close bond linked us with the ground crews," Peter Townsend describes the quick turnaround. "They held our lives in their hands."

The fourth sortie of the day sees Townsend's 85 Squadron patrolling over Dungeness, a hamlet at the very tip of England's eastern coast. France can be seen across the Channel from ocean level on a clear day.

"Bandits in your vicinity," the air controller says calmly over the radio to Townsend.

---

* The Neutrality Act of 1937 stipulated that countries could purchase nonmilitary items from the United States, provided that they paid cash and transported the goods on their own vessels. President Franklin Roosevelt demanded this clause be included.

The pilot does not need to be told. The habit of scanning his eyes to the right, left, and straight up into the sky is ingrained. Nothing worse than being surprised.*

A lone Spitfire joins 85's formation, giving Townsend a start. Fighters often lose sight of their squadrons during a dogfight. This appears to be the case. The Spit is flying "arse end Charlie," weaving around at the rear of the formation, whose job is to prevent attack from the rear. Townsend prefers that the unknown pilot fly to either the right or left of 85, where he can see him. The squadron already has a plane flying in what is more formally known as the "tail guard" position.

"Watch him very closely," Townsend warns 85. From a distance, both Spitfires and Messerschmitts can look the same. As a staunch advocate for the Hurricane, Townsend has a mild disdain for Spitfires, particularly since German pilots find it more honorable to be shot down by a Spit than by a Hurry. Even when captured Luftwaffe fliers are presented with evidence that they were shot down by a Hurricane, many still insist it could only have been the more graceful Spit that did them in.

Suddenly, Arse End Charlie disappears.

"Look out, Messerschmitts!" yells Pilot Officer William Hodgson. New Zealander. Nineteen years old. Lightly freckled. Large ears. Fighter ace with less than one year to live.

The official squadron after-action report will describe precisely what Hodgson sees: "Three Me 109s, the leader of which was not identified until he was within range on account of the previous presence of the Spitfire and the strong resemblance at a certain distance of a Spitfire and Me 109 from front view."

Townsend and Hodgson hurl their fighters into steep left turns. One Messerschmitt comes so close that its square wingtip flies just over

---

* The constant head rotation of pilots is one reason many wore silk scarves while flying. The process originated as a means of World War I pilots staying warm in the open cockpits. But this practice maintained its functional use after canopies enclosed cockpits. Wrapped around the neck, they prevented chafing against a collar or flight jacket during times of frequent head movement.

Townsend's cockpit glass. Another collides with a Spitfire flown by the Red section leader, shearing off its right wingtip, even as an Me 109 cannon blast destroys that plane's tail.

Even while turning and soaring through the hazy blue at top speed, Peter Townsend sees death: "Straightening out, my heart sank."

The pilot of Red One is a good friend. Same guy who gave Townsend a hard time for getting shot down by a Dornier. "Hammy's Hurricane was heeling slowly over, wreathed in flame and smoke. Then it tipped downward in a five-mile plunge to earth."

Flight Lieutenant H. R. Hamilton crashes near the ruins of a fortress built centuries ago by King Henry VIII known as Camber Castle, near Winchelsea.

Peter Townsend is furious. This death is not an act of war but an example of great stupidity on the part of the mysterious Arse End Charlie, Townsend believing "had it kept on the flank where we could see it," Hamilton would never have died.

"If this Spitfire pilot can be identified, I would like these facts brought home to him," Townsend writes in his combat report. "His . . . action contributed to the loss of one of my flight commanders."

44

HANDSOME RICHARD

Perhaps the most amusing though painful experience which I had was when I was shot down acting as arse-end Charlie to a squadron of Hurricanes," Richard Hillary jokes about finding his way back to base.

Blue-gray haze and cloud cover. Alone in the sky with a broken radio. Setting sun behind him. The pilot settles in at the rear of the Hurricane formation, weaving back and forth in an attempt to offer security. He's enjoying himself, glancing into his rearview mirror to make sure no German planes surprise him. Hillary sees himself as the last line of protection between the Hurricanes and horrible enemy surprise. He's just six weeks into his tenure as a Spitfire pilot, and the specter of being alone and unprotected is daunting. A band of Me 109s could swarm on him without warning. It's nice to join good company and return the favor by providing a friendly service. Hillary does not know the number or home base of the squadron he is following. Nor is he aware that Squadron Leader Peter Townsend is mightily annoyed by his presence.

Bullets suddenly rake his left wing. Hillary feels the pneumatic jolt and turns to look at the damage. He stares for an instant longer than he should, later comparing the experience with "getting charmed by a snake." But then he knows to get the hell out of there. Pushing the stick forward and kicking down hard on the rudders, Hillary goes into a spin.

Three Messerschmitts appear behind him—"Beware the Hun in the sun," pilots like to warn one another—but the Germans lose interest as he loses altitude; they're focused on attacking the Hurricanes.

The Merlin is hit, too. Hillary levels out, smoke pouring from the engine. Oil coats his windscreen, making it impossible to see. The cockpit smells of sweet glycol. He will be lucky to make it far with this coolant puncture. Burning oil streaming a long trail of white smoke adds to the calamity.

RAF Hornchurch is out of the question. Rochford is dozens of miles closer but still too far. Thinking quickly, he alters course, attempting to find the airfield at Lympne. The storied base has hosted everything from student pilots to the Royal Navy's air fleet. Hillary knows that airstrip well, having landed at Lympne back during his Oxford summer flights. Yet Stuka dive-bombers laid waste to those runways and hangars two weeks ago. Repair is underway, but the base is temporarily evacuated.

It doesn't matter.

Even that broken field is beyond his reach. Richard Hillary's Spitfire is failing rapidly. Stall speed is just less than 80 miles per hour and he's only going 90—but the emergency procedures manual stipulates 150 is minimum speed for a forced landing, meaning something catastrophic might happen at any instant. Hillary calmly searches for a new place to settle down to earth. He has just enough horsepower not to crash, but not enough for limping into Lympne.

A cornfield will have to do. Wheels up. Flaps down to reduce stall speed—but only after the Spitfire is close enough to glide. Power on to maintain airspeed and angle. Booster pump switched off. The young pilot guides the Spitfire down on its belly. Hard shock of impact and then high-speed chaos as the metal fuselage slides through soil and tall green stalks of unharvested sweet corn. Ninety miles per hour in the air is pedestrian but ninety out-of-control miles per hour on the ground is terrifying.

The Spitfire slides to a halt in the rich brown soil. Hillary quickly turns off the engine to reduce the risk of fire, slides back the canopy, and pulls himself up out of the cockpit. In just minutes, he has gone from four miles in the air to flat on the ground. Not an ideal landing, and the aircraft is probably beyond salvage. But things could have gone much worse.

"Fortunately, nothing caught fire," he will soon joke to a roomful of fellow officers. "I had just climbed out and switched off the petrol, when to my amazement I saw an ambulance coming through the gate. This, I thought, was real service."

But the orderlies aren't looking at Richard Hillary. Instead, their gaze is directed straight up into the sky, where Hillary's good friend and fellow member of the triangle of friendship Colin Pinckney dangles beneath a parachute canopy, floating to earth. The fellow Spitfire pilot, Trinity College alum, and 603 Squadron member was forced to bail out seconds ago at just one thousand feet. Pinckney's aircraft has come to earth much quicker than its pilot, already colliding with the planet on St. Mary's Road in Dymchurch.

So this is an extraordinary coincidence.

Of all mankind, one of his favorite people in the world lands just fifty yards from Hillary. Both cheated death this afternoon. Like Richard, Colin earned his first victory, winning one dogfight before getting shot down in another. "He was a little burned about his face and hands but quite cheerful," a relieved Hillary will tell his story tonight.

And what a celebration it will be. Through yet another stroke of enormous good fortune, the two have landed right next to Lympne Castle, where a Thursday afternoon cocktail party is in full swing. "We were at once surrounded by a bevy of officers," Hillary will fondly recall. As he clung to his helmet and parachute, a "salvage crew from Lympne took charge of my machine, a doctor took charge of Colin, and the rest took charge of me, handing me double whiskies for the nerves at a laudable rate."

Laudable enough Hillary gets so pie-eyed that the local brigadier puts him up for the night. He will never know that Squadron Leader Townsend holds him to blame for the death of a Hurricane pilot, nor that today is a time of incredible coincidence—not just having Colin Pinckney literally fall out of the sky into the same cornfield where Hillary crash-landed, but also that Flight Lieutenant H. R. Hamilton hit the earth right next to one medieval castle while Hillary is now spending the night in another.

Such is war.

Flight helmet and parachute once again adorning his athletic, hung-over frame, Richard Hillary is back in the air the next afternoon.

45

THE VETERAN

S quadron Commander Peter Townsend desperately wants back into the air.

Anything to stop the Germans on this long, terrible day.

Germany owns the skies. Luftwaffe bombers hold supreme deadly power over everything above and below. Not even battleships are safe: A German bomb severely damages the thick steel hull of the modern new HMS *Prince of Wales* during shipyard outfitting, yet another sign that naval power is deeply vulnerable from the sky.

And all the more evidence that Fighter Command must win the Battle of Britain.

Now Townsend impatiently awaits authorization to rejoin the fight. An interrupted lunch. Entire squadron called to readiness twenty minutes ago. Hurry up and wait. Deafening drone of a dozen eager Merlins. Townsend's Hurricane at the front of a long fighter takeoff line. Dorniers attacking bases in two separate waves. The pilots of 85 need to get off the ground this very instant.

Yet the order to take off isn't coming.

"For God's sake, let us go!" Townsend barks over his radio to the controller in Kenley, four miles south.

"Wait a bit, old boy" comes the arch response.

The pilot is exhausted. Townsend's squadron has seen great success in the past few days, though at a cost. Yesterday morning just after ten thirty, eleven Hurricanes of 85 Squadron were scrambled and told to circle over Dungeness at eighteen thousand feet. From this high vantage point, the British fighter pilots witnessed an enemy formation—Heinkels and Me 110s, almost eighty in total—assembling for an attack all the way across the Channel in France. Townsend patiently watched their approach, wisely hiding 85 in the sun, attacking only when the German convoy crossed the English coast. The squadron commander personally led the surprise attack, charging at the bombers head-on, waiting for their opponents to flinch and try to climb away, showing their aircrafts' vulnerable underbellies. The German formation split up in the fight but 85's Hurricanes found their targets. Two Heinkels were destroyed and several more damaged. At least seven 110s were shot down, with other wounded German birds disappearing into clouds, their fates unconfirmed.

But over the last two weeks, fourteen pilots from 85 have also been shot down. It is two days since "Hammy" Hamilton went in. Despite that heart-numbing loss, the discipline and aerial skill of his men show Townsend that his leadership is having a positive effect.

So now, hungry for the lunch he has not eaten, impatiently awaiting the order to launch, the squadron commander indulges in a moment of satisfaction. "I glanced back at my squadron, which had formed up behind me! They looked superb, all those Hurricanes—straining against the brakes with their long, eager noses tilted skywards and the sun glinting on their whirling propellers," he will remember this moment. "Every pilot was watching me, waiting for the signal."

Kenley control finally grants permission: "Off you go."

Townsend turns into the wind and powers into the sky, taking off to the east. The large green parks and the fat, snakelike river and the iconic buildings and the barrage balloons of London are visible in the far distance. Wheels come up. But then the Hurricane's engine falters. A hard blast of sonic wind makes the fighter shudder. Looking back once again, Townsend is stunned to see black smoke billowing from the runway. One by one, 85 Squadron emerges from the oily cloud. Townsend's sudden shock is replaced by fury as he looks up and sees Me 110s with 109s in escort circling high above.

It was Dorniers that did the bombing, but they aren't sticking around to fight.

"After them," he orders angrily, eyes focused on the 110s. "But look out for the 109s."

Townsend sees RAF Biggin Hill in the distance, also consumed in smoke and rubble. He pushes full throttle to chase the Messerschmitts, not caring whether or not anyone from 85 is close behind. He will do the job alone. "Get those ill-mannered bastards," he commands himself.

Townsend throws his Hurricane into a defensive circle of German fighters, though quite aware he is too eager. Foolish perhaps. "Down they came, and a violent cut-and-thrust combat followed, which I vaguely felt must end badly for me."

Yet on this afternoon, Squadron Commander Townsend remains fearless.

The pilot depresses the gun button. His bullets find the undercarriage of an Me 109, and he instantly searches for another, not taking the time to confirm his victory.

Townsend finds what he is looking for, enraged at this violation of English airspace by an enemy who "disturbed our lunch, smashed our airfield, invaded our sky."

The rest of 85 find their commander and join the fight. On this day, the squadron will lose no pilots and claim seven enemy kills.

Peter Townsend fixes a third 109 in his sights. So close he can see the pilot. Townsend places his left thumb on the tit and waits for the split second when his bullets will not miss.

But Townsend has narrowed his focus too much. An unseen Me 110 hides in his blind spot. Too late, the veteran pilot sees the wink of machine-gun fire.

Something hard tears a hole in the bottom of the Hurricane and slams into Townsend's left foot. BAM 100 pours into the cockpit, the gasoline smell unmistakable, high-octane fuel almost sure to burn. Above him, fellow 85 pilot Tom Gleave is right now dealing with a roaring cockpit fire after taking a round from one of the Dorniers that bombed Croydon. Flames bubble the skin of his hands, nose, eyes, and legs.

Yesterday, Gleave, the handsome husband and father shot down five Me 109s. Now he is contemplating whether or not to kill himself with his revolver.

But Townsend's fuel tank does not explode. Instead, the stunned pilot goes into a steep dive—rule number one when dogfighting Me 109s is never to dive or climb, only turn. His bulletproof windscreen is starred with deflections, but the glass holds.*

Squadron Commander Townsend needs to quit this fight and land.

Right now. This plane is about to burn.

But Croydon is gone. So is Biggin Hill.

No other choice.

Townsend bails out—over land this time. "I say, would you mind giving me a hand when I get down?" he calls out to two young girls playing in their backyard as he nears the earth. The pilot comes to ground in a soft patch between a cluster of stately oaks and young firs. He lights a cigarette but remains sitting on the soft soil. Something is wrong with his left shoe.

The children have gone for help. Now that assistance arrives in the form of a local constable. A quick drive to Hawkhurst Cottage Hospital follows. "Just a superficial wound," the country doctor sniffs about the pain in Townsend's toe, removing the tip of a 20mm cannon shell from the hole in his shoe. Forty-one RAF fighters have been shot down today. Nine pilots died. Townsend's flesh wound is a blessing compared to the fates of those lost men.

Then it's straight to the pub for an impromptu fighter pilot reunion.

---

* The Messerschmitt was powered by a fuel-injected engine. The Merlin utilized carburetors. This created a problem of fuel delivery during the initial moments of a climb or a dive. Spitfires and Hurricanes tended to stall briefly, giving the advantage to the Messerschmitt. However, the British fighters had a much tighter turning radius.

The Royal Oak Hotel in Hawkhurst. Low beamed ceilings. Brick walls. Beer on tap at a reasonable price. Townsend is joined at the bar by Bill Millington, an Australian pilot shot down twice today. Flight Officer Pyers Worrall from 85, hit when a 110 blew away his rudder and elevator controls, joins them. When it comes time to be driven back to base, a crowd presses in around the besotted pilots and asks for autographs.

"Lovely people," Townsend realizes, letting the moment sink in. "Good and warm and solid."

But the ride is not easy. All three fliers are hurt in some way. Their shock is only now wearing off. Each wraps his deflated silk parachute around himself to stay warm, but the men shiver nonetheless. Townsend notices that the driver wears a light red toupee and distracts himself from the throbbing pain by watching "that ginger wig bobbing up and down."

Little does Squadron Leader Peter Townsend know, but his Battle of Britain is over. Instead of the dispersal hut, he is delivered to Croydon General Hospital. Dr. Brayn-Nicholls, the house surgeon, removes his left big toe.

The last sound Townsend hears as the anesthesia mask is clamped over his face is a "wailing air raid siren fading into oblivion."

It is 10 p.m. Somewhere, a Hurricane or Spitfire pilot is transitioning from readiness to takeoff.

On this night, for the first time in months, Squadron Commander Peter Townsend does not answer that call.

. . .

MEANWHILE, AT CHEQUERS, Prime Minister Winston Churchill and Air Marshal Hugh Dowding are engaging in debate about the Battle of Britain's progress. A late dinner is being followed by brandy and Stilton cheese. Unlike the normal weekend guest list of diplomats and government officials, Stuffy Dowding gives as good as he gets—much to the delight of Churchill's staff.

The air marshal suggested German pilots are entitled to shoot RAF pilots parachuting over Britain since they will be able to return to combat missions after they land. Dowding, however, believes British pilots should *not* fire upon their opponents, because German pilots would soon be prisoners of war if they land on British soil. Churchill is appalled.

"Dowding is splendid," Churchill's private secretary writes in his journal. "He stands up to the P.M., refuses to be particularly unpleasant about the Germans, and is the very antithesis of the complacency with which most Englishmen are infected."

Then, in a prescient tone, John Colville will add: "He told me he could not understand why the Germans kept on coming in waves instead of one mass raid a day which could be effectively parried."

It is as if Hermann Goering himself is in the room, overhearing Dowding's words. That mass Luftwaffe raid is soon to come.

46

HANDSOME RICHARD

SEPTEMBER 3, 1940
RAF HORNCHURCH, ENGLAND
8 A.M.

Richard Hillary has dangergous trouble with his canopy.

Twelve miles east of London. Low fog across the airfield. Silent parked Spitfires looming in the mist. One year to the day since Britain declared war. Tea for breakfast—though not too much. One never knows how long a flight might last.*

It's been a week since a German fighter came out of the sun and surprised him from behind, shooting up his port wing and forcing a crash landing.

Hillary enters the hangar and climbs up onto a wing to inspect his fighter. Blue pilot's tunic, flight badge sewn on the chest; calf-high, black leather, fleece-lined flying boots. The ground crew has replaced the canopy since Hillary's last flight. But the fit is imperfect. Rather than slide easily backward along its groove, the new cockpit hood will not open. Left unsaid in this frantic effort to fix the problem is that Hillary will not be able to bail out, should his next flight come to that.

So Hillary gets to work. Before the war, the twenty-one-year-old didn't

---

* A relief tube is commonly used by pilots to urinate while flying. A funnel in the cockpit is connected to rubber tubing, which exits through a hole at the bottom of the fuselage. The tubing had a tendency to freeze at high altitudes, which had a greater impact on the long-range bomber crews when the tube backed up. It is said that pilots unpopular with their ground crews could expect the same fate from an intentionally stoppered tube—a fact that remains true to this day.

take much seriously, preferring to focus his attention on "friends, sports, literature, and idle amusement." The idea of picking up a file and performing manual labor like a workingman might never have crossed his mind. But now, because he already knows the sensation of enemy bullets riddling his aircraft, the potential imprisonment of being trapped inside a cockpit as his plane plummets to earth is enough to make him set aside class distinctions.

Takeoff will come as soon as the fog lifts. Maybe an hour. Hillary frantically works with a corporal from the maintenance department to get the canopy unstuck. They alternately file and lubricate the reluctant metal track, to no avail.

Morning mist is gone by 10 a.m., replaced by pale yellow late-summer sun. The canopy will open only halfway. But that must do. Fifteen minutes later, the controller's voice echoes over the loudspeaker, ordering 603 to take off and await further instructions.

The pilot already wears his Mae West flotation vest. He dons a B type leather flying helmet and an oxygen mask, grabs his parachute from the tail of the airplane, where he has left it overnight, then squeezes through the small opening between the canopy and the forward windscreen. As usual, he chooses not to wear gloves because they make his hands sweat in this warm August weather.

Sitting atop his chute, Hillary tightens the straps around his chest and legs, then buckles his Sutton restraint harness.

Hillary's D type oxygen mask made of green melton wool dangles from one side of his helmet. He connects the air hose to the valve on his right, trusting that the ground crew has replaced the pressurized bottle of oxygen located behind his seat. Finally, after plugging in his radio transmitter, the flight lieutenant is ready to launch.

The Merlin's twelve cylinders kick to life as Hillary presses the starter. There's no time to warm the engine or check the guns. The corporal steps off the wing and makes a show of crossing his fingers for good luck.

Canopy still partially open, Hillary rolls down the dirt taxiway, then takes off.

At ten thousand feet, the pilot places the oxygen mask over his face.

The chamois lining is smooth and soft. Many British pilots wear a large mustache as a playful homage to World War I pilots. Yet Hillary's youthful skin remains clean-shaven, allowing a tighter seal for his airflow.

The eight Spitfires of 603 emerge from a cloud bank at Angels 12. Hillary squints in the bright sun, unable to see even the next plane in formation. Yet he keeps his MK.IV goggles pushed up against his forehead, preferring not to wear them because they make him feel even more claustrophobic in the cramped cockpit.

The sun casts cloud shadows over the dark gray waters of the English Channel as the formation leaves land behind. Over the radio, the Dowding System enters its next phase as a controller warns 603 that coastal RDF has picked up a formation of fifty enemy fighters.

Then there they are.

It's not fifty, but it's enough: six German Dornier bombers escorted by a dozen Messerschmitt Me 109s. Another twelve Messerschmitts fly escort a thousand feet above.

The Germans dive to attack.

There is no order to the battle that follows. In the random and impulsive three-dimensional world of aerial combat, pilots on both sides seek out enemy aircraft while plunging, spinning, climbing, and rolling. Tight turns make stomachs drop and sphincters pucker from intense gravitational pull. Straining engines, smell of cordite, deafening clatter of guns being fired in two-second bursts. Fire and smoke. Never fly level for more than a second. Hillary latches onto a stray Messerschmitt, its nose painted bright yellow. His Brownings stitch holes in the enemy wings. Black smoke billows from its engine.

Rather than plunge into the Channel, the German pilot turns for France, desperately fleeing Hillary's pursuit. The RAF pilot depresses the gun button once more. He lets the burst linger for more than three seconds. This leaves him almost out of bullets. Making matters worse, he pauses to admire his handiwork. Following a kill is one of the greatest mistakes a pilot can make. But Hillary can't help himself.

Richard Hillary almost gets away with this conceit.

He stares, enthralled, as fire envelops the Messerschmitt. The German plane begins an uncontrollable dive into the sea. Hillary does not hear the emphatic shouts over the radio telling of the enemy aircraft locked onto his tail. Unlike the Spitfire, which fires only the Browning .50-caliber, the Me 109 is armed with machine guns in the wings and cannon in the propeller hub.

Messerschmitt *gruppenkommandeur* Erich Bode opens fire with both.

A sudden explosion yanks the control yoke from Hillary's grasp. The Spitfire trembles like a large stricken beast.

One of the most distinct safety differences between the Spitfire and Messerschmitt is the location of the fuel. The German aircraft features an L-shaped tank beginning underneath the pilot and stretching into the fuselage to an area behind the pilot's protective armor plate. The Spitfire gas tank is directly in front of the pilot. Should the Spitfire fuel tank receive a bullet, the resulting flames will rise up and get pushed backward by the wind, consuming the canopy area. Luftwaffe pilots have no such worries.

Hillary's fuel tank has just been hit.

The cockpit is on fire within seconds. Flames lick Hillary's face and hands. He smells his own scorched flesh as he desperately fights to bail out.

Clawing free from his safety harness, Hillary yanks down the latch inside the top of the hood. He lowers his seat for a quick departure, then uses his elbows to push the canopy outward and back. But the thick glass won't open. His bare hands burn as fire spreads. Little by little, the metal tracks slide backward. There's a crowbar stowed in the spring clips on the cockpit door for an emergency *just like this*—but the flames and Hillary's burned hands make him forget all about it.

Not that a crowbar would do any good.

A Spitfire cockpit is barely wider than a man's shoulders. This small space is now a cauldron. Flames lick at Hillary's goggle-less face, burning away his eyelashes, then his eyelids, too. His mask protects his mouth, but the seal is not perfectly tight. The pilot's lips are severely burned as the flow of oxygen combines with flames from the burning engine to scorch his mouth—and go beyond: with every breath, fire shoots down his throat.

So even as the canopy opens enough for Hillary to bail out, the metal comprising the cockpit and the aircraft's outer skin is far too hot for him to place his hands on the sides of the cockpit and push himself up and free. In vain, he reaches for the control stick, hoping to turn the Spit onto its back so gravity will drop him out. But it is impossible to grasp the metal column, now engulfed in flame. The vulcanized rubber spade grip cover is melting.

There is no dignity in the death that is coming for Flight Lieutenant Richard Hillary.

The unconscious flight lieutenant is five miles in the air as his Spitfire flies nose first toward the English Channel.

47

HANDSOME RICHARD

SEPTEMBER 3, 1940
ENGLISH CHANNEL
10:04 A.M.

Richard Hillary regains consciousness.

Gravity sucks him down to earth. English Channel silver and blue straight below. British coast visible in the distance but too far for a swim. Fellow pilots watching his plane dive toward earth breathe a sigh of relief as Hillary slides out of the downward spiraling Spitfire at Angels 10. Left pants leg burned away.

Hillary pulls the rip cord.

A violent upward jerk as the parachute blossoms above his head. The rapid descent toward the Channel abruptly slows. He scans the horizon from his high vantage point, searching for fishing boats or rescue craft but seeing none. There are also no signs of German fighters, which is good news because even Stuffy Dowding believes the Luftwaffe is entitled to shoot at British airmen swaying beneath a parachute canopy.

He wonders if the water will be cold. Despite severe burns on his face and hands, Hillary does not yet feel pain as he goes into shock. Twenty feet above the water, thinking the parachute might drown him, the pilot clumsily struggles to undo his straps. But his burned fingers are bent like claws and will not retract. He fails. Hillary splashes into the Channel, going under the swells, then bobbing right back to the surface, where he floats easily, thanks to his life vest. He tries once again to free himself from the shrouds, but the pain is beginning to set in. Parachute straps dig into his flesh. Hillary grows nauseous from the smell of his own burned skin, an aroma like sizzled pork. He goes to check the time but his watch is gone. He sees for the first time the skin on his hands hanging down in white sheets. He cannot look at his face but the morning sun feels too hot on his skin, so he assumes that smooth flesh is also burned.

One hour passes.

Not wishing to suffer any longer, the pilot chooses death. Hillary opens the valve on his flotation vest, releasing all the air. His head goes under.

Hillary resurfaces. He chokes on a large mouthful of seawater and thinks of his mother and his squadron. The pilot's burned face and hands, as well as his approaching death, do not cause him to cry out to God for deliverance. As an atheist, Hillary finds this to be a comforting sign of strength. The water grows colder, but that is a blessing because it numbs his body, so the pain is manageable. His parachute and its shrouds make for an unlikely life jacket, keeping him buoyant at a time when Hillary would much prefer a hasty demise.

By 11:45 a.m., Richard Hillary has been in the Channel ninety minutes. His exact position is seven miles out to sea, due east of London and the Thames Estuary. When the Germans launch their planned invasion sometime in the next few weeks, Nazi landing craft will churn right past his current location.

Richard Hillary finally lets go.

48

MURROW

"This . . . is London."

A city bathed in sunshine and smoke. Adolf Hitler has had enough of British defiance. The Blitz has begun. Two weeks after Winston Churchill had the gall to bomb Berlin, the führer, furious about "British arrogance" at not conceding to his surrender demands, is now laying waste to London. Three hundred forty-eight bombers escorted by 617 fighters swat aside Fighter Command's best attempts to defend the city, dropping 500 incendiary bombs, and killing 430 Londoners in a raid that begins in daylight and lasts well into the night. The firemen of six hundred fire engines now fight blazes across London.

"An air raid siren, called 'Weeping Willie' by the men who tend it, began its uneven screaming. Down on the coast the white puffballs of antiaircraft fire began to appear against a steel blue sky. The first flight of German bombers was coming up the river to start the twelve-hour attack on London," Edward R. Murrow tells his CBS audience. "They were high and not very numerous. The Hurricanes and Spitfires were already in the air . . . the German bombers, flying in V-formation, began pouring in."

The Luftwaffe bombers come over the Kent coast in waves, quickly met by Fighter Command and antiaircraft fire. London's docklands are the primary target, but German planes can be seen everywhere. A train

The London Necropolis Railway Station   *Wikimedia Commons*

is blown off the tracks. Four thousand spectators at a football match turn their attention from the game to the dogfights overhead. Bombs strike a greyhound track, one falling near the kennels but killing no animals. The racing is discontinued as shrapnel rains down on the grandstand.

In London streets, these deadly bombings are once again a spectator sport. Thousands of men assigned to fire brigades rush to their posts. One hundred tons of explosives fall on London today.

The all clear is sounded at six thirty-five. But sirens wail again soon after. As the night sky blackens, the German strategy becomes clear: A few bombers lead the way, dropping incendiary devices to start fires. Then comes the real attack: hordes of Luftwaffe fighters and bombers following the flames to find their London targets.

"It was like a shuttle service, the way the German planes came up the

Thames, the fires acting as a flare path," Murrow continues. "Often, they were above the smoke. The searchlights bored into that black roof but couldn't penetrate it. They looked like long pillars supporting a black canopy... the shrapnel clicked as it hit the concrete road nearby, and still the German bombers came."

. . .

THE BOMBINGS WILL continue for fifty-seven consecutive days before London gets a night's reprieve. The Blitz gives new urgency to Murrow's reporting. He prowls the streets relentlessly, searching for a scene or a story to share with his listeners. He describes a trench dug into a London park as a makeshift air raid shelter, where there are "a half hundred people, some of them stretched out on the hard wooden benches. The rest huddled in their overcoats and blankets . . . the big stuff the Germans were dropping rattled the dust boards underfoot."

British prime minister Stanley Baldwin's 1932 words about the bomber always getting through are prophetic. The Thames Estuary is the meatiest target, but the Luftwaffe will drop a bomb on anything: St. Paul's Cathedral, Buckingham Palace, the Natural History Museum. Pubs, hospitals, homes, children.

Edward R. Murrow tells his listeners all this.

He informs America about the shell casings to be found on the streets each morning after a long night of antiaircraft fire. About delayed-action bombs that shut down a street long after German planes have flown back to their bases, the people of London waiting for the bomb unit to come out and defuse the device. And about what Londoners now call a "routine" night: an air raid alarm followed by on and off bombing until dawn. He and Janet sleep most nights on mattresses spread out on the studio floor with other members of the broadcast staff. When the bombs fall, they take cover under a thick wooden table. Murrow sometimes even goes on the air in the early-morning hours as others sleep all around him.

"Today I went to buy a hat," Murrow describes to America. "My favorite shop had gone, blown to bits. The windows of my favorite shoe store were blown out. I decided to have a haircut—the windows of the barber shop were gone, but the Italian barber was still doing business."

Murrow closes one broadcast with a new sight seen as German bombs force the city underground.

"The sundown scene in London can never be forgotten—the time when people pick up their beds and walk to the shelter.

"Good night and good luck."

49

AMBASSADOR KENNEDY

The last three nights in London have been simply hell," Joseph Kennedy writes to wife, Rose, back home in Massachusetts.

The ambassador is not one to prowl the streets after dark like Edward R. Murrow, but he cannot withstand the allure of watching the German attacks. He roots for the Nazis.

"Last night I put on my steel helmet and went up onto the roof of the Chancery and stayed up there until two o'clock in the morning watching the Germans come over in relays every ten minutes and drop bombs, setting terrific fires.

"You could see the dome of St. Paul's silhouetted against a blazing inferno that the Germans kept adding to from time to time by flying over and dropping more bombs."

The ambassador flees to Windsor most nights, but those times when he remains in London, Kennedy finds himself growing awed by the determination of the British people. He has even requested signed copies of Churchill's speeches from this arduous summer, believing they will become important historical documents.

Somewhere deep down, Joseph Kennedy is starting to think Britain might win this battle.

"It is amazing to see all these flares and these bombs dropping and yet as you ride through the streets there is little indication of their effects except in the devastated areas. I am completely a fatalist about bombing accidents."

Kennedy misses America very much right now. These bombings could be the start of something serious. "There is a very definite feeling in the minds of both the Prime Minister and Beaverbrook"—and here Kennedy makes reference to the Canadian newspaper baron who was asked by Churchill to redirect his energies to increasing the production of Spitfires and Hurricanes—"that Hitler will try an invasion very soon.

"Barges and ships are lined up at all the ports from Norway to the southern point in France."

. . .

WINSTON CHURCHILL AGREES with Ambassador Kennedy. These attacks are the obvious prelude to invasion.

Now, more than ever, Londoners must gird their loins.

"We must regard the next week or so as a very important period in our history," the prime minister tells London in a BBC broadcast. Winston Churchill reads every war report he can get his hands on. Britain's top meteorologists weigh in daily. He knows Channel weather far more thoroughly than any German meteorologist. England just needs to hold out a little longer. Winter waves will soon make invasion impossible. One more week might make a very big difference.

He can't say that now. But the PM's "next week" hint gives London something to think about.

For the first time, Churchill's address tonight is aimed specifically at the people of England's capital. These bombings of innocent civilians, already leaving thousands homeless and dead, are now very personal for everyone within the city. He must not let them believe these harsh attacks will go on forever.

"It ranks with the days when the Spanish Armada was approaching the Channel, and Drake was finishing his game of bowls; or when Nelson stood between us and Napoléon's *Grand Armée* at Boulogne," Churchill tells London.

"These cruel, wanton, indiscriminate bombings of London are, of course, a part of Hitler's invasion plans. He hopes, by killing large numbers of civilians, and women and children, that he will terrorize and cow the people of this mighty imperial city, and make them a burden and an anxiety to the Government and thus distract our attention unduly from the ferocious onslaught he is preparing."

Churchill makes it a personal habit never to speak the führer's name— a policy from which he has just veered. But he wants London to know he is one of them, an angry resident of this city who holds Adolf Hitler personally responsible for this horrendous catastrophe.

Warns Winston: "This wicked man, the repository and embodiment of many forms of soul-destroying hatred, this monstrous product of former wrongs and shame, has now resolved to try to break our famous island race by a process of indiscriminate slaughter and destruction."

Fighter Command is doing its part. Until last week, London watched the desperate daily battle unscathed. No more. Every citizen is a warrior.

London does not need to hear these next words, but Churchill adds them just the same.

"This is a time for everyone to stand together, and hold firm."

Everyone.

50

PRINCESS ELIZABETH

SEPTEMBER 13, 1940
LONDON, ENGLAND
11 A.M.

Aperfect day for bombing London.

And for launching a future monarch into the spotlight.

The attacks begin at breakfast. Cloud banks hang low over the city, concealing German aircraft seeking fresh targets. Spitfires and Hurricanes scramble to intercept the intruders, but Luftwaffe pilots drop their payloads with precision, finally able to see targets in the clear light of day after a week of nighttime attacks. Londoners race into the safety of Tube stations, packing subway platforms as bombs rain down. Red double-decker buses pull to curbs. Riders spill out. Explosions. Fires. Air raid sirens and antiaircraft chatter. The final all clear does not sound until 4:13 p.m.

Yet casualties are few. As the bombings end, Londoners lucky enough to own a car pull up to bus stops and call out their destinations, offering stranded strangers a ride home. Compared to the horrific poundings London has taken since the Blitz began, today's attacks have left the city relatively unscathed.

And yet five German bombs will make this morning quite unforgettable.

A twin-engine Heinkel bomber evades low-level barrage balloons hanging over Central London. Buzzing Nelson's Column and hugging treetop level over St. James's Park, the German pilot takes aim at Buckingham

Palace. The Heinkel bombardier fixes his sights on a prominent balcony at the front of the building. King George VI is in residence. As the Heinkel approaches, the sovereign stands next to a window so his wife, Elizabeth, can remove an eyelash stuck to his cornea. The king has adamantly refused to leave London during the bombings, despite Adolf Hitler's wish that George be murdered. The sovereign hopes to show solidarity with his subjects.

The king's behavior is in marked contrast to that of American ambassador Joseph Kennedy, who has fled to the countryside. This does not go unnoticed. "I thought my daffodils were yellow until I met Joe Kennedy," cracks Randolph Churchill.

· · ·

BUCKINGHAM PALACE IS the most symbolic target in all London.

"All of a sudden we heard an aircraft making zooming noises above us," the king will write in his journal. "Saw 2 bombs falling past the opposite side of the Palace, & then heard 2 resounding crashes as the bombs fell in the quadrangle about 30 yds away. We looked at each other, & then we were out into the passage as fast as we could get there. The whole thing happened in a matter of seconds."

Buckingham Palace is extensively damaged. The Royal Chapel is decimated. A water main is destroyed. Four workers are hurt, one of whom will later die.

Twenty-three miles away at Windsor Castle, George's daughter—also Elizabeth—has no idea that the bombing is taking place or that it will soon mark her first foray into the role of hands-on monarch, a job she will perfect over her long life. Young Elizabeth is still twelve years away from being crowned queen of England. She and her younger sister, Margaret, have been sent to Windsor, spirited out of Britain's cities like three million other children for reasons of personal safety.

For Elizabeth, that life of seclusion is about to end—for good.

The British public rallies around George VI after the September 13 bombing. He responds by traveling throughout London to visit bomb-damaged homes. The people love it. Seeing the surge in public morale, the king seeks to bolster this connection between his monarchy and the British people. He decides Princess Elizabeth is the answer. George requests she make her first-ever address to her future subjects. The princess's audience: children just like herself separated from their parents during time of war.

Making the matter more poignant is a reminder that until this fight is over, British children will remain in harm's way. The evacuation ship *City of Benares* sailed out of Liverpool this afternoon, taking British children to safety in Canada. A German U-boat will sink the vessel on September 17, leading Winston Churchill to immediately halt all overseas evacuations.

On October 13, 1940, speaking on the BBC show *Children's Hour* in a voice that listeners will describe as "charming" and "lovely," Elizabeth delivers her address, which is an enormous success: "Thousands of you in this country have had to leave your homes and be separated from your fathers and mothers," she says into the microphone from a Windsor Castle drawing room. The message is broadcast in Britain and America. "My sister Margaret Rose and I feel so much for you, as we know from experience what it means to be away from those we love most of all. To you living in new surroundings, we send a message of true sympathy and at the same time we would like to thank the kind people who have welcomed you to their homes."

Not so long ago, Elizabeth was a child without responsibilities. An innocent. The notion of speaking to her entire nation would have been unthinkable.

September 13, 1940—and five well-placed German bombs—changes all that.

51

HANDSOME RICHARD

SEPTEMBER 15, 1940
ROYAL MASONIC HOSPITAL, LONDON
10 A.M.

Richard Hillary is in a morphine haze.

A face so deformed, nurses faint at the sight. Burned body coated in a thick black crust of tannic acid. Fingers oozing pus and still curled like claws. Blind eyes covered in gauze. Third-degree burns on the verge of turning septic. It's a week since the long ambulance ride from Margate Hospital, where the rescue boat crew came to visit in the days after fishing him out of the sea, his mother and father quietly listened to him make bad jokes about a neighbor girl who had been disfigured by burns as a child, and the hospital smelled of ether.

The crewmen aboard the lifeboat *J. B. Proudfoot* were just about to give up their search, when they sighted Hillary's chute floating on the water two weeks ago. Hypothermia was pulling him in and out of consciousness. The world was a delirium. Hillary imagined a rope falling upon him without warning. The coarse hemp sliced into his scalded palms as he reached to grab hold, so he let go. Then something pulled at his arms and took off his parachute. A rum bottle was pressed between his aching lips. An ambulance waited back on land, ready with morphine to ease his pain and a short transport to Margate General Hospital. Treatments for burn patients are experimental; little is known about the best method of restoring lost flesh and facial features. The doctors at Margate did their best before transferring Hillary to this London hospital.

Richard Hillary's Battle of Britain is over.

His real fight is about to begin.

.   .   .

TODAY IS THE day Hermann Goering needs to make good on a two-month-old promise to Adolf Hitler. He is supposed to have crushed the RAF by now. The German invasion is supposed to begin at any moment. But the new Luftwaffe tactic of bombing cities rather than air bases has revived the Royal Air Force. New and repaired fighters take off from runways now devoid of bomb craters. The people of London are enduring horrific destruction and hardship, but Adolf Hitler's new focus on the British capital has saved Fighter Command. For the first time since the Battle of Britain began two months ago, Stuffy Dowding's chicks appear to have the upper hand.

Richard Hillary knows nothing of this.

He is in enormous pain, as he has been every day since being shot out of the sky. Today's agony ended temporarily fifteen minutes ago. The morphine makes the unrelenting ache go away, but it also gives him visions.

Here's what his mind imagines today: a hallucination so vivid that he could swear it's really happening. It's like he's there. In no world is this a fantasy.

Richard Hillary sees a Spitfire from the 603 chasing a Messerschmitt. The British pilot is Peter Pease, one third of the triangle of friendship. Hillary has previously dined with Pease's landed family, debated his fellow Oxford alum endlessly, and even taken sage advice from the thoughtful Pease. There was the one time when Hillary insisted on the daredevil stunt of flying a fighter beneath the low bridge over the Severn River. Pease found this to be a pointless and self-glorifying way for Hillary to prove himself.

"From now on, a lot of people are going to fly under that bridge," Pease cautioned Hillary. "From a flying point of view it proves nothing. It's extremely stupid. From a personal point of view it can only be of value if you don't tell anyone about it."

Stubbornly competitive, Hillary flew under the bridge—then, despite the temptation to crow about it to a rival pilot, followed his friend's advice.

It was the very next day when Richard Hillary, Colin Pinckney, and Peter Pease were assigned to Spitfires and Squadron 603. Hillary and Pease drove up to Scotland together to report for duty, engaged in debate the entire way. The two men could not be more different—the middle-class, irreverent Hillary and the cautious, wealthy Pease—but they have a deep common bond.

Flying under the Severn bridge actually happened.

But that memory is not Richard Hillary's morphine-induced hallucination.

What he sees through his mind's eye is this: Peter Pease is dying.

Richard Hillary is sure of it. In his opioid state, still blind from his burns, he has a very clear vision of "a tall figure leaning forward with a smile at the corner of his mouth. Suddenly, from nowhere, a Messerschmitt is on his tail about 150 yards away. For two seconds, nothing happened. I had a terrible feeling of futility. Then, at the top of my voice, I shouted, 'Peter, for God's sake look out behind!'"

Hillary's screams echo through the private ward. Nurses and a doctor come running, even as Hillary's nightmare continues. He sees the Me 109 open fire, then vividly witnesses the Spitfire of Peter Pease float into a lazy roll before plunging toward earth.

Hillary feels the weight of being physically restrained as he regains consciousness. A doctor tells him to calm down. The burned pilot orients himself to his surroundings, waking up in the burn unit here at Royal Masonic instead of chasing Peter Pease through the sky in a Spitfire.

It was all a bad dream.

Or was it?

.   .   .

THIS IS THE new life of Richard Hillary: gauze, morphine, delirium, and restraint. The tannic acid—coagulation therapy, as it is known—puts a crust over the burned skin, allowing it to heal. But healthy flesh for skin grafts is also destroyed. He is a man in the wrong place at the wrong time, third-degree burns covering his face and hands at a moment in history when medical science does not know how to treat the effects of 100 octane gasoline setting fire to human skin. But a solution must be found quickly.

In the past, little thought was given to flame and aviation. Pilots flew without parachutes in World War I. When they crashed, they went down with their aircraft. Those who survived very often died from a lack of antibiotics to treat their wounds. Now the forward location of fuel tanks in modern British fighters means extreme burn danger when that gasoline explodes. There are mysterious cases of pilots bailing out successfully from fiery cockpits, only to operate the quick-release lock on their parachute harness while descending, then fall to their deaths. Many believe these pilots were suffering from severe burns and could not tolerate the pain.

What is known for sure is that there are fighter pilots who did not choose death after a cockpit fire. There is a cadre of men known as the "faceless ones," so called for the damage fire does to noses, lips, eyelids, and facial skin. Tom Gleave of Peter Townsend's 85 Squadron, shot down August 31, contemplated shooting himself. Now he is here.*

"What on earth have you been doing with yourself?" his horrified wife demanded when she saw his once handsome face so horribly burned.

"I had a row with a German," he replied.

Yet even as the pilot so nonchalantly redirects the conversation, the fact remains that faceless men present not one, but two medical challenges: treating burns and rebuilding bodies.

Richard Hillary's worst burns are to his hands. But his forehead, nose,

---

* Tom Gleave will go on to become a founding member of the Guinea Pig Club. He will endure extensive plastic surgery and return to duty. He will write the air plan for Operation Overlord, the Allied invasion of Nazi-occupied France that was launched on June 6, 1944. D-Day. Gleave will remain in the RAF until 1953. He served as technical and tactical adviser for the 1969 film *Battle of Britain*. Gleave also served as the historian for the Battle of Britain Fighter Association, a position he held until his death in 1993.

and upper lip are also seriously scorched. Right now, in all of Britain, there are just four full-time plastic surgeons. The "Great Four" are more known for fixing cleft palates and faces scarred in car crashes than battle wounds.*

Yet in Ward III at Queen Victoria Hospital in East Grinstead, Sussex, plastic surgeon Archibald McIndoe advances the art of plastic surgery in miraculous fashion. The RAF has charged him with not only treating burn victims but also improvising new methods of repairing the bodies and psyches of fire-ravaged men like Richard Hillary. McIndoe saw just one patient in the first seven months of the war, but the Battle of France, Dunkirk, and now the Battle of Britain mean each of the forty beds is filled all the time.

Ward III at Queen Victoria Hospital
Queen Victoria Hospital NHS Foundation/East Grinstead Museum

Yet Ward III is not just a place for enduring brutal burn treatment. McIndoe sees this unusual hospital as a place for planning a return to normal life. The one-room ward has a communal feel, with two rows of beds located across from one another. Patients are encouraged to joke and swear, just as if they were back in the squadron. Off-color comments about their missing body parts—"you've got to keep a stiff upper lip, even

---

* Harold Gillies, Thomas P. Kilner, Archibald McIndoe, and Arthur Rainsford Mowlem. The term "plastic" surgery comes from the Greek word *plastikos*, a term for sculpting.

if you haven't got one"—are encouraged. There are also a piano, a radio, and a full keg of beer. Dr. McIndoe believes that all forms of hydration are a vital part of healing. The weekly "grogging parties" are legendary. He even takes these patients into town for a visit to the local pub. Moderation is an issue.

In this way, the forty-year-old New Zealander offers a holistic method of treatment focused on relieving a patient's anxiety about his new appearance as well as reconstructing noses, lips, ears, eyelids, cheeks, foreheads, eyebrows, and even necks. Noses are reconstructed from flaps of skin taken from the forehead, a technique first used in India in 800 BC. Some men need as many as fifty operations before their appearance returns to a semblance of their previous state—and McIndoe performs them all.

Hospital staff calls him the "Maestro."

Jowly, with a tender smile and an honest gaze that instills trust, the plastic surgeon uses terms like "total patient care" and "it takes a team to treat a patient." Each victim receives a personalized treatment plan. He seeks to promote "trust and confidence" in his work—and succeeds.

The men under McIndoe's care will, somewhat proudly, label themselves the Guinea Pig Club.

"It has been described as the most exclusive club in the world, but the entrance fee is something most men would not care to pay and the conditions of membership are arduous in the extreme," McIndoe will say to describe these graduates of his surgical theater.*

Just as Richard Hillary once looked forward to the steady advancement from officer training to getting his wings to advanced pilot training to squadron assignment, his new progression is from rescue boat to local hospital to preliminary burn treatment here in London to advanced care under Dr. McIndoe in Sussex. There, as a Guinea Pig, he will endure skin

---

* Seven hundred twenty men were treated at East Grinstead. Two hundred were severely disfigured. In all, of the forty-five hundred RAF pilots who survived plane crashes during the war, thirty-six hundred endured serious burns to their hands or face.

grafts and advanced burn treatments like saline baths. Gauze soaked in Vaseline is used instead of coagulation therapy. There will be no more thick black crusts of tannic acid, which McIndoe considers archaic and ineffective. Hopefully, the reconstruction of Hillary's burned body will make his physical features handsome again.

Yet Richard Hillary would like to take the process one step further.

He's a pilot. Pilots fly. Hillary wants to be back on flight status as soon as possible. His hands are curled so tightly, he can't grip a fork, let alone a spade grip, but he vows to fly in combat again.

·   ·   ·

An extremely depressed Richard Hillary is visited by Dr. Archibald McIndoe for the second time. "He started to undo the dressings on my hands and I noticed his fingers—blunt, capable, incisive," Hillary will remember. "He took a scalpel and tapped lightly on something white showing through the red granulating knuckle of my right forefinger. 'Bone,' he remarked laconically."

McIndoe says it is time for Richard to be treated in Ward III. He talks about the new eyelids the pilot needs. How much he wants to supervise Hillary's treatment personally.

But Richard Hillary has a more pressing question on his mind.

"How long before I fly again?" Hillary finally asks.

"Next war," says the doctor.

·   ·   ·

A letter arrives for Richard Hillary. The nurse reads it to him. Two weeks since Hillary was shot down in flames. Forty-eight hours since his very bad dream. Colin Pinckney is writing to pass along some terrible news:

Hillary's premonition was true after all.

Peter Pease is dead, shot down on September 15.*

---

* *Oberleutnant* Roderich Cescotti, a German bomber pilot, witnessed the courageous death of Peter Pease. "I saw a Spitfire dive steeply through our escort, level out, and close rapidly on our formation. It opened fire, from ahead and to the right, and its tracers streaked towards us. At that moment an Me109, that we had not seen before, appeared

This date will go down in history as Battle of Britain Day.

The fighter boys will remember it as the day when Air Marshal Hugh Dowding's fears of a single massive German raid finally came true.

---

behind the Spitfire and we saw its rounds striking the Spitfire's tail. But the Tommy continued his attack, coming straight for us, and his rounds slashed into our aircraft . . . at the last moment, the Spitfire pulled up and passed very close over the top of us . . . then it rolled on its back, as though out of control, and went down steeply trailing black smoke . . . the action lasted only a few seconds, but it demonstrated the determination and bravery with which Tommies were fighting over their own country."

52

CHURCHILL

SEPTEMBER 15, 1940
RAF UXBRIDGE
11 A.M.

Winston craves more action.

Sunday morning. Perfect flying weather. The prime minister thinks the air war might be busy under these ideal conditions. He and Clementine are spending the weekend at Chequers. Churchill calls for his driver.

On the off chance there might be some German activity, the Churchills pay a surprise return visit to RAF Uxbridge. The prime minister apologizes to commanding officer Keith Park and even offers to "sit in the car and do my homework" if this is not a good time.

Air Vice Marshal Park has also been enjoying this beautiful morning, calling it "one of those days of autumn when the countryside is at its loveliest." The World War I fighter ace would love nothing more than a walk in the sun. Yet intercepted intelligence, from a source soon to bear the code name Ultra, states that Germany has been planning a massive air strike in advance of the coming invasion. Park is now certain this is that day. Just after breakfast came more news of Luftwaffe aircraft and personnel activity in coastal French bases. "This, I think is what we have been waiting for," he tells himself. "I think that it is about to happen."

RAF fighter pilots woke this morning to the warning that there might be "a flap on," leading some to believe this is the date of German invasion. September 15. The English Channel is going to be too rough for invasion any day now. This morning has to be the ultimate attempt to destroy the RAF.

Having the prime minister and his wife make a surprise appearance is not ideal under the best of circumstances, but particularly not today. Park is so focused on his intended counter-maneuvers that he forgets to wish wife Dorothy a happy birthday. Yet he is calm with the Churchills, telling the prime minister, "I don't know whether anything will happen today." Park adds, "At present all is quiet."

Air Marshal Park invites Winston and Clementine into the bunker under one condition: no cigars. The air filters of the underground command post can't handle tobacco smoke.

Churchill has no choice but to agree.

"My wife and I were taken down to the bombproof Operations Room, fifty feet below ground," he will write.

Churchill has been here several times before. The small chamber is two stories tall. Filterers and plotters surround the large map table. Churchill counts twenty of them, some wearing telephone headsets hung around the neck. Others use the lull to knit or read. An enormous blackboard covers one wall, "divided into six columns with electric bulbs, for the six fighter stations, each of their squadrons having a sub-column of its own, and also divided by lateral lines. Thus, the lowest row of bulbs showed as they were lighted the squadrons that were 'standing by' at two minutes' notice," Churchill will write.

The prime minister thinks quite highly of 11 Group and their commander, "on which our fate largely depended. From the beginning of Dunkirk all the daylight actions in the South of England had already been conducted by him, and all his arrangements and apparatus had been brought to the highest perfection."

The affable, forty-eight-year-old New Zealander still flies quite frequently as he leads 11 Group. On days when fighting is minimal, he pilots his own Spitfire to observe the squadrons under his command rather than drive by car. The primary responsibility for 11 Group is London, but the twenty-five squadrons under Park's command cover all of Southeast

England. This is the second step in the Dowding System, one notch removed from Fighter Command. Just as at Bentley Priory, those lighted bulbs also show which squadrons are "In Readiness" and "Available." There are also red lights for those aircraft who report seeing the enemy in the distance, those currently fighting, and those flying back to base.

Calm before the storm. Park has no time to babysit. He shows the prime minister to a viewing area.

The Churchills take a seat and wait for those bulbs to become illuminated.

"On the left-hand side," Churchill observes, using the quiet moments to appraise every aspect of this war room, "in a kind of glass stage box, were the four or five different officers whose duty it was to weigh and measure the information received from our Observer Corps."

To the right, the prime minister observes army officers in contact with antiaircraft batteries.

The Churchills study the quiet action as if watching a play. Fifteen minutes pass. Then subtle new movement from the players as reports from Chain Home stations and the Observer Corps are plotted on the board. Planes are launched to patrol the coast. Bulbs on the board light one by one.

Then the onslaught. Large waves of German aircraft approach England, forty, sixty, and even eighty strong. The map table becomes a frenzy. Churchill makes out the French coast, the Channel, then England as discs and triangles and arrows slowly converge. The board is almost completely lit. Dorniers and Heinkels aiming for London make landfall in the gap between Dover and Dungeness.

Between 11:05 and 11:42, twenty-two complete RAF squadrons are launched to repel the daylight attack. Geoffrey Wellum, the young Spitfire pilot from 92 Squadron nicknamed The Boy, is among the pilots flying up to join the fight. His Battle of Britain will not end today.

Park gets on the phone with Stuffy Dowding, who is watching the battle from his own bunker at Bentley Priory. He requests that Dowding send fighters from 10 Group and 12 Group to join the fight. This is an extraordinary request. Park and Air Vice Marshal Trafford Leigh-Mallory's avowed rivalry grows stronger by the day. Their animosity has often led them to avoid calling upon each other for help. Requesting that Leigh-Mallory divert his fighters to Park is an enormous ask.

Yet this is no time to be petty.

Permission granted.

The Churchills watch for an hour, spellbound. Aboveground, the people of England crane their necks skyward, shielding their eyes from the pale September sun to see for themselves the fighting as it takes place. The bombings of London are taking an enormous toll, yet citizens never cease delighting in watching British fighters shooting down German bombers—even to the point of risking their lives by not descending into shelters. The *Daily Telegraph* will report that through the first half of September, "2,000 civilians had been killed and about 8,000 had been injured—three quarter of these had been in London during air raids on Britain."

Yet warning sirens deter few on a day meant to be spent outdoors.

Citizens go about their business. The aerial combat almost seems a form of entertainment. "We heard guns, machine guns and the air was full of sound," one eyewitness will remember. "We thought we might see the fun, so we went to where we could see the sky. We saw little white specks moving about and suddenly my friend said look up there and we did . . . we saw a plane . . . coming down. I will never forget it . . . it caught the sun with a trail of smoke coming from it twisting and turning."

The action subsides. Air Vice Marshal Park explains to the Churchills that British fighters are on the ground again, refueling and rearming. Average flight time on a full tank of gas is eighty minutes. A fine balance is being struck by those taking this necessary break and those remaining in the sky.

By 12:45, RDF shows the Germans returning to France. Skies clear.

The Luftwaffe has never bombed London twice in one day. So the RAF lands. Pilots grab lunch in their squadrons' dispersal huts and hope that's enough fighting.

Just as the bombing ends, Squadron Leader Peter Townsend is released from the hospital. He requires a walking stick to hobble to his car, but successfully engages the clutch with the heel of his left foot. He is thrilled to be away from the "charnel house" as he drives to his mother's home for further recovery. Amputated toe or not, he plans on returning to 85 Squadron within the week. Whether he can find a way to get back into the cockpit remains to be seen. "Transcending all the hideous slaughter," he will write of the burned and mutilated men filling the hospital's beds and then his own moment of escape, "was the eternal, immaculate purity of the blue heavens and the notion, which these days on the ground had sharpened, that we were dying for a country we loved which had nourished us and breathed its formidable, unconquerable spirit into our souls."

Then, even before driving off the grounds, Townsend hears a new round of air raid sirens.

The Germans are coming back.

In the bunker, a spellbound Winston Churchill watches the big map as reports show bombers again approaching Dover, due to cross the coast between 2:14 and 2:20. Squadrons from 10, 11, and 12 Group are scrambled between 2:00 and 2:15 to meet them.

"A subdued hum arose from the floor, where the busy plotters pushed their discs to and fro in accordance with the swiftly changing situation," Churchill will write.

These are not normal German raids. By every appearance, the Luftwaffe is throwing every available aircraft into the bombing of London. In fact, *Reichsmarschall* Hermann Goering is personally directing the action from Boulogne, just across the Channel. The vainglorious Goering, desperate to keep his promise to Hitler, insists that the Battle of Britain will be won today.

In the underground command post, Winston Churchill watches pensively as Park personally takes control of the action. "The Air Marshal himself walked up and down behind, watching with vigilant eye every move in the game, supervising his junior executive hand, and only occasionally intervening with some decisive order, usually to enforce a threatened area.

"I became conscious of the anxiety of the Commander, who now stood still behind his subordinate's chair. Hitherto, I had watched in silence. I now asked, 'What other reserves have we?'"

Park has no choice but to answer. "There are none."

Churchill has played out this drama before. Back in May, while visiting a doomed Paris, he asked the same question and received the same answer from French general Maurice Gamelin as German troops overwhelmed the French Army. That lack of a reserve force doomed France. The prime minister was as "dumbfounded" by Gamelin's poor judgment as he is right now.

Yet the prime minister has no choice but to trust that Park knows what he is doing.

A hard look crosses Churchill's face. Keith Park will describe it as "grave."

One by one, British squadrons land to refuel, once again putting them at risk from German bombs before they hurriedly return to the sky. In London, a Dornier tries another attack on Buckingham Palace but is rammed by a Hurricane and crashes through the roof of Victoria Station. The Dornier crew is taken into custody shortly after parachuting onto the Kennington Oval cricket ground, though not before pilot *Oberleutnant* Robert Zehbe is savagely pummeled by a crowd of irate Londoners. The twenty-seven-year-old Zehbe will die from wounds received from both the ramming and the public beating.

In all, an estimated one hundred German bombers successfully pound the British capital. Yet their effect is muted by a wide separation between targets.

Churchill sees none of this. His entire view of the fighting comes from the lit bulbs on the board and the tokens on the map table. He has no idea whether the British are winning or losing. The prime minister is exhausted from the drama, his body drained. As the Germans are driven off once again, Churchill can only reflect on how close Fighter Command had come to utter defeat.

"It was evident that everywhere the enemy had pierced our defenses," Churchill will write. "Many scores of German bombers with their fighter escorts had been reported over London. About a dozen had been brought down while I was below, but no picture of the results of the battle or of the damage of the losses could be obtained."

Now he can only wait for the after-action reports to tell him the score.

Winston and Clementine depart the underground command post for the return to Chequers. The prime minister needs a nap.*

And a cigar.

. . .

IT IS WINSTON Churchill's daily habit to enjoy an afternoon bath and a brief rest. Today, wrung out by the very real fact that the Royal Air Force was pushed to its very limit, he sleeps almost four hours. He wakes up to a litany of bad war news from John Martin, his private secretary. "It was repellant," Churchill will write. A number of British ships have been sunk by U-boats. "This had gone wrong here, that had been delayed there."

But Martin saves the good news for last.

"However, all is redeemed by the air. We have shot down one hundred and eighty-three for a loss of under forty."†

. . .

"THIS IS NOT the end. Not even the beginning of the end," Churchill will tell his people with caution after a victorious tank battle over the German Army in the North African desert two years from now. "But it is perhaps the end of the beginning."

Those words can just as easily describe the Battle of Britain. Fighter Command continues to hold the line, no matter how many planes Nazi Germany throws at them. The time for dire worry is passing. The

---

* Beginning in 1943, services to give thanks were held to celebrate September 15 as Battle of Britain Day, marking the date on which the tide turned in Britain's favor. Annual commemorations now also include parades and flyovers.

† Actual losses are constantly being revised, even to this day. The Royal Air Force gives the numbers as sixty German aircraft lost versus twenty-nine British losses. Thirty RAF pilots were killed or wounded versus almost two hundred killed, wounded, missing, or captured Luftwaffe personnel.

Luftwaffe is licking its wounds, restricted to bombing London by night even as RAF Fighter Command gets stronger every day. Winston Churchill told them it would be like this; in speech after speech after radio message, he told them.

And though this day is perfectly marvelous for a walk through Hyde Park, the Channel is already turning rough.

Across the low fog and haze of those turbulent waters, all those landing craft lining the shores of Western Europe are still empty.

And will remain so.

53

CHURCHILL

Winston Churchill is almost killed today.

A daytime raid. German bombs just miss 10 Downing. Nearby St. James's Park is also hit. Buckingham Palace is bombed again, the London centerpiece an easy visual target for Luftwaffe bombardiers. The prime minister now sits at a conference table for the evening meeting of his chiefs of staff. The safest place is "the Hole," as the underground command post adjacent to No. 10 is known. Ventilation is negligible, but ashtrays are everywhere on the great conference table.

Churchill chews on a long cigar as the agenda is presented. Among the items is a top secret message intercepted by British code breakers. The missive is from the German General Staff, intended for a logistics officer in the Netherlands. The recipient is responsible for the loading and un- loading of aircraft deemed vital to the cross-Channel invasion. The mes- sage states that the officer should begin dismantling the cranes and other equipment utilized for this purpose. Without these apparatus, there can be no invasion.

Churchill is confused. The message has been rushed to the prime minister with urgent priority. It means something spectacular, but he cannot discern what.

The prime minister turns to Air Marshal Cyril Newall for his inter- pretation.

Newall was informed earlier about this message. He has had time to study the wording and figure out exactly what this means. The chief of air staff tells the prime minister that this note means there will be no Sea Lion. At the very least, Great Britain will get a reprieve until there is better weather. Or the operation could be called off altogether.

Along the French coast, Nazi Germany has huge artillery pieces that can drop shells all the way across the Channel into England. It has the most elite parachute units in the world. Hitler has at his disposal almost four million soldiers eager to do as he orders. Even in the prisoner of war camps throughout Britain, downed German pilots await the news of invasion, already preparing to escape and join the fight for control of England.

Adolf Hitler has all those things at his disposal.

But he does not have control of the skies.

"September 15 was the crux of the Battle of Britain," Winston Churchill will write, also noting Hitler's postponement on September 17. "It was not till October 12 that the invasion was formally called off until the following year. In July 1941 it was called off by Hitler again till the spring of 1942."

Churchill adds: "On February 13, 1942, Admiral Raeder had his final interview on 'Sea Lion' and got Hitler to agree to a complete stand-down. Thus, perished Operation Sea Lion.

"And September 15 may stand as the date of its demise."

54

MURROW

This . . . is London."

The Battle of Britain is over, but night is never a safe time. The German bombings continue. "I'm standing tonight on a rooftop looking out over London, feeling rather large and lonesome," says a pensive Edward R. Murrow. "In the course of the last fifteen or twenty minutes there's been some considerable action up there, but at the moment there's an ominous silence hanging over London."

German attacks on England are far from over. The Luftwaffe is taking advantage of Fighter Command's inability to locate Luftwaffe bombers in the dark. Daylight raids are becoming a rarity as cities are bombed in a relentless attempt to break the will of the English people. But Winston Churchill's determination to seek victory at all costs buoys the nation, and Hitler's tactic is proving futile. "I've seen some horrible sights in this city during these days and nights," Murrow will tell his American listeners. "But not once have I heard man, woman, or child suggest that Britain should throw in her hand. These people are angry."

Some forty-three thousand civilians will die in the next nine months of Blitz. Coventry is flattened. In London, the House of Commons is hit by bombs fourteen times. These poundings become so regular that Londoners will be pleasantly confused on November 3 and 28, nights without air raid sirens or German attacks.

More common are nights like May 10, 1941, when over a seven-hour period under a full moon, 505 German bombers drop seven hundred explosive bombs and eighty-six thousand incendiary devices on London. When the roof of Westminster Hall catches fire at the same time as Commons that night, it is decided to save the illustrious structure, which has played a vital role in English history for almost nine hundred years. The hall smolders but still stands when the sun rises.

But the House of Commons Chamber burns to the ground. The casualties that night in London are 1,364 killed and 1,616 wounded, the most of any night during the Blitz.

It will also be the last.

Adolf Hitler, seeing the futility of trying to force a British surrender through aerial bombing, calls off the Blitz the next day.

He has other battles to fight.

Six weeks later, on June 22, 1941, the führer turns his military attention from England to the Soviet Union. Nearly four million Wehrmacht soldiers massing in the East pour across the border, bound for Moscow. Fighter Command had done their job so effectively that Hitler prefers to send his Wehrmacht, the greatest and most modern army in the world, across the thousand miles between Berlin and Moscow rather than risk crossing the twenty short miles of English Channel to take London.

Adolf Hitler believes the invasion of the Soviet Union will turn the tide of war.

And it will.

But not in his favor.

.   .   .

EDWARD R. MURROW continues his September 22 broadcast. His fondness for London shines through in his attention to detail and hope for a return to the city's normal routine.

"Down below in the streets I can see just that red and green wink of the traffic lights; one lone taxicab moving slowly down the street. Not a sound to be heard. As I look out across the miles and miles of rooftops and chimney pots, some of those dirty gray-front buildings look almost snow white in this moonlight here tonight."

Murrow takes a breath. A little moisture in the air. Searchlights on the horizon. Faint smell of smoke from smoldering distant fires. The incredible lack of enemy aircraft and falling bombs feels like a respite. He spies a watcher, specially trained to report aircraft sightings.

"And the rooftop spotter across the way swings around, looks over in the direction of the searchlights, drops his glasses, and just stands there. There are hundreds and hundreds of men like that standing on rooftops in London tonight watching for fire bombs, waiting to see what comes out of this steel-blue sky. The searchlights now reach up very, very faintly on three sides of me."

Murrow takes a quick drag on a Camel. His speech tonight is spontaneous. No prepared notes. He will stay in London as long as the bombings continue, with no thought of fleeing with Janet to somewhere safer.

"There is a flash of gun in the distance, but too far away to be heard.

"Good night. And good luck."

55

THE BOY

The Boy lives.

The youngest pilot to fly in the Battle of Britain is at one with his machine. Somewhere over the Channel. Sun already below the horizon. Heading 350 degrees. Just survived a dive that separated him from 92 Squadron. The Merlin feels smooth, even sounds quiet. Though he is flying at more than 300 miles per hour, it feels as if his fighter is suspended motionless over the world. "This is a type of peace and tranquility that, to my mind, is utterly beautiful," he will write about this moment forty years from now.

Wellum knows that "only men who fly will understand."

He learned the Spitfire at Uxbridge for a time, way back in May, then returned to 92. The squadron spent much of the summer training in Wales, only becoming operational the first week of the London bombings. On September 11, Wellum scored his first victory, destroying an He 111. On September 27, he shared a kill. On November 2, he will damage two Me 109s, then damage another on November 17.

Wellum does not know this lies in his future. Nor can he know about the wife and children, the successful careers, the high acclaim for his bravery, the moment he will share a laugh with Prince Charles, a future king of England, both men sporting vibrantly colored rows of medals commemorating their bravery. He cannot possibly know that he will be one of the last surviving members of The Few, elevated to iconic status in Great Britain for their great victory.

Because at this moment there is no future.

Right now Geoffrey Wellum revels in just one thing: flight.

It's a shame having to think about the ground and having to get back on it. If only I could go on flying like this forever.

This is the Spitfire experience R. J. Mitchell envisioned during that first test flight in 1936. Cancer killed him one year later. Spitfire's inventor never saw his brilliant design challenged in combat.

Obituaries were effusive, front-page. Yet none compared Mitchell to legendary national heroes like Sir Francis Drake, who saved England from invasion in 1588 by thwarting the vaunted Spanish Armada.*

Nor did newspapers think to mention R.J. alongside Admiral Horatio Nelson, the steadfast naval commander who saved Britain from invasion by defeating Napoléon's navy at the Battle of Trafalgar in 1805. The same Nelson whose column rises over Trafalgar Square.

The führer has never heard of R. J. Mitchell. Nor will he ever lay hands on that column.

Yet R. J. Mitchell's Shrew, along with Sydney Camm's Hurricane, robbed Hitler of the one thing Nazi Germany needed most to take London in this summer of 1940: the big blue British sky.

In which Geoffrey Wellum is having one hell of a good time right now.

In years lived, the teenage Wellum is still a boy. On leave, he still returns to his parents' home and sleeps in his childhood bed. But he has killed, and perhaps just moments ago did so once again. His thoughts turn to God and prayer as he flies through the purple dusk. "It was strange and wonderful and I feel a great contentment," his memoirs will state.

Wellum brings the plane to a lower altitude to check visibility. At one thousand feet, he sees a railway line he knows, and uses it for a navigational aid. He gets lost for a moment but finds his way back on course and

---

* Drake was well known for leading that success but was actually second-in-command behind Lord High Admiral Charles Howard.

comes in to land. His ground crew, Davy and Bevington, wait at Wellum's parking spot, their jobs still to be done after he lands—refueling, rearming, slapping red tape over the gunports.*

You've survived until dawn tomorrow, he tells himself.

What on earth shall I find to do when I am not able to fly a Spit anymore?

Pilot Officer Geoffrey Wellum (right) with Flight Lieutenant Brian Kingcome

WikiWand/Original image housed at the Imperial War Museums

---

* Taping over gunports before flight prevented weapons from freezing during the climb to high altitudes. When fighting began, fired rounds shot a hole through the tape. This was also a quick way for a ground crew to know whether or not a pilot had fired the machine guns during a sortie—aircraft landing with the red tape intact had not engaged the enemy.

ONE SUMMER LATER

56

CHURCHILL AND ROOSEVELT

Canada.

A gray Sunday morning. A harbor far from London. A low fog. A flat sea. A quiet fishing village filled with a fleet that will change the world.

A very important meeting.

After so many months of phone calls and telegrams, Winston Churchill and Franklin Roosevelt have traveled to this remote harbor to meet in person for the first time since the war began.

Adolf Hitler would despise this extraordinary moment.

Distant green oceanfront pine forests. Gray-hulled American and British naval vessels at anchor. HMS *Prince of Wales*, that great new addition to the fleet and largest vessel in this remote fishing village, is the exception, painted in swirls of tropical camouflage. *Prince of Wales's* reputation precedes her. Less than three months ago, the destroyer and a squadron of Swordfish torpedo bombers participated in a landmark British naval victory: the sinking of Germany's fearsome new battleship *Bismarck*.

President Franklin Roosevelt, on crutches and with legs encased in metal braces, sweats as he struggles to cross the gangplank and come aboard. Sailors and admirals alike hold their breath, praying the president does not fall.

Dark blue suit and gray hat. A nearby bank of photographers knows better than to take pictures of the president's infirmity. Few in America know what polio has done. FDR sailed to this conference aboard the USS *Augusta* in total secrecy. The presidential yacht *Potomac* still plies the waters off the New England coast as a decoy for those believing he is still on board.

Winston Churchill waits on *Prince of Wales*. A salute and handshake to greet the president. Dark blue Royal Yacht Squadron uniform. Shiny brass buttons. Peaked blue cap. He looks like a railroad conductor.

The prime minister left London in complete secrecy, traveled under guard to Scotland, then boarded *Prince of Wales* for the crossing. The destroyer charged alone across the Atlantic at maximum speed to elude German submarines. Roosevelt arrived a day earlier. The president waited patiently on board *Augusta*, protected by a tight cordon of US Navy vessels. *Prince of Wales*'s arrival was far from ceremonial, the proud camouflaged monster floating into the bay like an all-powerful dreadnought of old.

The Royal Navy band strikes up "The Star-Spangled Banner." Roosevelt and Churchill move slowly to their seats for this morning's religious service. They sit in the black chairs. Behind them, standing, are the great diplomats and military leaders of Britain and the United States: Admiral Ernest King, General George Marshall, Field Marshal Sir John Dill, Admiral of the Fleet Sir Dudley Pound, and top Roosevelt advisers Harry Hopkins and Averell Harriman, and on.

A single German U-boat could kill the highest levels of Anglo-American leadership with a single well-placed torpedo.

Churchill has personally chosen the hymns for this morning's celebration. "Eternal Father, Strong to Save" and "Onward, Christian Soldiers," now sung by a thousand-strong chorus of British sailors on the afterdeck. The music stirs Churchill's heart. The pulpit is adorned with the Union Jack and the Stars and Stripes. Chaplains from Britain and America take turns reading the prayers. Those same high-ranking dignitaries standing behind the president and the prime minister press close together in order to share hymnbooks.

"Our God, Our Help in Ages Past" closes the service. The singing carries across the quiet waters of Placentia Bay, the twining of the British and American forces now complete.

"It was a great hour to be alive," Churchill will write.

. . .

THE UNITED STATES has not declared war on anyone, but President Roosevelt is most definitely taking sides. The days of neutrality are over. FDR ignored Ambassador Joseph Kennedy's anti-British sentiments back during the dark days of the Battle of Britain, knowing he needed Kennedy's support to get reelected. On September 2, 1940, when the aerial conflict was still far from decided, the president approved sending those fifty destroyers requested by Winston Churchill, overriding Ambassador Kennedy's isolationist stance.

On October 6, Kennedy requested permission to return to America. By then he had earned the nickname "Jittery Joe" for his fear of being bombed. President Roosevelt requested a meeting upon the ambassador's arrival on October 27. It was FDR's hope to reconcile policy issues between himself and Kennedy. Though the end had been coming for months, a November 1940 interview with the *Boston Globe* in which Kennedy stated that "democracy is finished in England. It may be here" sealed his fate.

On November 6, one day after being reelected for a third term, FDR received Joseph Kennedy's letter of resignation.

On December 1, President Roosevelt accepted it.

Yet Joseph Kennedy remains a defiant isolationist. "Ambassador Says He Will Now Help Roosevelt 'Keep the United States Out of War,'" the *New York Times* headline about his resignation will scream on December 2, 1940.

. . .

BUT THE UNITED States will enter the war just four months from now. The sinking of HMS *Prince of Wales* will follow two days later, halfway around the world from this Canadian fishing village in hostile waters off the Malayan Peninsula. That is all to come. The elegant warship seems indestructible on this quiet Sunday morning. With its paneled wardroom and bar for its officers, fifty-eight guns, eighty rocket launchers, two bag-pipers for entertainment, and complement of 1,521, there is a revived sense of British naval strength in her appearance.

But the bomber always gets through.

For Winston Churchill on this overcast Sunday morning off the coast of Canada—a place to which Hitler once predicted he would flee, never dreaming that the prime minster would travel to in triumph to cement a powerful alliance with America rather than defeat—it is enough that his great nation no longer stands alone.

The Battle of Britain has shown Great Britain's strength. "The Royal Air Force," he will write, "was triumphant. A strong flow of fresh pilots was provided. The aircraft factories, upon which not only our immediate need but our power to wage a long war depended, were mauled but not paralyzed. The workers, skilled and unskilled, men and women alike, stood to their lathes and manned the workshops under fire as if they were batteries in action—which indeed they were."

Churchill concludes: "The stamina and valor of our fighter pilots re-mained unconquerable and supreme.

"Thus, Britain was saved."

EPILOGUE

The correspondence between **Winston Churchill** and **Franklin D. Roosevelt**, which began on September 11, 1939, lasted until Roosevelt's death from a cerebral hemorrhage at the age of sixty-three on April 12, 1945. Churchill wrote 1,161 letters and telegrams to the president. Roosevelt penned 788 of his own. Despite the prime minister's aversion to the telephone, Churchill and Roosevelt also called each other frequently. Visitors to the Churchill War Rooms in London can see the secret phone the prime minister used for the specific purpose, even as German bombings forced him underground. Churchill led Great Britain almost until the end of the war, when a weary Britain voted for a leadership change. He would remain in Parliament, serving once again as prime minister from 1951 to 1955. He died at the age of ninety on January 24, 1965. He is buried at St. Martin's Church in Oxfordshire. **Clementine Churchill** outlived her husband by thirteen years, dying of a heart attack on December 12, 1977. She is buried with her husband and son, Randolph.

. . .

JOSEPH P. KENNEDY remained in political limbo after resigning as ambassador to the Court of St. James, destined never to fulfill his dream of becoming president of the United States—although his son John would be elected to that post in 1960. Joseph Kennedy had a most undesirable legacy, being best remembered for the tragic lives of his children: eldest son, Joe, killed in a wartime airplane explosion; daughter Rosemary lobotomized by order of Ambassador Kennedy without first consulting wife, Rose; death of daughter Kathleen "Kick" Kennedy, who died in a plane crash four years after her older brother; and sons John and Robert killed by assassins' bullets. On December 19, 1961, Joseph Kennedy suffered a stroke that left him paralyzed on the right side of his body and barely able to speak. He died on November 18, 1969, and is buried with Rose in Holyhood Cemetery in Brookline, Massachusetts.

. . .

EVEN AS THE Nazi Blitz pounded London, **Air Marshal Hugh "Stuffy" Dowding** was relieved of his duties at Fighter Command on November 24, 1940. The Big Wing theory advocated by his political enemies played a pivotal role. Dowding rightfully believed this was a conspiracy begun by opponents in the Air Ministry who disapproved of his tactics during the Battle of Britain, despite his masterminding the surprise victory. Secretary of State for Air Archibald Sinclair, Air Vice Marshal Trafford Leigh-Mallory, and Squadron Leader Douglas Bader questioned Dowding's tactics, in particular his refusal to practice the Big Wing theory of attack. To prove the effectiveness of the Big Wing, Leigh-Mallory conducted a simulated exercise to show its effectiveness against enemy attack. The Big Wing failed miserably, allowing RAF bases to be "bombed" before the fighters could arrange in formation.

This makes it clear that Dowding's tactics won the Battle of Britain.

"Churchill told me that I was to be replaced as C-in-C Fighter Command," Dowding will relate. "He told me of his surprise that this recommendation should have been made 'in the moment of victory,' but did not indicate any personal opposition. It seemed natural enough to me: The Air Council had been anxious to be rid of me since before the start of the war, and this seemed to be an appropriate moment."

A shocked Winston Churchill tried to make up for the Air Ministry's decision by appointing Dowding to a role in the Ministry of Aircraft Production, then sending him to the United States to research new types of aircraft. Dowding's direct manner of communicating won him few friends during this trip. He retired upon his return in July 1942 and was named Baron Dowding of Bentley Priory on June 2, 1943. Dowding laid the foundation for the RAF memorial at Biggin Hill in 1951. He also re-married that same year. Dowding died on February 15, 1970, and was cremated. Air Marshal Hugh Dowding's ashes are located in the Royal Air Force Chapel in Westminster Abbey.

. . .

R. J. MITCHELL is buried at South Stoneham Cemetery in Hampshire, England. It is worth noting that the British Postal Museum mentioned Admiral Horatio Nelson and R. J. Mitchell together in a 2015 blog post on its official site. A stamp showing the image of a Spitfire along with Mitchell's name was issued in 2009. Fighter Command leader Air Marshal Hugh Dowding received his own stamp in 1986.

. . .

THE **FOUR PILOTS** suffered vastly different fates. **Richard Hillary** returned to flight status, despite his burns. The rebellious pilot's confidence never left him, and despite his disfiguration, Hillary had an affair with Hollywood actress Merle Oberon and then a girlfriend named Mary Booker, a relationship lasting from 1941 until his death on January 8, 1943. Hillary was killed in the nighttime crash of a Bristol Blenheim fighter-bomber, along with his navigator, during a training exercise. His ashes were scattered over the English Channel. Hillary's good friend **Colin Pinckney** was transferred to the Far East in 1941. He was killed in action over Burma on January 23, 1942. **Peter Pease**, the third member of Hillary's triangle of friendship, who was shot down and killed on September 15, 1940, is buried at St. Michael and All Angels in Middleton Tyas, Yorkshire. In 1990, a lime tree was planted in Kingswood, marking the spot where Pease's burning Spitfire impacted the ground at 3:05 p.m.

. . .

PETER TOWNSEND RETURNED to 85 shortly after the amputation of his big toe. Though unable to walk properly or return to flight status, he commanded his squadron from the ground. The unit was reassigned to Yorkshire for a period of rest after the Battle of Britain. There, he was helped into a Hurricane cockpit shortly before a visit to the base doctor. "It will be some time before you can fly again," the physician is said to have told Townsend. "I've just been flying," the pilot responded, formally resuming his flight career. On October 25, he shot down a Dornier in a Hurricane newly outfitted with De Wilde exploding bullets.

Townsend married twenty-year-old Rosemary Pawle on July 17, 1941. Their son, Giles, was born nine months later. In 1944, the pilot was named air equerry to King George VI, a position that saw him come into weekly contact with distinguished Buckingham Palace visitors such as Winston Churchill.

It also led to one of the more infamous scandals in royal history.

Townsend and his wife, Rosemary, divorced in 1952. By then he had fallen in love with the king's younger daughter, Princess Margaret. When her sister, Elizabeth, became queen upon George's death, she refused to allow the couple to marry; Townsend's divorce was at odds with the teachings of the Church of England. This attracted widespread notoriety, causing Margaret to break off the relationship in 1955. Townsend married again in 1959. He died of stomach cancer on June 19, 1995, at the age of eighty. He is buried in St.-Léger-en-Yvelines, France.

· · · ·

GEOFFREY WELLUM BECAME a minor celebrity at the age of eighty when *First Light* was published. During his wartime service, he flew sweeps over France in the summer of 1941, then became an instructor pilot for a time. He was promoted to flight commander in March 1942. Soon after, he led eight Spitfires in a rescue mission for the besieged British garrison on the Mediterranean island of Malta, taking off from the deck of the aircraft carrier HMS *Furious*. By 1943, Wellum was exhausted from three years of aerial action and was reassigned as a gunnery instructor. Over the course of World War II, he was credited with six German aircraft either shot down or damaged.

Geoffrey Wellum remained in the Royal Air Force until 1960, whereupon he became a commodities broker. The success of *First Light* led to public hopes for a sequel, but he never wrote another book. Wellum, whose first marriage ended in divorce after three decades, died in Cornwall on July 18, 2018, at age ninety-six.

. . .

THE MEMORY OF **Billy Fiske** lives on through memorials, various books, and a foundation bearing his name. On July 4, 1941, a plaque in his honor was unveiled in the crypt at St. Paul's Cathedral. The inscription reads: "An American citizen who died that England might live." Sir Archibald Sinclair, secretary of state for air, dedicated the small monument, stating: "Here was a young man for whom life held much. Under no compulsion he came to fight for Britain. He came and he fought, and he died."

There is widespread belief that Winston Churchill played a quiet role in ensuring that Billy Fiske would be long remembered for his sacrifice.

Rose Greville (née Bingham) died in London on December 29, 1972, at the age of fifty-nine.

. . .

FLIGHT LIEUTENANT **ALAN Deere** would go on to an illustrious Royal Air Force career. The New Zealander flew in the Battle of France, in the Battle of Britain, and in the June 1944 Normandy invasion. He is credited with twenty-two aerial kills. By the end of the war, he was held in such high esteem that the fuselage letters on his personal Spitfire bore his first name: AL. Deere would remain in the RAF until 1967, holding a number of command positions and also serving for a time as aide-de-camp to Queen Elizabeth II. Upon the death of Winston Churchill in 1965, Deere led the cortege of Battle of Britain pilots during the funeral procession. The legendary pilot died of colon cancer on September 21, 1995, at the age of seventy-seven. A Spitfire flew over the Thames River to scatter his ashes.

. . .

DR. ARCHIBALD MCINDOE kept in touch with members of the Guinea Pig Club for the rest of his life, and served as club president. He was knighted in 1947 for his advances in plastic surgery and service to Great Britain. McIndoe resumed his private practice after the war and even farmed for a time in East Africa. Monuments to McIndoe can be found at his former flat in Chelsea and in East Grinstead. Ward III still stands, though it is now a research facility. McIndoe died in his sleep from a heart attack on April 11, 1960, at the age of fifty-nine. His ashes are located at St. Clement Danes in London, a place of worship also known as the "Royal Air Force Church."

.   .   .

THE MARRIAGE OF **Randolph Churchill** and **Pamela Digby** did not last. They had one child, Winston, named for the boy's grandfather. The couple divorced in 1945, but Randolph's long absences during his military services led Pamela to have several affairs with wealthy men, including CBS chairman William Paley and Ambassador Averell Harriman, a practice that earned her a reputation as a courtesan. Among her lovers was Edward R. Murrow, who broke off their relationship after his wife, Janet, gave birth to their first child. Pamela married again in 1959 to Broadway producer Leland Hayward. After his death in 1971, she rekindled her relationship with Harriman, whom she married the same year. Pamela Harriman became a US citizen and later served as ambassador to France. She died there in 1997, after suffering a cerebral hemorrhage while swimming in the pool at the Ritz Hotel in Paris. She was seventy-six and is buried at the Harriman family estate in New York.

Randolph Churchill served for a time in Parliament and worked as a journalist. He died of a heart attack in 1968 at the age of fifty-seven. Randolph is buried with his parents at St. Martin's Church in Bladon.

.   .   .

EDWARD R. MURROW briefly returned to New York in December 1941, where he was honored by CBS chairman William Paley with a testimonial dinner at the Waldorf Astoria Hotel. The crowd of eleven hundred rose in a standing ovation to honor the newsman. Five days later, on December 7, he and wife, Janet, dined at the White House with President Roosevelt, where Murrow received a personal update from the president about American losses in Hawaii.

Murrow would return to Europe and broadcast throughout the war, then remain with CBS News afterward for the entire length of his twenty-five-year career. He would go on to several postwar broadcasting triumphs, but Murrow's reporting from London in the early days of bombing is his greatest legacy. The lifelong smoker had a lung removed in 1963 and died two years later at the age of fifty-seven. His wife, **Janet**, survived him and passed away in 1998. The couple is buried next to each other at Worthington Center Cemetery in Massachusetts.

. . .

DIARIST **CHIPS CHANNON** served in Parliament for twenty-three years, until his death in 1958 at the age of sixty-one. Channon was widely loved and loathed for his ambitious behavior. He died of a stroke after years of heavy smoking and drinking.

. . .

AMERICAN PILOT **FLOYD Smith** and his adventurous wife, **Hilder**, deserve more than a footnote. The former trapeze artist's 1914 parachute design and his wife's subsequent death-defying test saved countless lives in the Battle of Britain—and forever after. Test pilot Smith would go on to make the first simulated aircraft carrier landing in Coronado, California, in 1917, advancing naval airpower in ways that still affect modern warfare.

Yet Smith's passion was always parachute development.

By 1942, silk in parachute canopies had been replaced by nylon, with Smith also leading the design process. His parachutes would be used in NASA astronaut landings and the dropping of large munitions and vehicles.

Hilder Smith was an aviation force in her own right. She would become the first woman to pilot a plane from Bennett's bean field, which would later become known as Los Angeles International Airport (LAX). Despite her near-death experience in April 1914 during that first parachute jump, Hilder Florentina Youngberg Smith survived her husband by twenty-one years and lived to the age of eighty-six. Husband and wife are interred at the Portal of the Folded Wings Memorial at Valhalla Memorial Park in Burbank, California.

. . .

THE CIRCLE OF **Princess Elizabeth's** World War II service came full at Buckingham Palace in May 1945. London was celebrating the end of the war in Europe. Princess Elizabeth stood on a balcony overlooking thousands of cheering citizens; she was standing in her ATS uniform next to Prime Minister Winston Churchill and her parents. It was the same balcony at which the unnamed Heinkel pilot once aimed his stick of bombs.

King George VI slowly increased Elizabeth's royal duties throughout World War II. The teenager was trained to be an active monarch, connected with Britain's people through words and deeds, just like her father. A year after her radio address, she was photographed growing vegetables in her Windsor Castle garden as part of the nation's "Dig for Victory" campaign to prevent food shortages. In 1942, at the age of sixteen, the princess inspected troops at Windsor Castle in her guise as an honorary colonel of the Grenadier Guards. Two years later, upon turning eighteen, Elizabeth stepped beyond the bonds of "honorary" and truly joined the military. She enlisted in the women's branch of the British Army, known as the Auxiliary Territorial Service. Rather than allow his daughter to be granted a high rank due to her royal standing, George VI insisted that she be treated like any other soldier. Training as a second subaltern, Elizabeth became an ambulance driver and learned to fix engines and change tires.

Elizabeth would lean on her father's dogged refusal to leave London during wartime as an example of steadfast leadership and morale boosting.

But Queen Elizabeth's own wartime service molded her sense of duty. "She took immense pride in the fact that she was doing what other girls of her age had to do," royal governess Marion Crawford once commented. "She kept strictly to the routine of the mess, taking her turn with the others as duty officer, doing inspections, and working really hard on the maintenance of cars."

Elizabeth ascended to the throne on February 6, 1952, upon the death of her father. The coronation was June 2. In 2022, after seventy years as queen, she celebrated her Platinum jubilee on that famous balcony, standing in almost the exact same spot.

But on the night of that V-E Day celebration in 1945, all that was to come. Elizabeth stepped from the balcony, pulled her green uniform cap low over her eyes, and wandered with the crowds through London. She described this as "one of the most memorable nights of my life." No one knew a princess and future queen walked among them.

There were later rumors Elizabeth ended the night at the Ritz Hotel, where she was reported to have anonymously danced in a conga line.

NOTES

Hundreds of pilots flew in the Battle of Britain. Many wrote excellent books about their experiences. I went through a great number of these when deciding which pilots to feature in *Taking London*, but in the end, it was the writing of Peter Townsend (*Duel of Eagles*), Richard Hillary (*The Last Enemy*), and Geoffrey Wellum (*First Light*) that provided the most insight into the actions and thought processes of fighter pilots. Billy Fiske did not live long enough to write his story, but the American's journey was so unique that he made a perfect fourth. Thank you to Alex Kershaw for his assistance with the Fiske research.

Michael Korda's *With Wings Like Eagles* and Paul Richey's *Fighter Pilot* are also outstanding. Alan Deere's *Nine Lives* is a gem, written in straightforward fashion. All three books will transport you into the Battle of Britain with a very you-are-there feeling.

Len Deighton's significant work *Fighter* is astounding in its detail and entertainment.

Edward R. Murrow's *This Is London* brings the Battle of Britain to life.

It's worth noting that Hillary, Wellum, and Townsend wrote their memoirs at different stages in their lives. Hillary's book came out in 1942 and became an instant wartime classic. Townsend published in 1971, after spending a great deal of time tracking down his old Luftwaffe opponents to add their stories to his own. Wellum wrote *First Light* in the early 1980s, but kept it to himself. It was not published for twenty more years. I heartily recommend all these books, each told in the voice and style unique to its author.

. . .

Writing a work of history is an adventure unto itself. It seems simple to retell a story that has already taken place, but the questions on whom to feature, the arrangement of chapters, and what facts to leave in and what facts to leave out make for some interesting weeks of mental searching before the actual writing begins. Of course, writing history is not all struggle. One of the true joys of immersion into a historic subject is travel, and with it the opportunity to walk in the footsteps of the people I'm writing about. I always find an excuse to include London in my journeys, both for the history and the excellent hands-on research. Thanks to the magic of cell phone cameras, it's now possible to take much of the information home by snapping pictures of museum displays for use throughout the writing process. The old practice of filling a notebook with handwritten comments still exists, but it sure is nice to have a photo of the verbatim transcript to explain things months after a visit.

The Battle of Britain is a cottage industry, with museums, memorials, and famous places I've described in this manuscript that still exist. I sat on the stoop of Morpeth Mansions, visited Stuffy Dowding's office in Bentley Priory, paid my regular visit to the Churchill War Rooms (a must for anyone visiting London; if you've been there before, go again—the exhibits are constantly changing), and dragged my wife through the large number of airfields and museums with displays about the Battle of Britain. As someone who grew up on air force bases as the son of a pilot, I greatly enjoyed the many museums dedicated to flight, in particular the Royal Air Force Museum and the Imperial War Museum Duxford, with its incredible static displays of historic aircraft and regular daily Spitfire flights.

It is also worth noting that the 1969 film *Battle of Britain* was a seminal influence on my young life (much of it filmed at RAF Duxford), leading me to build model airplanes of Hurricanes, Spitfires, and Me 109s, which I hung on my bedroom ceiling engaged in a mock dogfight. As you can imagine, I was something of a history geek. My other childhood curiosity was adventurers, which ultimately led to me writing books about Captain James Cook and Dr. David Livingstone. I cannot explain how the events of childhood play into the creative process, nor can I explain a childhood fascination for all things epic and British, other than to say the mind works in mysterious ways.

Thirty-five years after *Battle of Britain*, when the British comedy duo of Alexander Armstrong and Ben Miller unveiled their comedy sketches portraying two nonsensical Spitfire pilots who have utter disdain for the Hurricane ("them's shit planes"), I became nostalgic about my youthful passion for those single-seater fighter aircraft and the Battle of Britain. It took a while, but I finally realized all those emotions were coalescing into the need to write this book.

Two events in particular made researching *Taking London* unique. The first event was of enormous international significance: the death of Queen Elizabeth II. By sheer coincidence, her passing on September 8, 2022, took place just one day before a scheduled research visit to London. Her body lay in state for almost six days in Westminster Hall—the same section of the Palace of Westminster saved from fire on the night of May 10, 1941, and the oldest building on the parliamentary estate. The BBC was predicting that mourners wishing to pay their respects should anticipate waiting in line for twenty-four hours. But my wife, Calene, and I joined the queue anyway, starting a mile past Tower Bridge. It took only eight hours (this was the second day; those daylong lines came on the fifth and sixth days). It was midnight when we finally went through the final security checkpoint. Our feet hurt from standing too long and jet lag was kicking in, but as we ascended the steps into the hall, that was all forgotten. The cavernous room was bathed in strong light. Beefeaters stood vigil around the catafalque, on which rested the crown jewels, glittering in that way only diamonds and precious gems can. It was one of the most moving scenes I've ever witnessed. At the front of the queue, every person had the chance to stop for an instant to pay final respects. Some men saluted, other mourners made the sign of the cross. Calene curtsied. I just offered a small bow and wiped away a tear, strangely overcome by the death of a woman who had played such a prominent role on the world stage for as long as I've been alive.

Left unsaid was that this powerful scene might never have taken place if the Battle of Britain had been lost.

The other event was also something I'll never forget. There exists a company operating out of Biggin Hill Airport—next to the former WWII RAF base—known as Fly a Spitfire. On the morning of the very same day that Calene and I joined the line to see the sovereign, I had the opportunity to fly in the rear seat of a Spitfire (Supermarine designed a two-seat training version of the plane). I wore a parachute and had to pass a test on emergency-egress procedures, which I can still recite. After takeoff, pilot Adam Green took me through dives, rolls, breaks, and any number of maneuvers used by Battle of Britain pilots through the course of a dogfight. For the briefest of instants, I was allowed to take the controls. The flight was forty-five minutes long but felt like ten. I could not wipe the smile off my face. As we came in to land, using the same wide approach R. J. Mitchell's test pilots used so long ago, I wondered aloud if we might make one last victory roll. Commander Green happily turned us upside down in the manner of RAF pilots returning to base after a win during the Battle of Britain. He then brought the aircraft back to a smooth and level flight for a pinpoint landing.

I tend to choose my book topics based on places I'd like to visit or events I'd like to know more about. In the case of *Taking London*, I must admit that the subconscious desire to fly over the English countryside in a Spitfire was a strong motivation. I was not disappointed.

ACKNOWLEDGMENTS

The process of writing a book can feel so solitary, especially somewhere in the middle, when the beginning seems very long ago and the end is tens of thousands of words away. I sometimes compare that part of the process to being alone on a rowboat in the middle of a vast lake, drifting, unable to see the shore. But soon enough, as the final pages get written, that boat has floated back to shore, and there's quite a crowd waiting on the dock. The truth is that writing may require hours of lone endeavor, but publishing takes a team. A pretty big team, actually.

Taking London is no exception.

At Dutton, great thanks to the leadership of Ivan Held, Christine Ball, John Parsley, Benjamin Lee, Amanda Walker, and Stephanie Cooper. I appreciate your belief in my work and rock-solid support for the Taking series.

I'm lucky enough to have two amazing editors for *Taking London*. The insightful, thoughtful, and passionate Brent Howard and his assistant, Grace Layer, began the process and challenged me to expand the story in directions I had not imagined. Jill Schwartzman and assistant Charlotte Peters brought a new set of eyes to the project, inspiring me to add more nuance, story, and suspense. As you may have guessed, I revel in these sorts of challenges. Enormous thanks to you all. Jill, your enthusiasm is contagious.

But there's more to the *Taking London* team: thanks to publicist Sarah Thegeby, marketer Nicole Jarvis, production editor LeeAnn Pemberton, text designer Tiffany Estreicher, art director Jason Booher, copy editor Frank Walgren, and proofreader Phil Bashe, who was particularly insightful in his comments on the manuscript.

I cannot say enough marvelous things about my agent, Eric Simonoff. His wit, even keel, and incredible body of knowledge make him the ultimate pro.

Mike Di Paola is amazing in his attention to detail in all aspects of the printed word. Much thanks for the footnote ideas and for thoughts on the umlaüt.

The past couple years have presented challenges beyond the written word, the sort requiring the extremely raw humor of dear friends. I would be wandering in a desert without all these guys.

I am lucky enough to be uplifted by two such groups. The first are my longtime brothers in the Tough Guy Book Club (so named for the Tough Guy race in England): Mark Burkhardt, Gregg Hemphill, Alan Mariconda, Mike Brough, JC Abusaid, John Herold, and John Burns.

The other is the Diamond Dogs (yes, we stole it from Ted Lasso), a collection of fellow track coaches who spend way too much time on text threads having nothing at all to do with running: Sean Zeitler, Ricky Martinez, Tim McCintosh, Mark Gardner, Jim Roldan, Mike Powers, and JT Ayers.

To my assistant, Nikki Nguyen. I admire your genius and energy. Your suggestion about blogging every Sunday reminded me how much fun it is to riff and let the words fall where they may.

To the distance runners at Santa Margarita Catholic High School. Thanks for letting me push you to do hard things, knowing some form of greatness lies on the other side.

Kristina Burkhardt, Martin J. Smith, Terry Johnson, Tim and Bethany Cody, Sean Scott, Liz Terry, and the iconic Toby Walker.

To my dad. What a life.

To my sons: Devin, Connor, and Liam. No words can say how much I love you, other than a simple acknowledgment that you guys are the absolute best.

And finally, to Calene. It's been a long time since I stole a Tom Petty line to tell you that if you held on to me, there'd be magic when I held on to you. I had it all wrong. It's you who brings the magic.

INDEX

Note: Italicized page numbers indicate material in photographs or illustrations.

ABOUT THE AUTHOR

Martin Dugard is the *New York Times* bestselling author of several works of history, among them *Taking Berlin*, *Taking Paris*, *Into Africa*, and thirteen books of the Killing series, which has now sold more than ten million copies. Mr. Dugard is also a Fellow of the Royal Geographical Society. In addition, he spends afternoons coaching high school cross-country and track and field near his Southern California home. He has indulged in this avocation for the past twenty years—as documented in the essay collection *To Be a Runner*. His website is www.martindugard.com, where he writes the weekly *Paper Kenyan* blog. He can be found on Twitter, Instagram, and Facebook.

Mr. Dugard and his wife, Calene, live in Rancho Santa Margarita, California. They have three sons.